EFFECTIVE PRACTICE IN SPATIAL PLANNING

In the past, planning's role was to provide overarching policy and to regulate delivery. This has now changed to one that is centrally engaged with the local investment decisions of all, with a particular emphasis on the public sector. This book sets out these underlying changes in the system and how spatial planning is now engaged in delivering places.

Looking at the key elements of spatial planning, including community engagement, the use of evidence and taking an integrated approach to local infrastructure planning and delivery, this book discusses the increasingly important role of project management in delivering effective spatial planning. It addresses spatial planning at local, sub-regional and national scales, includes a discussion on developments in Scotland, Wales and Northern Ireland, and considers spatial planning within its European, North American and Australian context. Spatial planning's role in delivering major change such as urban extensions or redevelopment is discussed, concluding with a forward look at what is likely to follow the effective creation of inspiring and successful places using spatial planning as a key tool.

Particularly useful for students of planning, this will give an essential background for anyone interested in the practice and outcomes of spatial planning whether as participants, local authority councillors, professionals or the private sector.

Janice Morphet is a Visiting Professor at the Bartlett School of Planning, UCL. She is also a member of the Planning Committee of the London 2012 Olympic Games. Janice spends much of her time as an academic and practitioner working on spatial planning and its interrelationships with local governance.

THE RTPI Library Series

Editors: Robert Upton, Infrastructure Planning Commission in England and Patsy Healey,
University of Newcastle, UK

Published by Routledge in conjunction with The Royal Town Planning Institute, this series of leading-edge texts looks at all aspects of spatial planning theory and practice from a comparative and international perspective.

Planning in Postmodern Times
Philip Allmendinger

The Making of the European Spatial Development Perspective
Andreas Faludi and Bas Waterhout

Planning for Crime Prevention
Richard Schneider and Ted Kitchen

The Planning Polity
Mark Tewdwr-Jones

Shadows of Power
An Allegory of Prudence in Land-Use Planning
Jean Hillier

Urban Planning and Cultural Identity
William JV Neill

Place Identity, Participation and Planning
Edited by Cliff Hague and Paul Jenkins

Planning for Diversity
Dory Reeves

Planning the Good Community
New Urbanism in Theory and Practice
Jill Grant

Planning, Law and Economics
Barrie Needham

Indicators for Urban and Regional Planning
Cecilia Wong

Planning at the Landscape Scale
Paul Selman

Urban Structure Matters
Petter Naess

Urban Complexity and Spatial Strategies
Towards a Relational Planning for Our Times
Patsy Healey

The Visual Language of Spatial Planning
Exploring Cartographic Representations for Spatial Planning in Europe
Stefanie Dühr

Planning and Transformation
Learning from the Post-Apartheid Experience
Philip Harrison, Alison Todes and Vanessa Watson

Conceptions of Space and Place in Strategic Spatial Planning
Edited by Simin Davoudi and Ian Strange

Regional Planning for Open Space
Edited by Terry van Dijk and Arnold van der Valk

Crossing Borders
International Exchange and Planning Practices
Edited by Patsy Healey and Robert Upton

Effective Practice in Spatial Planning
Janice Morphet

EFFECTIVE PRACTICE IN SPATIAL PLANNING

JANICE MORPHET

Routledge
Taylor & Francis Group

LONDON AND NEW YORK

First published 2011
by Routledge
2 Park Square, Milton Park, Abingdon, Oxon OX14 4RN

Simultaneously published in the USA and Canada
by Routledge
270 Madison Avenue, New York, NY 10016

Routledge is an imprint of the Taylor & Francis Group, an informa business
© 2011 Janice Morphet

Typeset in Akzidenz Grotesk by
GreenGate Publishing Services, Tonbridge, Kent

Printed and bound in Great Britain by
CPI Antony Rowe, Chippenham, Wiltshire

British Library Cataloguing in Publication Data
A catalogue record for this book is available from the British Library

Library of Congress Cataloging-in-Publication Data
Morphet, Janice.
Effective practice in spatial planning / Janice Morphet.
p. cm. -- (The RTPI library series)
Includes bibliographical references and index.
1. City planning--England. 2. Regional planning--England. I. Title.
HT169.E5M67 2010
307.1'2160942--dc22 2009046101

ISBN: 978-0-415-49281-2 (hbk)
ISBN: 978-0-415-49282-9 (pbk)
ISBN: 978-0-203-85183-8 (ebk)

For Charlotte, Sophie and Robin

CONTENTS

FIGURES AND TABLES

TABLES

FIGURES

PREFACE

I began my career in planning in June 1969 and over the 40 years that have followed, I have been engaged in discussing planning practice and its future in many different ways and places and in a variety of different roles – practitioner, academic, chief executive, central government advisor and consultant. In the period 1996–2006, I focussed my attention on local government and when I returned to look at spatial planning in more detail, I was surprised to see how close the relationship had become. The opportunity to explore this relationship emerged even further through the leadership of the *Effective Practice in Spatial Planning* (EPiSP) project that was commissioned by the RTPI, CLG, GLA and the Joseph Rowntree Foundation in 2007. This demonstrated spatial planning's integration with the emerging local governance architecture. Its role in delivery for places was central but there were considerable barriers to understanding this. The EPiSP report identified these and made some recommendations about the ways in which they could be addressed. It was the Planning Advisory Service, through Jackie Leask, a member of the EPiSP Steering Group, supported by Sarah Richards, that started to address these barriers and brought me back to the central activity of spatial planning.

This book sets out the spirit of spatial planning, its purposes, its energy and its ability to bring an integrated delivery approach to places. It also identifies the formal processes of preparing Local Development Frameworks and how these fit within wider partnership working. The book sets spatial planning within its wider governance context and shows how place is the policy narrative of our time. It concentrates on English spatial planning at the local level but also includes discussions about other spatial scales, notably regional and sub-regional. It also sets English spatial planning within the context of spatial planning developments in other parts of the UK where practices at regional and sub-regional scales are evolving. Finally, it discusses the provenance of English spatial planning, with its focus on delivery, and its debt to the spatial planning systems in Europe, North America and Australia.

This book would not have been written without the invitation from Robert Upton, former Secretary-General of the RTPI, and I am grateful to him for this opportunity. Thanks are also due to many other individuals who have provided help, stimulating and invigorating discussions and the opportunity to develop my thinking on spatial planning. These include Bill Neill, Steve Barker, Will French, Marco Bianconi, John Pounder, Dominic Hewson, David Morris, Richard Blyth, Faraz Baber, Kay Powell, Tony Burton, Dave Shaw, Vincent Nadin, David Massey, Anne Doherty,

Janet Beaumont, Matthew Carmona, Nick Gallent, Mark Tewdwr-Jones, Cecilia Wong, Stephen Hill, Dru Vesty, Celia Carrington, Viv Ramsay, Richard Ford and Niel Williams. My thanks also go to the many local authorities where we have discussed spatial planning, how it works and how to implement it with planners, other officers, councillors, members of the Local Strategic Partnership and Chief Executives. My thanks, as ever, go to my family for their support, encouragement and practical help along the way. Any errors or omissions are my own.

Janice Morphet
Wandsworth, London
May 2010

ACKNOWLEDGEMENTS

Figure 6.1 is reproduced with the kind permission of the Planning Advisory Service and the Improvement and Development Agency.

ABBREVIATIONS

AAP   Area Action Plan
AGMA   Association of Greater Manchester Authorities
AMR   Annual Monitoring Report
CAA   Comprehensive Area Assessment
CDA   Comprehensive Development Area
CIL   Community Infrastructure Levy
CLG   Department of Communities and Local Government
CPA   Comprehensive Performance Assessment
CPO   Compulsory Purchase Order
CSR   Comprehensive Spending Review
DETR   Department of Environment, Transport and the Regions
DfT   Department for Transport
DH   Department of Health
DPD   Development Plan Document
DTLR   Department of Transport, Local Government and the Regions
EIP   Examination by an Independent Person
EiP   Examination in Public
ESDP   European Spatial Development Perspective
EU   European Union
FOI   Freedom of Information
GOs   Government Offices of the Regions
HCA   Homes and Communities Agency
IDP   Infrastructure Delivery Plan
IPPR   Institute for Public Policy Research
JSNA   Joint Strategic Needs Assessment
LAA   Local Area Agreement
LDF   Local Development Framework
LDO   Local Development Order
LDP   Local Development Plan
LDS   Local Development Scheme
LSP   Local Strategic Partnership
MAA   Multi Area Agreement
NLGN   New Local Government Network
NPF   National Planning Framework

ODPM   Office of the Deputy Prime Minister
OECD   Organisation for Economic Co-operation and Development
PAG   Planning Advisory Group
PDG   Planning Delivery Grant
PPG   Planning Policy Guidance
PPS   Planning Policy Statement
PSA   Public Service Agreements
RDA   Regional Development Agency
RDS   Regional Development Strategy
RES   Regional Economic Strategy
RPG   Regional Planning Guidance
RS   Regional Strategy
RSS   Regional Spatial Strategy
RTPI   Royal Town Planning Institute
SA   Sustainability Appraisal
SCI   Statement of Community Involvement
SCS   Sustainable Community Strategy
SHLAA   Strategic Housing Land Availability Assessment
SHMA   Strategic Housing Market Assessment
SPD   Supplementary Planning Document
SRO   Senior responsibility owner
SRS   Single Regional Strategy
SUDS   Sustainable Urban Drainage Systems
ToS   Tests of Soundness
UDP   Unitary Development Plan
VfM   Value for money
WCS   Water Cycle Studies
WSP   Wales Spatial Plan

CHAPTER 1

WHAT IS SPATIAL PLANNING?

INTRODUCTION

This book is about spatial planning in England. The formal introduction of spatial planning in England was marked through the implementation of the 2004 Planning and Compulsory Purchase Act, although much of the development in the thinking about the role of spatial planning came before this and there has been more since. Many have attempted to define spatial planning, and it is most frequently characterised as being integrated and concerned with delivery. Its origins are usually seen as being within the European spatial planning context but, as this book shows, English spatial planning has a more international provenance. A new form of spatial planning is developing that could be described as hybrid or transitional and, in this emergent form, it is likely to shape spatial planning in England for the next ten years.

The spatial turn in 2004 in England represented a significant shift in planning's role within the local governance structure shifting from a set of regulatory policies to being a delivery mechanism. Years of Thatcherism's promotion of the market and undermining the state from 1979–1997 resulted in planning's retreat. Achieving the proposals of development plans was primarily in the hands of the private sector, whilst in the public sector, the economic crisis meant that delivery was through regeneration. Yet, both in 1947 and 1970, planning had been secured as a key delivery tool, particularly for expenditure and investment in publicly funded infrastructure. In the longer term, the abdication of the direct delivery mode for planning between 1979–2004 may be seen to be the deviant period. History will decide.

The shift from delivery to policy in the post-1979 period has left a legacy which continues to work through the system. The residualisation of the proactive role of planning and the foregrounding of private sector planning proposals, often at the margins of planning policy, meant that the planning system was conducted in a regulatory space. Once policy and plans were prepared, the focus in the system was directed towards upholding them. Developers sought to stretch them to their limits. The benefits of exploiting the conditions of an imperfect market came from the private sector, where breaking a plan policy could considerably increase land and development values.

For many planners, the regulatory phase of planning has been their only experience of practice. In more economically buoyant areas, planners have left the role of implementing development to the private sector. Alongside this, the planning role has been focussed on extracting developer surplus to mitigate the effects of development. In less economically buoyant areas, the leadership for development has been primarily through public sector regeneration. In England, most local authority areas have as much social and economic variance within them as between them, so both approaches to development were frequently run in parallel. In 1979, most planners were employed in the public sector but by 2009, more members of the Royal Town Planning Institute (RTPI) were employed in the private sector, albeit many working for public sector clients as the mixed economy has developed. The introduction of spatial planning in 2004 was not accompanied by any major fanfare. Those involved in implementing the new system, at all spatial scales and in all sectors, were unprepared for what was to follow. As a response, Government has had to make its intended role for spatial planning clearer whilst planning practitioners are beginning to develop this new role and the associated activities that it brings.

Yet this is not a completed story. The history of planning is one of change, progression and, at times, returning to recapture old skills and experience. Planning's history is one of adaptation and change. Planning has held the thread of improving places and ensuring the best use of land and buildings, whether through development or protection, through regulation or promotion. The era of planning when regeneration led to delivery, particularly in the 1970–1990s, was critical at the time, but the underlying Nimbyism and revolt of middle England against planning represented not only an attack on change but also something deeper. It was a concern that places had become secondary to the market. Places were perceived as being less important. Those areas not in the main focus for change were somehow second best or received less attention. Planning's regulatory character allowed less time to consider the cumulative impact of many individual decisions in localities apart from those that had specific designations such as Conservation Areas. Spatial planning can address this in its new role in which, together with a fresh approach to development management, provides a key opportunity to 'make everywhere somewhere' (Morphet 2007b). Spatial planning brings together the multiplicity of decisions about place, whether through planning or through the activities of other organisations; it makes places more than the sum of individual decisions. Spatial planning is a key component in this approach to shaping and making places.

SPATIAL PLANNING: THEORY AND PRACTICE

Spatial planning has a wide range of theoretical underpinnings from the meta-theories which locate it within a general social movement to middle range theory which attempts to set out what spatial planning is and how it works. In terms of this text, the key concern is to understand where spatial planning sits within its theoretical context and then to identify ways in which this theoretical underpinning can be used to predict outcomes, particularly in practice. Theories vary in their type and role, and much that has been written about spatial planning could be called 'intuitionism', or normative, identifying what the role of spatial planning 'ought' to be, based on some self-evident moral position, with equitable principles (Alexander 2009). This is particularly true of communicative planning theory which identifies the key role of spatial planning as being concerned with the inclusive mode of planning. It has a concern for redistribution and with an emphasis on discourse analysis as a means of determining the relative outcomes for those with differential access to power. As such, the theory sets a model of what some, e.g. Healey (2006; 2007), argue planning should be about. It is a high level theory, and works through case study approaches although it does not relate to detailed practices of spatial planning within an operational context. In these terms, communicative planning theory can create a critical discourse about the outcomes of spatial planning based on the key principles included within it. Overall, it is generally useful and is one means of considering the role and purpose of planning and evaluating its progressive and reformist role.

A second approach to spatial planning theory is one that has concentrated on the political dimensions that it involves and can be described as structuralist in its approach. This is based on the arguments that all planning processes have redistributive outcomes based on class/power relations. This approach to planning theory does not concentrate on process, but rather judges whether it has been successful within its theoretical framework. Those discussing spatial planning theory within a political context are more concerned to look at the interaction between spatial planning and the levers of distribution exercised within it by political process (Massey et al. 2003; Sandercock 2003; Friedmann 2005). This theoretical approach includes both the formal and informal political processes and the role of power interests from those who own property and other major capital assets, as well as local politicians who make specific decisions. The political explanation of spatial planning provides a model which may generally predict outcomes, based on a variety of other theories on the issue of power (Bevir and Rhodes 2003; Dryzek and Dunleavy 2009).

A third approach to spatial planning theory rests on decision making in governance. If a system is well regulated and managed, these theorists such as Hood and Peters (2004), Pollitt and Boockaert (2004) and 6, P. et al. (2002) argue that there are generally better outcomes for individuals if decisions are supported by more integrated administrative arrangements rather than taken by separate organisations with differing and internalised objectives. This approach takes a 'holistic' or joined-up approach and argues that public policy and service delivery should be shaped around individuals and places rather than organisational or administrative principles. This is frequently described as reflecting the difference between user- and producer-based views of policy and delivery. This theoretical approach has a profound influence on the underpinnings of spatial planning. In many ways, spatial planning is one of the ways in which this holistic approach is both most nec- essary and most likely to be able to be implemented, with its focus on place. The holistic approach can be characterised as horizontal integration and it deals with the issues of vertical integration between activities at different spatial scales by drawing them into the most local. Tett (2009) describes this as organisational 'lattice' which she argues is more resilient than silos or strata.

A fourth approach to the theory of spatial planning is one which is based on the predictability of spatial planning as a model of delivery of outcomes, locally and nationally. In this approach, the wider aims of redistribution and equity are embedded in its priorities and in the way it operates to ensure some specific outcomes. In one approach to the use of this theory, Government is assuming that providing more houses will reduce the blocks on economic growth that have been caused by a housing market which seems to reduce the potential for labour mobility (Barker 2004; 2006; Gibb and Whitehead 2007). However, a more developed form of this approach to the theory of spatial plan- ning assumes that specific actions such as joined-up investment will have measureable outcomes and a cumulative impact on places. This then becomes an empirical or positiv- ist model of spatial planning, with a series of expected outcomes that are specific and measureable (Wong 2006).

In considering these theoretical positions, spatial planning is generally placed within the normative mode, although frequently failing to meet the expected outcomes of integrating multi-scalar actions (Albrechts 2006). This approach assumes that plan- ners are the actors making these changes on predetermined approaches based on shared value systems. However, Alexander (2009) and Newman (2008) take another view. They argue that a positivist approach which recognises the institutional context and the motivations of the actors, including planners, provides a closer assessment of what planning can achieve. Alexander argues that it is the people in any area that should decide what the best is for them. Spatial planning offers an approach to deliver- ing better places, within a framework that is set nationally. However, it is the local use and interpretation of this which is of value. Newman argues that:

> we suggest a shift in emphasis in our approach to contemporary planning
> practice from a search for ideal strategic planning to a greater concern with
> tactics and the perception by planners of institutional and political constraints
> and opportunities.

> (2008: 1373)

Spatial planning provides more opportunities to actively deliver change but suc- cess will depend on how appropriate the actions are for localities and how engaged communities have been in selecting them. Spatial planning's dependence on an evidence-base suggests that delivery can be integrated within local solutions that are verified and triangulated with communities and partners, rather than being focussed entirely within a regulatory context.

All four theoretical approaches underpin spatial planning in different ways, but it is the third and fourth approaches which are currently more predominant. When considering the application of the positivist version of spatial planning in practice, it is also important to understand the context in which it will be operating. Government also uses theories or meta-narratives to explain and justify the actions that are being taken directly and through others. The choice of narratologies will generally swing between those based on people and those based on places. During the Thatcherite period, the narrative of Government was about individualism and the state restricting the individual's progress. The individual is the key focus of neo-liberalism and places were also seen to hold people back in 'those inner cities' (Lawless 1989; Imrie and Raco 2003) whereas, in Thatcher's view, the apogee of individualism was home ownership. Similarly, the entrepreneurial spirit of companies that wanted to locate in the green belt or on green field sites was considered to be frustrated by planning processes that were supporting places (Boddy *et al.* 1986; Hall 1973). The restructuring of major parts of British industry were undertaken without any recourse to their effect on place.

In the first period of the Blair government, 1997–2001, this focus on individuals continued. The relationship with place was part of the 'old Labour' cannon, where places had to be saved at all costs and where people were shielded from change. In pursuing targets for health and education outcomes, Blair focussed on the potential of the individual, how they could be better supported by the state and their lives have improved outcomes? During this period, some of the 'places' that had long-running problems were tackled through neighbourhood renewal, but again there was a focus on support to individuals and their life chances through joined-up government.

The second period of the Blair government, 2001–2004, started to move away from a focus on people to a focus on place as the overriding governance narrative (Morphet 2006; 2008). Through the new place-based policy, 'new localism', the intersection between people and place became paramount and represented a paradigm shift back to place which had not occurred for over 20 years (Ball 2003; Corry 2004). Why did this shift back to place replace individualism in the narratology? As Blair remained a solid individualist throughout his period of office, it can be assumed that there were wider forces at play which encouraged this shift. This influence towards place came from various sources. First, there was an assumption that the scale of support for an individualistic approach had probably run its course and that the rump of social deprivation, poverty and other social problems could not be helped on an individual basis. What was required to tackle these issues was a change in local cultures (HM Treasury 2004). Poor educational attainment, truancy, crime, drugs and unemployment became a hard set of problems to shift through individualistic means. Those that could be helped had probably taken advantage of what was on offer. How could people clustering together in problem estates, in deprived wards and families be tackled? Under the influence of Robert Putnam's notion of the positive effects of social capital as a means of effecting localised cultural change (2000), the area-based approach was seized upon. Targeted spatial intervention coupled with other initiatives has been predicted to have beneficial economic and social outcomes. An early trial in Kent showed that cross-agency intervention could make a difference. What stopped it were organisational silos and attributions of costs and savings (Bruce-Lockhart 2004).

Another key issue that emerged as a challenge driving the second Blair period was that of climate change, particularly manifested through flooding. During 2007, there were numerous instances of flooding without any warning and outside the parameters of existing risk assessments (Cabinet Office 2008). The need to deal with climate change through mitigation and adaptation at all spatial scales emerged as a major priority. Coupled with this, the growing concerns about the globalised supply of energy and its role in international security policy brought consideration of energy production and a policy for potential self-sufficiency into sharp focus (Wicks 2009). These issues have had a shaping influence on spatial planning in England at all scales. They have included a focus on energy supply, water management and consumption. The push towards sustainability, carbon reduction and meeting climate change targets has also suggested a more local economic approach, where goods and services are produced and consumed locally. In England, the creation of the Infrastructure Planning Commission in 2009 to determine nationally significant infrastructure projects within government guidance on an independent basis, and is another outcome of the risk assessments that events such as flooding have caused (CLG 2009f).

The importance of this agenda meant that it was taken to the heart of Government for consideration. The future for planning in England was reviewed by the Cabinet Office, the Treasury, the Prime Minister's Delivery Unit and, perhaps unsurprisingly as a result, a more corporate role for planning emerged. This had to be communicated to the country and thus a change in name to spatial planning also signalled a change in role and meaning.

SPATIAL PLANNING: AN ENGLISH APPROACH

Spatial planning does not have a common definition that everyone can agree on. As a concept, spatial planning operates at different spatial scales and can be defined in different ways at national, regional and local levels. The introduction of the term 'spatial planning' in England marks a distinct break with the past and as an indicator of wider policies for the future. The use of the term spatial planning denotes a change away from 'land-use planning', which is commonly taken to mean the designation and use of land. Land-use planning is often equated with regulatory planning and the basis of all planning activity. It is also a restricting term, implying no intervention or delivery and a disassociation from the distributional nature of land-use activities and how these might be delivered with other public policy outcomes. The term land-use planning, when used on its own, is primarily Thatcherite in its scope and limiting in its meaning. On the other hand, it also represents a clearly defined activity; it is what planners can claim to do and whilst other types of planning activity have been scaled back, land-use planning has been regarded as the basis of all planning activity.

Following the 2004 Planning and Compulsory Purchase Act, the term spatial planning was subsequently defined in PPS 1(2005):

> spatial planning goes beyond traditional land-use planning to bring together and integrate policies for the development and use of land with other policies and programmes which influence the nature of places and how they function. That will include policies which can impact on land use, for example by influencing demands on, or needs for, development, but which are not capable of being delivered solely or mainly through the granting or refusal of planning permission and which may be implemented by other means.

So spatial planning in England is defined to include these wider concepts. Any definition needs to include a number of assumptions of joined-up working and as Nadin (2007) suggests, the planning process is the nexus for decision making and delivery through which all other policy transactions regarding place will occur, but it goes further than this and is:

1   Different from land-use planning (Nadin 2007; Allmendinger and Haughton 2007), representing a paradigm change (Harris and Hooper 2004: 151).
2   Spatial translation of vision and policy objectives (OECD 2001).
3   Quality of place (Harris and Hooper 2004: 151).
4   Related to integration (Nadin 2007; DTLR 2001b; Morphet 2004).
5   Primarily concerned with delivery (Morphet 2009b; 2010).

> Spatial planning refers to the methods used largely by the public sector to influence the future distribution of activities in space.
>
> (CEC 1997: 24 quoted in Amdam)

One of the key questions to consider is why the term 'spatial' was adopted and what implications there might be of the use of this new term for the English planning system. Until 2004, the development planning system was described as being part of the land-use planning system (Cullingworth and Nadin 2006). This approach had persisted since the introduction of the 'plan-led' approach to planning in 1991. The plan was primarily cast as a policy document which was then interpreted on a case by case basis. It included some specific locations where development would be permitted or where specific areas would be protected but, in the main, it was a catalogue of policies which together provided the means of delivering the future objectives for the area. These policies were then interpreted in relation to any specific location or planning application. Some issues were not included in this process despite planners identifying them as being important to delivery. Among these was a consideration of housing need by tenure rather than the provision of an overarching housing target.

The development plan in this form was not concerned with the delivery of the policies or proposed land-use allocations that it contained. When originally introduced in 1947, and then as revised in 1970, the development planning system was conceived as a mechanism for identifying local investment requirements and, for the public sector, the resources with which to deliver them. Planning was primarily an interventionist task which included the implementation of the development plan's objectives through a variety of tools including Comprehensive Development Areas (CDAs), land assembly and development including the use of Compulsory Purchase Orders (CPOs) and Action Areas. In some ways, it was the over vigorous application of these processes in many inner city areas such as London, Liverpool and Birmingham that led to change, as redevelopment accompanied by dispersal of employment policies laid waste land which was not being taken up by the market (Lawless 1989).

This concern led to a range of outcomes. One was a review of the 1947 Development Planning system by the Planning Advisory Group (PAG) Review of Development Plans (1968) and its subsequent emergence as a more strategic corporate tool for guiding investment in 1968 Town and Country Planning Act and the Development Plans Manual (1970). The economic context had also changed and public sector funds for housing development and other infrastructure investment were drying up. Inner city areas became a major cause for concern not least when emerging examples of 'hollowed out cities' from the US began to emerge (Neill 2004). The role of regeneration and economic development emerged as the key means of achieving intervention at the local level, still using the same tools but with a separate skills base in market and property-led implementation and delivery. Planners were also among the first professionals to espouse public consultation, following the publication of the Skeffington Report in 1969.

For development plans, the more corporate approach which had been set out by PAG and in the Development Plans Manual was proving difficult to achieve in the 1970s. During this decade, the world suffered a number of economic crises and the UK had to negotiate a loan from the International Monetary Fund

(Morphet 1993). These difficult economic crises led to a structural reform of many industries with plant closures and growing unemployment. These changes occurred in formerly prosperous areas such as the West Midlands (Spencer *et al.* 1986) which was then the subject of studies and policy initiatives such as the Inner Urban Areas Act 1978.

Despite many studies showing that the effects of the application of multiple policies in localities had dysfunctional effects, different agencies were not willing to work in a coordinated framework and there were no tools available to encourage them to do so. Yet during this period, there was still a fundamental adherence to the principle that development should be managed on sustainable principles. The Greater London Development Plan (1969) and the subsequent Layfield Inquiry identified strategic town centres across London, based on public transport nodes. Much of the debate at the inquiry was not about whether centres should be designated but their locations, as local authorities perceived (rightly in retrospect) that without such a designation their centre would be likely to decline in significance and its ability to attract investment.

The rise of Thatcherism from 1979 meant that the private sector had a much greater influence than at any time in the post-1945 period. The planning system was increasingly regarded as a major impediment to economic growth and was close to being abolished by Margaret Thatcher and Nicholas Ridley, the then minister in charge of planning, in the mid-1980s. Instead of abolition, planning decisions were increasingly made through the planning appeal system. National policies allowed edge of town and green field development. The inner cities were left without investment. Underused infrastructure and a stranded population were seen to be in some way responsible for these failures but not given any tools to adapt to these changes. By the early 1980s, Michael Heseltine, then a senior member of the Government, started to develop a more interventionist approach to inner city areas which included redevelopment and 'boosterism'. Regeneration through garden festivals, the creation of Canary Wharf and other Dockland developments, and the provision of sporting facilities started to offer some means of developing jobs and new places. Some of these initiatives were short lived, such as the Liverpool Garden Festival, where the site still remains unused some 30 years later, but other changes have occurred in Liverpool that started in this period. Liverpool had the confidence to win the title of European City of Culture in 2008. In other locations such as Gateshead, the creation of a new art gallery in the Baltic Flour Mills, the Millennium Bridge across the Tyne that has won awards, the Sage Concert Hall and the Angel of the North have all improved local pride and attracted visitors and other investment to the area. Much of this thinking started then.

Planning outcomes created by planning appeal decisions led to the potential for uncoordinated investment and a fear that development was being delivered in an unsustainable way. This more sporadic development frequently meant that major new housing areas did not have access to public transport or community facilities. Increasingly, the expectation was that people would access their jobs by car. The completion of major motorway investment including the M25 around London and the motorway system around Manchester led to new commuting patterns which were exacerbated by two-job and two-car families where both partners travelled long distances to their jobs, frequently in opposite directions.

The review of the planning system and the introduction of the plan-led approach in 1991 was a way of ensuring that adequate locations for investment were identified and that this could be more coordinated at the local level. In this approach, planning was given a minimalist role; it was not expected to deliver or to coordinate the investment of other organisations. In a plan-led system, the plan had a primacy in decision making about the location of development and the determination of planning applications as set out in s54a of the 1990 Town and Country Planning Act as amended by the 2001 Planning and Compensation Act (Cullingworth and Nadin 2006: 113). However, this also depended on up-to-date plans being available for this to work. This period did not see a significant speeding up of the plan making process. The concerns about the role of plans in providing more housing land and delivering locations for investment also caused delays and many politicians could see that progressing plans at the local level was unpopular and could lead to electoral defeat.

Throughout the period 1947–2004, the mechanism for adopting the development plan remained constant in character. It consisted of numerous specified and formal stages in development plan preparation leading to an Examination in Public (EiP). Here the proposals and policies in the plan were tested through an adversarial process by an independent planning inspector, who determined the merits of each argument on a quasi judicial basis. Although organisations and businesses were involved in the plan making process, the EiP formed the main focus of the debate on the evidence that underpinned the appropriateness of policy. Issues, such as housing numbers, and their consequent link to potential development sites were the main focus of interest in this process. It is unsurprising that these EiPs frequently took many weeks to complete and were costly in time and advocates' fees.

In the period 1991–2004, the development plan came in two forms. In areas with unitary local government, the Unitary Development Plan (UDP) was prepared. In areas of two-tier governance, county councils prepared a structure plan and district councils prepared local plans. These two plans worked together at the local level in providing the policy by which decisions were made. Both types of development plan sat within the regional planning context supplied in Regional Planning Guidance (RPG) that was prepared for each region. During the period to 2004, RPGs had become increasingly focussed on the number of new houses to be built and where these should be located. Although regional housing strategies were introduced in

2003 (ODPM 2003b), RPG increasingly became concerned with housing delivery above all other strategic, economic and investment considerations in the period to 2004 and beyond, frequently representing a centralised view of new housing requirements, expressed through Government Offices or Panels sitting at EiPs of the RPGs.

The Planning Green Paper (DTLR 2001b) addressed the need for reform of the system through a restatement of planning's role. It summarised the key issues that the planning system was facing as being:

- complexity – no one could understand it and with too many spatial layers;
- speed and predictability – the system was seen as regulatory and negative, providing no certainty on where development could go and this was creating delay and inefficiencies in the system;
- community engagement – people and communities felt disempowered by the system;
- little customer focus – need for better skills in the delivery of the planning service;
- enforcement – need to strengthen for those who avoid planning processes.

The Green Paper proposed a new role for planning that was more integrated with the rest of the local governance structure. Community strategies now set out the vision for the local area and each local authority had a duty to prepare one (Local Government Act 2000). Planning was about to take on a new role in the proactive and direct delivery of change. The development plan's role as an independent policy document for the determination of planning applications was being transformed into a spatial planning process. Although little observed at the time, the Planning Green Paper was published alongside a Local Government White Paper, *Strong Local Leadership, Quality Public Services* (DTLR 2001a) which was setting the organisational context for the future of local governance arrangements. It built on the foundations of an earlier White Paper, *Modern Local Government In Touch with the People* (DETR 1998) which promoted greater joined-up working between agencies at the local level. The 2000 Local Government Act placed the promotion of economic, social and environmental well-being as a duty on local authorities and also established a duty to prepare a community strategy – a vision and delivery document for each area. The 2001 White Paper continued this more joined-up approach, paying particular attention to the role of the community strategy and the Local Strategic Partnership (LSP).

The LSP was a newly established local advisory body, not set up through legislative means but through strong formal advice. Many local authority politicians were not supportive of LSPs, as they saw them as undemocratic and potential rivals for the exercise of power. However, since their creation in 2001, they have become increasingly important elements in the local governance landscape. LSPs now 'own' much of the local governance territory, including oversight of resources, consultation, performance management, and scrutiny (CLG 2008d). They also now have a leadership role in relation to the context and operation of development plans.

The Local Government Act 2000 set up a process of drawing development planning closer into these converging local governance structures. The publication of the White Paper on local government and the Green Paper on planning in 2001 further developed this intention, although very little attention was given to it at the time (see Box 1.1). In the Planning Green Paper, it stated that:

> arrangements for preparation of local plans are being overtaken by new local authority policies and programmes. Local authorities have to prepare Community Strategies ... in addition, at a more local level, there are regeneration and neighbourhood renewal initiatives. The arrangements for putting such strategies in place are more flexible and inclusive than the local plan process. We need to ensure that local plans are better integrated into this new framework, enabling them to become the land use and development delivery mechanism for the objectives and policies set out in the community strategy.
>
> (§4.7)

The reasons for the changing role of planning to one that is delivering the objectives set out in the community strategy tied more closely to the European model of planning, as set out in the European Spatial Development Perspective (ESDP) (CEC 1999) and the spatial approaches to delivering sectoral policies in Europe. The EU has also been evolving a spatial approach to all its policy making through the concept of *territorial cohesion,* which has been growing in influence. But this was not all. Like all public policy development in the period 2000–2006, there were also strong influences from other parts of the world including South Africa, Australia, New Zealand, United States and Canada, and all became the combined provenance of English spatial planning which was introduced following the Planning Green Paper to the 2004 Planning and Compulsory Purchase Act. Planning was now to have a new, integrated role as spatial planning.

Planners focussed on specific planning processes, rather than understanding the contextual changes in which planning was being designed to operate. As Allmendinger and Haughton state, the planning system that operated between 1992 and 2004 had three axes of 'irresolvable tensions' (2006: 17) which were as follows and needed to be solved:

- speed of preparation and adoption vs. public involvement;
- detailed prescription vs. flexibility;
- acknowledging complexity in the real world whilst wanting to foster simplicity in planning practices.

So the change in name to spatial planning was important. It represented a break with the immediate past. It moved planning back into a delivery mode and a corporate role. However, this was not without its difficulties. The change in name was not supported by a communications plan and reskilling programme. As Shaw and Lord point out, this involved not only a change in practice but also of value systems of practitioners and stakeholders (2007: 75–6). The Planning Delivery Grant (PDG) that was paid to each local authority in 2005–2008 was used to improve the performance of the planning service in determining planning applications through more staff or new IT systems rather than to address culture (Newman 2008; Alexander 2009). Whilst central government concentrated on performance management as the most important planning deliverable, PDG was aimed at this. There was no clear communication about planning's delivery role to those operating the wider governance system. As can happen with government initiatives, the picture is complete at the end but the uneven delivery of specific initiatives and components can be confusing and delay successful implementation. This has been the case with spatial planning in England.

THE PROVENANCE OF SPATIAL PLANNING

The role of spatial planning is now integrated within a wider system of local governance architecture and changing to have more emphasis on delivery than policy leadership which derives from the SCS. The introduction of spatial planning in 2004 marked this shift more formaly, and it can be argued that the provenance of this shift came as much from planning as from new models of

Box 1.1   The Planning Green Paper 2001 and Development Plan Reform

---

Reform – key issues for 2001 Green Paper

- More timely plan and decision-making processes that enable planning authorities to positively shape rather than to report on outcomes.
- A more inclusive and effective process of participation and consultation that lends more public confidence to plans and decisions.
- More effective collaboration with policy-makers in other sectors and stakeholders that leads to integrated objectives and joined-up policy.
- More positive, evidence-based reasoning in the formulation of strategies and policies, and in managing change.
- A focus on delivery of wider priority outcomes defined at national, regional and local levels, so that planning can contribute more effectively to wider government objectives.

Source: Nadin 2007: 45

public management (Hood and Peters 2004; Pollitt and Bouckaert 2004). This may be because there has been a wider emphasis in the components of public service and delivery across many countries and new integrated formations are still emerging (Barca 2009).

The development of integrated spatial planning, introduced by the 2004 Act, has three distinct policy origins, creating a hybridity which is now emerging as the dominant form of integrated spatial planning in England. These policy provenances are derived from different traditions and geographies. The first is European in origin and is related to policies for spatial cohesion and integration. The second is primarily economic in focus and derives from a more Atlantisist view of economic growth and regeneration (Brenner 2004). The third derives from the use of the planning system to more systematically manage assets, including contributions from developers, and is widely practised in South Africa, Australia and New Zealand. As in any system, these three components work separately but also overlap and interact. In practice, they provide a means of understanding the shift in the function and role of planning in England that is now underway.

The origins of spatial planning and its associated role of integration are frequently identified as deriving from the wider political and governance pressures for integration within the EU. As Gleeson states (1998: 221), this has origins in the Single European Act (1987) and the harmonisation of regulation that started in 1992 and is emerging as a key component in EU policy development such as Territorial Policy Integration (TPI) (Faludi 2004; Schout and Jordan 2007: 836). In this approach, spatial planning is an important component in integrating layered spatial policies within EU delivery programmes which have an overt EU source such as INTERREG and the structural funds, or an indirect EU source such as neighbourhood renewal or transport projects. In England, vertical integration of policy has been one of the key principles of the land-use planning system, and has primarily been focussed on the delivery of state objectives through the filter of regional and local plans, and increasingly through performance management regimes (Hood *et al.* 2000).

Since 2004, horizontal integration has also been introduced as part of the spatial planning process in England, although its role has not really been discussed or understood. Horizontal integration is apparent in the new system in two main ways. Firstly, Local Development Frameworks are required to be consistent and coherent with neighbouring areas on policies which are relevant. This also extends to the provisions of services and facilities which support communities across administrative boundaries (Planning Inspectorate National Service 2005; 2009). More recently, spatial planning outcomes have been included in LAAs which run from 2008–2011. In this model, local authorities have 'contracted' to deliver specific outcomes within a policy vehicle that has as its main purpose the achievement of horizontal integration between agencies to deliver specific outcomes for localities.[1] In this process, spatial planning has been more strongly tied to the regional targets which have been identified through a new government agency, National Planning and Housing Advice Unit (NHPAU) as well as regional planning processes, but also horizontally, in a contracted delivery format with local partners.

In this single move, the nature of planning in England has changed from being one that is derived through an adversarial process to one that is delivered through a contract that is agreed at an earlier stage in development plan preparation. Local planning authorities have moved from being engaged in a plan approval process which has been tested through a quasi-judicial process to one where they are contracted to deliver specific outcomes. These include housing, reductions in CO_2 and waste and improving access to public services among others drawn for a list of 198 National Indicators together with local targets. The Local Area Agreement (LAA) is 'owned' by the Local Strategic Partnership, which is made up of stakeholders from private, public and voluntary sectors (CLG 2007c). Within this, the public sector has some specific roles and responsibilities. First, the local authority is identified as the 'convenor' and other public bodies have a duty to cooperate with the delivery of the LAA target outcomes. Also, the LSP now has oversight of some key local processes such as public sector expenditure in any area, performance of the achievement of the LAA targets and consultation. Spatial planning has accountabilities to the LSP for each of these three responsibilities. This marks a considerable change to the previous system where the local planning system's accountabilities were through a vertical integration model with accountability to meeting regional targets being held through the Examination in Public process for adopting the development plan.

This new system of LAA contracts for planning has been little discussed and is continuing alongside more traditional modes of local plan formation and adoption. However, the process leading to plan adoption has changed into one that is 'inquisitorial' in its nature (Planning Inspectorate National Service 2008) and concentrates on administrative tests rather than an examination in public. Now EIP stands for examination by an independent person, the planning inspector, whose report on the 'soundness' of the plan is binding. These tests of soundness have applied from 2005 and feedback on their use in practice was given in 2007, when it was increasingly clear that some aspects of the these tests were being given less emphasis in practice. In the revised version of PPS 12 (CLG 2008c), published in 2008, these tests were re-emphasised and put into two categories of deliverability and flexibility. The deliverability test emphasises the link to infrastructure planning (ibid.: §4.8 and 4.9), and the need to demonstrate that partners and stakeholders can deliver, that there are no legal impediments and that delivery will be coherent across boundaries (ibid.: §4.45). The European approach to spatial planning as vertical, horizontal and operational integration can be located within the version of spatial planning within the 2004 Act but it does not provide a complete explanation for the role of integrated spatial planning as it is currently being developed.

The second major influence on the role of spatial planning in England post-2004 has been economic. This is part of an international trend in relating spatial competitiveness and governance. As Brenner states, this can be understood as 'an outcome of complex, cross-national forms of policy transfer and ideological diffusion' (2003: 306) and, although Brenner relates this approach primarily to Western Europe, it is also a key policy strand of the OECD through their Local Economic and Employment Development Programme (LEED). The UK Government's interpretation of the way in which the world economy operates in the UK, and, in this case specifically, England, has been set out in a number of reports (HM Treasury 2004; 2006) including most recently the Sub National Review of Economic Development and Regeneration (SNR) (HM Treasury 2007a) and accompanied by the 30 Delivery Agreements for central government departments that reinforce this interpretation of the role of the economy at sub-state level in generating growth (HM Treasury 2007c). The approach to economic growth has been identified as being most successfully managed at local level, through both encouragement to more local entrepreneurship and increased pressure on those who are underperforming in the labour market to improve their skills and to enter employment. These policies are based on long-term estimates of costs to society of those with poorer skill levels and a wish to promote more sustainable production and consumption within local markets.

Although the global economic position has changed between 2007 and 2008, the local approach to economic growth has been strengthened as a policy tool. English local authorities have been given a new economic duty and have already started to exercise some leadership in this area through the local coordination of responses to the current economic crises. This policy of economic prioritisation is now emerging in spatial planning, particularly at a regional level, where there are regional strategies which will have a leading economic focus (CLG and BERR 2008a; GLG and BIS 2009).

The economic role of spatial planning has not so much been in its identification of land for employment or associated infrastructure requirements, but rather understood as a need to provide more housing, which is viewed as one of the main drags on economic growth (Barker 2004; 2006) and remains so, despite the current recession. Where infrastructure is required, it is primarily the social, physical and green infrastructure that supports housing. None of this represents a concern for the supply of land for employment, although there are non-planning incentives being introduced to encourage local authorities to support the location of new businesses in their areas (HM Treasury and CLG 2009). The new legislative duty requires local authorities to make an economic assessment of their areas and they will also be able to establish sub-regional economic improvement boards (2009 Local Democracy, Economic Development and Construction Act). Both measures, set out in the response to the sub-national review (CLG and BERR 2008a) appear likely to have a considerable effect on the content and focus on spatial plans, although any response to economic conditions or economic improvement would not only be achieved through these means. Again, the spatial plan will be integrated within wider public sector governance and delivery structures and not the key integrating mechanism.

The last, and possibly as yet least recognised, key influence on the role of spatial planning post-2004 is that deriving from a late Blair approach to public services which asks the question of how much worth public services are delivering (HMG 2007a). Much of the focus of this discussion has been on education and health services, but the continued focus on planning delivery, that has been a key concern of Government since 1997, has started to view the role of planning in a different light. Initially frustrated by what was termed as planning's poor performance in determining planning applications and its seeming failure to produce enough land for Government-projected housing requirements, this has now developed in ways that are based in practice in Australia and New Zealand. Planning is not only being asked to deliver change on the ground through its normal processes of plan-making and development regulation but also has to go beyond this in two ways. The first is to manage infrastructure delivery in a more integrated and 'transformational' way and the second is to achieve a more consistent level of contributions from private sector investors. Planning is also being asked to add value through regulation, which has been marked through the changing use of 'development management' to replace the term 'development control' in English practice.

When spatial planning was introduced into England in 2004, the assumption was that integration was primarily focussed on broader policy ends and, as Bishop *et al.* (2000: 312) indicate, spatial planning covers a number of categories of activity (which in practice may overlap):

- urban and regional economic development;
- measures to influence the population balance between urban and rural areas;
- the planning of transport and other communications infrastructures;
- the protection of habitats, landscapes and particular natural resources;
- the detailed regulation of the development and use of land and property;
- measures to coordinate the spatial impacts of secotoral policies.

But there was little or no expectation that spatial planning would be part of these local horizontal measures.

In England, this approach has been translated into a consideration of what contribution planning makes in exchange for the public funding which it receives (Morphet 2007b). This has generally been interpreted as being a more detailed understanding of how the planning process maintains property values, protects specific environments and identifies land for new housing. Planning is now being asked

'what is its public worth'? In this approach, an assessment of the financial investment in planning through public support for staff and democratic processes is being
weighed against greater measurement of the financial and community returns which
flow from planning activity.

This new evaluation of planning has led to it being given a more proactive role
in the use of existing assets and resources. At present, there is no local calculation of
the value of annual capital investment at the local level from all three sectors and this
is now emerging as a key interest for the integrated spatial planning task. Up to now,
planning's main role in this process has been through the development control process, where it has been central to achieving developer contributions, although this has
been more of a sporadic process than is generally recognised with only 14 per cent
of new dwellings generating development contributions (Audit Commission 2008b).
The deliverability role of spatial planning is concerned with the management of local
investment, including the public sector, whilst development contributions are a more
systematic part of the process through the adoption of Community Infrastructure Levy
or more rigorous applications of current approaches.

Making better use of existing assets and investment is also being implemented
at central government level, where government departments are now required to
report on their asset use on a quarterly basis as set out in Public Service Agreements
(PSA) 20 (HM Treasury 2007c). This process is designed to bring greater alignment
and integration to government spending and has profound effects on public sector
funding streams.

The first step to spatial planning is through infrastructure planning and delivery
through proper planning of existing and new areas (CLG 2008c). This includes managing existing resources, public sector investment and private sector contributions. To
this has been added the location of new public service delivery to changing populations. Further, planning has to deliver what is known as the transformation agenda, that
is a joined-up service delivery between public agencies to improve public service efficiency and improve citizen accessibility (HM Treasury 2007b). All this can be viewed
as a layered approach to funding that rests on the Local Development Framework
(LDF), as Figure 1.1 illustrates.

In England, approaches to more systematic collection of development contributions have been made by local authorities that have introduced a 'roof tax' or
tariff such as Milton Keynes, Ashford and Chelmsford, all pilots for a new approach
supported by central government. These approaches were expected to be translated into the Community Infrastructure Levy (CLG 2008e) which builds up a
practice of consistency in negotiating developer contributions based on the size
and type of all development. In this new model, spatial planning is integrating the
delivery of infrastructure on the ground as well as integrating financial investment
in a new way.

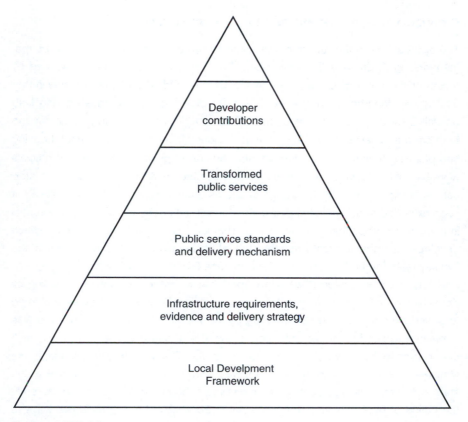

Figure 1.1 LDF delivery process

Source: the author

This approach is similar to Australia, where development contribution plans are used to generate contributions from developers and are made under s94 of the Environmental Planning and Assessment Act 1979 and as amended. The development contributions plans provide an administrative framework for contributions to ensure that public facilities are provided to address the cumulative demand from new development and ensure that the existing community is 'not burdened by the provision of public amenities and public services required as a result of future development' (Sydney (City of) 2006: 15). The development contributions plan is set at a baseline so that the current standards are maintained or improved. The infrastructure requirements in specified areas are identified and 'the works in the contributions plan are apportioned over all new development, large and small' (ibid.: 16). The contributions plan also includes a management charge for administration.

CONCLUSIONS: BRINGING IT ALL TOGETHER

The approaches to the reform of the planning system and the introduction of spatial planning in England that have been developed since 2000 have been led by teams at the heart of Government in the Cabinet Office and the Treasury rather than in the department with responsibility for planning. Senior ministers and lead officials have spent time in the Cabinet Office and Treasury working on reform and then been transferred to the department responsible for local government, housing and planning to lead their implementation. Australian political advisers and officials were part of the team formulating public service change. Although government interest in planning came initially through concerns about corruption (Morphet 2008), it soon extended to delays in the delivery of housing numbers and planning's potential impact on slowing down the economy. This lead came from the Treasury which developed a further interest when the state of the housing market became one of the five key tests for the UK's entry to the Eurozone (HM Treasury 2003).

The Treasury's interest was developed initially through a review on housing by Kate Barker, who was formerly on the Monetary Policy Committee and was appointed to undertake a review of housing supply by the Treasury in 2003. In 2005, she was appointed to conduct an independent review of land-use planning, which was also commissioned by Government and run from the Treasury. In parallel, the Prime Ministers' Delivery Unit, set up in 2003, was undertaking studies on the role of the state including reviewing evidence from a range of countries. This was undertaken in the Office of Public Service Reform between 2000–2007 which reviewed ways to improve customer orientation and delivery in public services. There were also studies on the role of the state at different spatial scales (HMG 2007b).

The word 'delivery' is pivotal here because in the post-2004 planning system, delivery means just that – completed development on the ground, rather than a plan which may or may not be implemented. All the government documentation about LDFs reinforces this delivery role, although a failure to hear this on the part of practitioners and the local governance apparatus is forcing Government to be ever more explicit about this in policy documents. The tests of soundness for the LDF (Planning Inspectorate National Service 2005; 2007; 2008b; CLG 2008c) reinforce this role through each test, whether it is that there should be an evidence base or that the LDF should be the spatial expression of the Sustainable Community Strategy (SCS) and the required alignment with other local authority plans. This is also shown in the preparation for the introduction of Community Infrastructure Levy (CLG 2008e; 2009g).

The translation of this approach into all scales of government is through a number of means including the harnessing of existing underused resources – people, property, investment and places. At the local level, the precedence of the role of the economy for the period 2009–2012, has been signalled through the economic duty on local authorities to promote economic regeneration (CLG and BERR; 2008a) and also through the National Indicator set. Although not communicated as a coherent policy stream by central government, the range of area-based initiatives that seek to link social housing with work, the identification of those areas which have the highest level of residents on incapacity benefit (HM Treasury 2004; HM Treasury 2006), the return of 14–19 training to local authorities and improving public transport within conurbations (Lucci and Hildreth 2008) all represent contributing elements to meeting these overall objectives.

It is possible to see a similar stream of activity emerging for the use of capital assets. The current pressure on health providers to manage their fixed assets in a way which contributes to the delivery of their services is now being set out for all government departments and agencies.[2] All political parties support this type of approach and its extension to the local level, particularly through the transformation agreement (HM Treasury 2007b). This approach views public assets primarily as a means of supporting delivery to citizens, businesses and other agencies rather than assets 'belonging' to any one agency or service (HM Treasury 2009b). Thus, the recent proposal from Essex County Council to manage post offices, the development of multiple service hubs in Ashford by the district council working with Kent County Council and single public agency service access in Wychavon District Council are all evidence of this new kind of approach in customer-focussed asset management. This thinking can relate to existing or new facilities. The development of a single capital programme for public and private investment at all spatial scales is now emerging, which will combine together with the means to will these changes. Although the market varies in different parts of the country, the variation within an authority can be as great as within regions and it is this kind of granular approach which is now expected to be used to harness investment through infrastructure planning, whether through the use of public resources or developer contributions.

Although it is difficult to identify how the policy strands which make up integrated spatial planning emerged from this nexus, it also clear that there was a wide search for successful public policy across the globe at the heart of Government during this period. The result has been an approach to spatial planning which is more integrated with other public services, has as its main focus the delivery of infrastructure and whose success will be measured by the extent to which it can deliver more effective public service investment at the local level which supports the attainment of wider objectives for the area. This approach has been put under a place shaping banner (Lyons 2007) although it also has much synergy with the original focus of planning in 1947.

CHAPTER 2

THE LOCAL GOVERNANCE CONTEXT OF THE ENGLISH SPATIAL PLANNING SYSTEM

INTRODUCTION

From 2000 it was clear that the local development plan would work within the vision set by community strategy rather than expecting the two plans to be equal and parallel, i.e. not overtly touching each other (Morphet 2002). A major reform of local government powers and constitutions in 2000 created a new operating environment for planning activity. It separated the development and delivery of planning policy from planning's regulatory role in determining planning applications. These reforms in local governance started a process of change that was to be the foundation of the 2004 Planning and Compulsory Purchase Act and to give spatial planning its new role. This chapter outlines these changes in more detail in order to provide greater understanding of the role of spatial planning post-2004. These reforms continue to be developed and implemented through new legislation such as the 2007 Local Government and Public Involvement in Health Act, the 2007 Sustainable Communities Act and the 2009 Local Democracy, Economic Development and Construction Act.

The introduction of spatial planning as part of the reconstructed planning system in 2004 inserted it as an essential component of the structure of local governance. The delivery role of spatial planning has been set out in more detail in government policy for planning and for local government, e.g. in PPS 1 (ODPM 2005e) and PPS 12 (CLG 2008c), Planning Together (CLG 2009a) and in the Local Government White Paper 2006 (CLG 2006a). However, there has been little consideration of how spatial planning works within these new arrangements which are more joined-up, evidence-based, place focussed and performance managed than ever before.

Before the 2004 reforms, development planning was frequently seen as something separate from the rest of local governance structures, partners and agencies. It operated to its own rhythm. Its long time scales and process-based approach often discouraged others inside local organisations from working with it. The focus on process inevitably overshadowed the role of planning and the wider contribution it could make. The slow speed frequently alienated others within the organisation. More importantly, the planning process was often regarded as being an impediment to taking any action and with it an inability to respond quickly to any changes in local circumstances, such as a closure of a major business or the availability of new funding or investment that was available on a competitive basis with other areas. Frequently, responses were developed by local, regional and national government agencies despite the planning system.

For those who were delivering the development planning system before 2004, the use of specialist language and processes led to separation and isolation. Planning services were increasingly incorporated within larger organisational groups of activities for management purposes as the strategic contribution of the development plan was perceived as reducing. Heads of planning services were frequently dropped from local authority management teams as their role and contribution appeared to be more procedural rather than strategic (CLG 2006a). Increased pressure from central government on local authority performance, including that of planning services, encouraged local authority chief executives to focus chief planners on improving the performance of development control. Those planners who were frustrated by this loss of status, the rule-based approach to the planning system and wider engagement, frequently left planning in order to move into the private sector or other public service roles (Durning 2007).

Planning was also operating within a changing local governance context, although this was not internalised within the local planning system. The scale and extent of these local governance reforms started to increase the distance between planning services and the rest of the organisation. The development plan had long served as the major strategic plan for the area and the local authority but, following the 2000 Local Government Act, this was replaced by the community strategy which every local authority had a duty to prepare. It was also identified as the 'plan of plans' for the area from the outset and this was recognised in the Planning Green Paper (DTLR 2001b). As the community strategy was not subjected to the same processes of examination and adoption as the development plan, many planners were slow to appreciate its strong and increasing role. It was, however, required to have a sustainability appraisal as an overarching policy document that would commit to priorities and expenditure for the area.

LOCAL GOVERNMENT: THE IMPLICATIONS OF THE 2000 REFORMS FOR PLANNING

(I) EXECUTIVE AND REGULATORY ROLES

The reform of local government is significant and wide ranging (Morphet 2008) and was high on the agenda of the incoming Labour Government and has been continuous since they took power in 1997. The reform programme continues with cross- party commitment and was described by Nick Raynsford (2004) as being at least a ten-year programme from 2004 onwards. After 18 years of a Conservative Government, this was one of a number of reforms that were ready to be implemented. Some of these, such as devolution for Scotland and Wales, had been long promised whilst the Labour Party had been in opposition and there was an immediate effort to move forward on implementation. For local government, the reforms were stimulated by a variety of reasons including past concerns about local government corruption on planning matters, a perceived sense that local government worked in an opaque, 'back room' environment and that the community's views were not sought or taken into account in a systematic way. The Government was also concerned that local government could become its Achilles heel, with poor performance and low election turn-outs, which would undermine success at any forthcoming national election (Morphet 2008). As the 1998 White Paper stated:

> People need councils which serve them well. Councils need to listen to, lead and build up their local communities. We want to see councils working in part-nership with others, making their contribution to the achievement of our aims for improving people's quality of life.
>
> To do this, councils needed to break free from old fashioned practices and attitudes. There is a long and proud tradition of councils serving their communi-ties. But the world and how we live today is very different from when our current systems of local government were established. There is no future in the old models of councils trying to plan and run most services. It does not provide the services which people want, and cannot do so in today's world. Equally there is no future for councils which are inward looking – more concerned to maintain their structures and protect their vested interest than listening to their local people and leading their communities.
>
> (Modern local government in touch with the people, DETR 1998)

The programme of change that commenced in 1997 culminated in the Local Government Act 2000. Following this, each council was to have its own written constitution and a new ethical framework. Each council had to separate the role of the executive from the rest of its functions, including regulation. This latter change had an immediate and direct implication for planning. Since 1888, each council had operated through a system that delegated power from the council to specialist committees. The exact distribution of responsibilities to committees was a matter for each council to decide but, before the 2000 reforms, the vast majority of councils had a committee that included planning policy and planning applications. The work of the planning committee was frequently broken down so that planning policy and key planning applications were considered by the committee, whilst the majority of planning applications were considered by sub-committees which could also be established to sit for different parts of the local authority area. Before 2000, the majority of planning applications would be determined by the planning committee.

After the Local Government Act 2000, the roles of councillors were divided into three separate elements and the powers of each were determined through this legislation. The main feature of the new governance model was the separation between that part of the council which made decisions and undertook the leadership role not just in the local authority but also for the area, to be known as the executive, and the rest of the council's members. The executive could take a variety of forms including a directly elected mayor or an executive of up to ten councillors or a mixture of the two. For those councillors no longer in decision-making roles on committees, their key functions were to be regulation, scrutiny and that of a ward councillor, continuing to represent the views and needs of their constituencies to the council. The role of the council, comprising of all the councillors, was one that agreed key strategies and plans and approved the budget. The governance of the local authority was now more like a three-legged stool, with power being allocated to each of its three-component parts and not providing the ability for any one of the three to exercise the powers of either of the other two parts. Thus, the individual roles of the council, the executive, (whatever its form) and scrutiny were established.

The separation of planning regulation from planning policy led to the break-up of existing planning committees. At the same time, the drive for speed and efficiency in processing planning applications led to increasing proportions of planning applications being determined by officers under local schemes of delegated decision making. These changes were significant and the underlying reasoning for them was not well understood. The separation between the executive and those councillors involved in planning regulation, making decisions on planning applications, was a means to implement a separation of powers that has been reshaping government since 1997. For example, this has included the separation of the Supreme Court from the House of Lords (HMG 2007b) and, for planning, through the establishment of the Infrastructure Planning Commission (CLG 2009f). A second reason was that the executive was now emerging to play a key leadership and promoter role for the local area (see Box 2.1). This separation would enable executive councillors to develop ways of working in partnership, to promote local investment and development schemes without then being seen to give planning permission for schemes that they had promoted. The increasingly clear code of conduct for councillors involved in making planning decisions also reinforced this separation (Planning Advisory Service 2008e).

However, for those councillors now comprising the executive, there was a degree of discomfort within this new political framework. Back bench councillors felt excluded and they lobbied to be incorporated into decision-making processes in an informal way through sounding boards or advisory committees. Although executive members could be permitted to exercise power and make decisions speedily and

Box 2.1   Responsibilities of executive in local authorities

> The responsibilities of the executive:
>
> *   translate the wishes of the community into action;
> *   represent the authority and its community interests to the outside world;
> *   build coalitions and work in partnership with all sectors of the community, and
>   bodies from outside the community, including business and public sectors;
> *   ensure effective delivery of the programme on which it was elected;
> *   prepare policy plans and proposals;
> *   take decisions on resources and priorities;
> *   draw up the annual budget including capital plans for submission to the full
>   council.

Source: DETR 1998: §3.39

on their own under the new legislation, many new council constitutions replicate the former committee system in some way and executive members frequently make decisions jointly in cabinet meetings.

Since 2000, the role of local authority executives has developed. Frequently, executive members are described as portfolio holders, with an overview of a range of services and activities which need to operate together. This role has moved away from a single issue lead as was common under the former committee system and developed as a thematic lead, e.g. housing and regeneration, the environment, neighbourhood and place. In some cases, this has further reduced the role of planning within the considerations of the executive. For planners, the leading councillor for planning is frequently the one who chairs the planning committee where planning regulation is undertaken. The requirements of the development plan and now the Local Development Framework, which are key components of the executive's delivery role, have been lost through lack of understanding and focus.

All these changes have evolved slowly and locally and without any real consideration of their implications. For planners, unaware of the wider changes that have been underway, there has been an attempt to cope with them by making them operate in ways that are understandable to them. Undoubtedly, this lack of parallel development, as the local governance system has changed, has had implications for planners in the public and private sectors alike. In the public sector, particularly in local government, the need to deal with change has sometimes been resisted or viewed as a loss of status. For planners in the private sector, there has been less understanding of the role of the executive in promotion and advocacy of change and delivery for the area.

Another form of the executive is that of the directly elected mayor. A mayor is an individual who is a figurehead for the place and provides transparent accountability.

A mayoral approach is also considered to be an essential feature of galvanising support and achieving economic growth based on the role played by the city mayors in the United States and Europe. The most well-known form of this executive governance model is the creation of a directly elected mayor of London that has been in place since 2000. A number of other local authorities have also selected this approach although it has not attained the popular support that was expected. In some locations, the directly elected mayor has had poor relationships with other councillors, e.g. Doncaster and Stoke. Nevertheless, all parties (CLG 2009d; Conservative Party 2009) continue to promote the mayoral option for the executive as their preferred approach, particularly for larger cities. A variation on this model was suggested in the 2006 Local Government White Paper (CLG 2006a) which would allow for one of the directly elected councillors to become the leader for the four-year period of the council through an indirect vote of all the councillors. More recently, this type of governance model has been proposed for city regions, alongside directly elected mayoral options (CLG 2009d).

In some smaller councils, a version of the pre-2000 local government system remains. In so-called 'fourth option' councils, the 2000 Local Government Act allowed a version of the former system to remain. Hoverer, the 2006 Local Government White Paper proposed that local authorities that adopted the fourth option should move into the same governance structures as other councils. A number of fourth option councils are fighting this move and wish to retain their current mode of operation. In these authorities, it is still possible to have a planning committee which combines policy and regulation, although other aspects of the councillors' code in making planning decisions still applies in these areas.

Concerns about the role of councillor codes in the determination of planning applications continue at the local level. All councillors are required to place their personal and financial interests on a public register and these include the interests of members of their close family and any business associates or community organisations they may serve. Underlying uncertainty and a risk averse approach to this system has had more serious effects at the local level. A failure to understand the need to achieve separation between promotional and regulatory roles of councillors has led to some local authorities not implementing the split in councillor functions for planning that were established in 2000. This has led to confusion in the implementation of the regulatory codes used by local authorities. Rather than attempt to separate executive and regulatory councillors as required, a mixed system has remained, giving rise to concerns that executive members cannot proactively promote development for which they are also regulators.

This reduces the potential effectiveness of the council in promoting those changes which they consider important through the executive and frequently alienates leading councillors from planning matters which they see more as a specialist interest than a major agent for change. Councillors interested in planning are frequently characterised as those who are interested in detail and process rather than having a strategic view. Serving on a planning regulation committee requires training and many hours spent together, including time on site visits. Councillors interested in planning regulation frequently develop a bond which is partly formed by the teasing of their colleagues not interested in planning regulation.

(II) VERTICAL INTEGRATION: THE ROLE OF TARGETS

A second significant feature of the new local governance arrangements implemented in 2000 was the introduction of greater amount of targeted delivery. This extension from the vertical integration has come primarily through the introduction of PSAs which have bound individual government departments to the achievement of specific outcomes. PSAs are established to deliver the targets set out by the Treasury within three-year periods of the Comprehensive Spending Reviews (CSRs). PSA targets are associated with specific performance measures. For a number of government departments, the achievement of their performance targets has depended on delivery through local authorities and other local organisations such as schools and hospitals. This has led to an increase in performance targets being set by government departments for public agencies including the police, Primary Care Trusts in health, schools and planning. This has inevitably led to a focus on vertical integration between government departments and local authorities where increasingly prescribed ways of spending money or setting outcomes and how they are measured have been established.

Until 2006, the development of PSA targets was largely individual for each government department. Central government departments have had separate targets without any interrelationship or codependency within or between them. Inevitably, the targets passed down to local authorities and other local agencies have also been set within a silo framework. This has resulted in the use of a target and performance culture which can be contradictory and self-defeating (Hood 2007). Targets set to focus on local outcomes have been more successful (Van de Walle and Bovaird 2007). Frequently, a number of different government targets have been set that measure the same outcome in different ways, such as that for teenage pregnancy rates which, according to central government folklore, had fourteen different measured targets across government departments in 2005.

Local government became increasingly concerned about the effects of these individuated targets at the local level. The targets were set centrally and had to be made to work within real communities and through staff who were not divided up in the same way as government departments. The targets were also frequently accompanied by restrictions on the use of funding, with some government departments putting 'golden handcuffs' on funding to meet their own objectives, despite increasing funding freedoms and flexibilities. This significantly reduced the potential to work on what was most important in the local area. The same was true of other local organisations. The police, for example, may have national targets to reduce domestic burglary, whereas car crime might be more important in an area; paying attention to a national target reduces resources to meet local issues.

Local authorities were also changing as a result of the introduction of the new governance regime in 2000. Performance in individual authorities was improving each year, whilst the freedoms promised at the outcome of this improvement seemed further away than ever. A ten-year review of local government was instigated in 2004 which was part of a move towards increased local governance. New localism, as this concept was labelled, was initially viewed as a political 'fad' and not something that was necessarily going to shape the future of the relationship between local and central government (Morphet 2006). Local government might want more power, and generated the right to expect it as their performance improved. However, there was a distinct difference between the local appetite for change and the views of civil servants in a number of central departments who wished to maintain control of what they saw as 'their' money and the achievement of the delivery targets that the Treasury had set for them. The move to a greater localism, or 'double devolution' a phrase coined by David Milliband (2006) was promoted by the then Office of the Deputy Prime Minister, the Treasury and the Cabinet Office. Other departments promoted different means to demonstrate some kind of devolved service but still retaining control (Blears 2002).

This targeted approach started to play a bigger role in planning. Through the PSA targets given to the department responsible for planning (ODPM 2002–2006), more housing delivery was required. ODPM was provided with funding to incentivise the achievement of these targets and this was paid to local authorities through Planning Delivery Grant (PDG). Planning was also being charged with delivering a speedier planning regulation service and this was the focus in the use of PDG. The role of the development plan in preparation for future housing delivery was largely overlooked at this stage.

(III) PLACE AND LOCALISM

Much has been written about the theory of place (Healey 2009) and its interconnected meanings with space (Soja 1996) – if place is the definite then space is the conceptual, belonging more to imagined communities (Anderson 2006). Places can be recognised, lived in but also 'other' in their ability to exclude either by formal means – barriers, gates or distance or by informal means of class, gender or race. Yet places are a point of identity and identification; they are meaningful in people's lives and much effort is expended in either improving them or maintaining them as they are (Neill 2004). Places are also important for personal well-being, as fear of crime or other anti-social behaviour in some places can mark out territory and exclude others.

In public policy over the last 50 years, there has been interplay between the preferred points of national policy intervention between people and places, although the predominant policy mode has always been accompanied by interventions on the other. For much of this period, place- or area-based policies have been the most effective approach from Educational Priority Areas (1968), Improvement Areas (1987), Housing Renewal Areas and neighbourhood renewal. The focus on the individual had some positive outcomes but the wider diseconomies of separate, nationally set targets led to funding and intervention silos that were never intended. A more holistic approach that was sought (6, P. et al. 2002). This led to a return to place as a key policy determinant.

The duty to promote economic, social and environmental well-being that was placed on local authorities in the 2000 Local Government Act provides a means of focussing on place. The Audit Commission (2004) found that the way in which local authorities were able to pursue this well-being duty was being hampered by the multiple targets and funding streams which were frequently contradictory and their national focus did not represent what was most important locally. The Audit Commission described this as a 'humpty-dumpty' effect, where Government's frag-mented approach to places had to be put together at the local level to make a more coherent and useful approach. The report also identified a series of key ways in which local leadership could improve local well-being and these have become an underpinning framework within which many subsequent initiatives have been located (2004: 3):

- developing coherent programmes of change that are based on local needs and opportunities;
- tapping into different funding streams without being driven by them;
- engaging with communities to ensure that interventions are responsive to local concerns;
- making the most of skills and resources of all sectors to ensure that the area has the capacity to deliver its ambitions and priorities;
- capturing learning from previous activity and transferring it to new interventions;
- paying attention to the sustainability of interventions, ensuring mainstreaming in the longer term.

The report influenced approaches to achieving these changes. The first was the development of a local contract between public sector bodies and the state for the achievement of place-based changes. This was in the form of a LAA and followed on from an earlier version of local PSA approaches. The second outcome was the emergence of the LSP as the focal point for joined-up local working. Although this shift in direction was clear, it also took a while for central and local agencies to appreciate that place had replaced individualism as the dominant national policy driver and that this would be enacted at local rather than national levels. In order to support this understanding, further narrative was supplied. It was the Lyons Report on the future of local government (Lyons 2007) which identified the key role of local authorities as 'place shaping', through their leadership convening and coordination of other agencies at the local level. The Lyons Report also established a new role for local government in England following the re-introduction of devolution in Northern Ireland and the introduction of devolution in Scotland and Wales. Lyons identified several components of the local authority's role in place shaping as:

- building and shaping local identity;
- representing the community;
- regulating harmful and disruptive behaviours;
- maintaining the cohesiveness of the community and supporting debate within it, ensuring that smaller voices are heard;
- helping to resolve disagreements;
- working to make the local economy more successful while being sensitive to pressures on the environment;
- understating local needs and preferences and making sure that the right services are provided to local people;
- working with other bodies to respond to complex challenges such as natural disasters and other emergencies.

Lyons identified local authorities as convenors in their areas. This included the coordination of agencies and initiatives to deliver a more joined-up approach to solving problems and promoting the economy at the local level. This leadership of the locality was identified as a positive role and one that was based on vision, evidence, delivery and convening together all those involved in achieving a better local place. Lyons also recognised that both citizens and central government departments had low trust and confidence in local government. This would make the development of this integrated role more challenging. Lyons identified that local authorities faced considerable barriers in the current system if they were going to take on this local leadership role. These barriers included limited flexibility on the use of resources, confused accountability and continuing pressures on services such as those for older people. Another potential barrier to achieving better places that Lyons identified is that local authorities do not appreciate the power of the tools they have that can be used to promote and develop places. In Lyons' view, local authorities have become overly dependent on central government for guidance and, on occasion, local authorities have also used this dependency relationship as an excuse for taking politically unpalatable actions. Spatial planning falls into this latter category, particularly in the provision of new housing, waste facilities and new roads.

Lyons' report on local government represents a new constitutional settlement for local government in England. It provides a secure role and identifies local authorities as those with lead responsibility at the local level. This was a significant change from the view that local authorities are the delivery arm of central government and that all their activities were controlled by legislation. The identification of 'place' as the delivery vehicle for this change in policy narrative was significant. It also underpins much of what spatial planning has been set up to deliver. The establishment of a constitutional role for local government was followed by a Local Government White Paper (CLG 2006a), *Strong and Prosperous Communities*, and acted as a second means of delivery for the place shaping approach. The White Paper was focussed on place and the communities which live in them and was described as a 'new settlement' for the future. It also introduced an increasingly 'bottom up' view of the way in which places work. This verges on the notion of a subsidiarity test which has also emerged as a potentially important tool in the local delivery of services (Hope and Leslie 2009). For a highly centralised state, which worked through the development and application of targets during the period 1997–2004, this all represented major change. It signalled a move away from a centralised way of developing and delivering policy and recognition that continuing centralisation was counter productive. It also failed to relate to local cultures and evidence of actions that are needed to achieve change and improvement. Localisation has now emerged as a concept that has political support across all parties. It has also been taken further in thinking by the Conservative Party which undertook its own policy reviews for the general election in 2010 (Conservative Party 2009).

So what role has spatial planning in the delivery of place? The White Paper identified the role of spatial planning, which draws together 'land-use, economic and social development, transport, housing and the environment as a critical underpinning to this place shaping approach' (§4.55). Each place faces different challenges and policy is designed to be more local. This further develops the role of spatial planning as a horizontal integration tool.

(IV) HORIZONTAL INTEGRATION: JOINED-UP PUBLIC SECTOR

The application of the localisation principle and place as the dominant policy driver has led to changes in the way that most local authorities work internally. There has also been a shift in the way in which local authorities work with their partners. The local authority retains legal responsibilities for its work but it is now the LSP, which it convenes, that takes responsibility for the relationships and performance of local bodies within the area. These changes came in the 2007 Local Government and Public Involvement in Health Act. The implications of these changes are significant for the local authority and the ways in which a more integrated approach to local delivery can be undertaken are being developed in many areas. A focus on place and the need to move away from silo-based targets have brought a new focus on horizontal integration between local agencies. Targets remain as a means of driving these changes but they have been reduced to 198 in each local authority area and many of them require cross agency working in order to be successful.

The LSP is at the heart of this local horizontal integration. The LSP is a non-statutory body which local authorities were encouraged to establish from 2001. The LSP is where all the key local stakeholders meet and determine how, through the actions of their individual bodies and increasingly jointly, they can improve the outcomes for the area. The LSP is convened by the local authority, although there may be a chair from one of the partners, e.g. police, health or the private sector. Informal guidance on how LSPs might operate and suggested membership was published in 2001. Since then, the 2007 Local Government and Public Involvement in Health Act has placed a duty on the public sector members of the LSP to cooperate with each other. This duty of cooperation has now been extended to schools. The LSP is not a corporate body and does not have its own staff, although there will be staff supporting it.

Since the 2007 Act, the LSP has been given some key lead responsibilities including:

- SCS
- Local Area Agreement (LAA)
- Comprehensive Area Assessment (CAA) (http://oneplace.direct.gov.uk)
- overview and alignment of resources
- joint use of evidence
- consultation
- performance management
- scrutiny.

The LSPs are required to have an executive board of decision makers, rather than place holders, and thematic groups which are cross cutting and made up of members from all sectors (CLG 2008d). These new duties and responsibilities for LSPs came into practical effect on 1 April 2009 and it is likely that many LSPs will not conform to these working arrangements as yet. This is assessed through CAA, where the successful joint working of localities to meet local needs is reviewed by the Audit Commission (2009a). There is likely to be a convergence of LSP practice over time.

The LSP has the role of bringing together the evidence and identifying how and what needs to be done and by whom in the area. This evidence base is comprised of contributions from all organisations working in the area and will include surveys, data analysis, scrutiny reports, parish plans and consultation reports. The SCS is the place where this combination of aspiration and action is expressed in a 20-year programme (CLG 2008a). Within the new local governance architecture, it is the SCS that provides the overarching framework, replacing what planners have traditionally identified as the role of the development plan. The role of the LSP at the local level is still a work in progress. Some government departments, particularly the Department of Health (DH), have understood the LSP's power for managing resources and have started to encourage health leads in chairing LSPs in a number of key localities (CLG 2008b).

Some of the local authority objections to LSPs, based on fears of loss of control that arose when first introduced in 2001, have diminished since the clarification of the local authority's 'convening' role. Whilst criticism of the lack of democratic mandate remains, the power of local authority scrutiny over health, the police and other public agencies is increasing. The duty of public bodies to cooperate contained in the 2007 Local Government and Public Involvement in Health Act will also have some effect. The final component in this local approach is pressure towards the devolution of central state activities to the local level in a call for government departments to have a 'duty to devolve', thus demonstrating a practical application of subsidiarity (Hope and Leslie 2009). As Bounds (2009) suggests, this move towards local integration that combines horizontal integration between local authorities and agencies through city regions is now being accompanied by reverse engineering, as city regions may potentially start running central government services that operate at the local level. A similar initiative is also being developed through Total Place (HM Treasury 2009a; Morphet 2009c), which is targeted at improving efficiency between all public sector providers through similar application of horizontal and vertical integration. This approach moves towards reducing the size of the central English state to one which is more comparable with Scotland, Wales and Northern Ireland.

This approach to local horizontal integration has been accompanied by three new interrelated regimes that are all target driven. They also all have a significant impact on spatial planning. These three are:

(a) Local Area Agreements (LAAs)
LAAs are 'contracts' between central government and places, which are represented by Local Strategic Partnerships. Each place has up to 35 individual targets which the local authority and its partners are committed to achieve within a three-year period. Each target has a senior responsible owner (SRO) and a delivery plan. The SRO and those working together on a particular target do not have to include the local authority.

The targets range over a number of issues, including health, CO_2 reduction, independent living and can be seen on www.localpriorities.communities.gov.uk for each area. Each individual LAA has numerical targets associated to the delivery of each of the 35 specific targets chosen for the LAA and these can be seen on www.idea.gov.uk.

The LAA is now part of the spatial planning process and local authorities have to demonstrate how the development plan is delivering the LAA (CLG 2008c). This includes all targets and not only those that have an obvious planning relevance, such as those on the provision of net additional housing (NI 154), gross additional affordable housing (NI 155) and available housing sites (NI 159). Targets such as those focussed on reducing obesity or active engagement in physical activity may have implications for the provision of adequate sports and leisure facilities. CO_2 reduction targets will be delivered through land-use allocations and policies.

(b) National indicators

The targets set out in each LAA are derived from a set of 198 national indicators. In addition to delivering the LAA, local authorities have to monitor their progress against these indicators on an annual basis.

(c) CAA (or One Place)

The progress of the local authority and its partners in delivering the LAA and improvement against the national targets is evaluated by the Audit Commission through CAA from 2009 (Audit Commission 2009a). This approach follows on from similar local performance-based systems such as Best Value (Carmona and Sieh 2005) and Comprehensive Performance Assessment (CPA). Unlike Best Value and CPA, CAA will provide reports on both the area and the local authority. The area-based report indicates how agencies are working together to deal with issues that they are facing. It will also review how resources are being used together to improve services and reduce other costs. It is also focussed on the use of land and building assets in a combined way through a 'use of resources' assessment. The oversight and ownership of these three performance processes now sits with the members of the LSP.

These regimes all focus the LSP on delivery. The LAA provides a short-term delivery focus, primarily aimed at changing people's behaviour by encouraging healthier or sustainable lifestyles over a three-year period. Longer-term delivery that involves investment in land, buildings and facilities is achieved through the Local Development Framework that lasts for 15 years. The LDF includes both a delivery programme of infrastructure requirements that have a good prospect of delivery and this is accompanied by a delivery strategy that includes the governance arrangements for coordinating decisions on local investment, particularly from the public sector, over the rest of the 15 yeas that is required for the LDF. The LSP is centrally engaged in the leadership of this process and the LDF is one of its main delivery mechanisms. These relationships are shown in Figure 2.1.

Figure 2.1 Local governance and delivery architecture

Source: the author

There are a number of indications that this increased focus on place and join-ing or integrating local public agencies to deliver it has support in all three main political parties in England. For the Conservative Party, a more local approach has been developed in its most detailed form in London. Here, the Mayor and London councils, the group that represents all local authorities in London, have signed a *London City Charter* (April 2009) which has some significant features, including:

- The application of the principle of subsidiarity, i.e. that 'local and regional deci-sions are made as close to people as is possible' (4).
- Reshaping the Mayor's role in relation to planning and the way in which he will exercise his powers.
- Establishing a series of key joint action areas between the Mayor and the bor-oughs to include:
  - transport
  - economic recovery
  - youth violence
  - climate change
  - improving police accountability
  - health care
  - winning resources for London.
- Establishing a Congress of Leaders for all the local authorities in London.
- Establishing a charter board of chief executives of local authorities and other public bodies which will meet at least quarterly in order to coordinate the work of London bodies, set annual priorities and advise the congress. It can also invite any other public service chief executive to meetings as an observer. The bodies on the charter board represented by their chief executives are:

- local authorities
- police
- fire and rescue
- transport commissioner
- London development agency
- homes and communities agency
- strategic health authority for London.

The wider landscape of Conservative policy at the local level is set out in two key documents, *Control Shift Returning Power to Local Communities* (Conservative Party 2009) and *Open Source Planning* (Conservative Party 2010). They set out to develop an approach to 'radical decentralisation' (2). These papers suggests a range of ways in which local people can be more in control of local decision making and revenue raising, including:

- helping local communities to benefit from housing development;
- retaining financial benefits from new business rates;
- providing a general power of competence for local authorities;
- abolition of targets;
- giving local people control of how central government money is spent in their area;
- phasing out ring fencing of funding;
- abolishing regional planning and housing powers and allowing local authorities to revise their LDFs in the light of the removal of these targets;
- abolishing government office for London;
- abolishing RDAs;
- replacing Infrastructure Planning Commission;
- promoting referenda for directly elected mayors in the major cities.

So if this is an all-party approach to delivering more local control, will this make horizontal integration more likely to happen? A key issue here will be the combination of legislative change and changes in control over the civil service. In the past, the civil service survival strategies have been ones which reduce the headcount and budget but retain control and include:

- establishing non-departmental public bodies;
- creating next steps agencies;
- inhabitation strategies where former civil servants take over leading roles in other agencies which work closely with them.

The new approach emerging as the next survival strategy seems to be the takeover of key posts in local government as set out by Hope and Leslie (2009). However, the pressure on localisation, whether through Total Place or City Regions initiatives, is moving towards a new form of horizontal integration that may not have been experienced in England before. In some ways, the new format may represent the structure of local government when it was created in 1888, with all-encompassing powers for raising funding and responding to local needs in a variety of ways. This unified approach was broken down as the state increased in size. It may return as the state reduces it scale to meet its wider economic objectives.

(v) MEETING WIDER NATIONAL OBJECTIVES

In addition to the general trends in the development of local governance that have been set out in this chapter, there have also been a number of key thematic issues which have transcended all of these and that keep reappearing over time. These are:

- housing supply
- efficiency in procurement
- shared services
- transformational services
- climate change
- economy.

In the period since 2000, many of these issues have been the subject of specific reviews undertaken under the auspices of the Treasury and frequently referred to as 'personality' reviews. They have been a means of allowing Government to receive advice upon which they have then shifted policy. The personality reviews are frequently undertaken by someone who is in business or who has particular knowledge of the issues. Hence, Sir Nicholas Stern has reviewed climate change (2009), Kate Barker housing and then planning (2004; 2006), Rod Eddington had reviewed transport (2006), Philip Hampton (2005) has reviewed regulation and Peter Gershon (2003) and now Michael Bichard (HM Treasury 2009a) have reviewed efficiency. These reviews are influential and can be pivotal in signposting changes in policy direction. The leaders of the reviews have teams of civil servants to work with them and to some extent they are a means through which Government can change policy direction without loss of face. If civil servants came up with radically different policies, it could seem as if the government had been on the wrong track and be subject to criticism. Commissioning an expert to provide an opinion which leads to change, on the other hand, can appear to be more responsible and accountable. This role is also undertaken by think-tanks, such as the New Local Government Network, the Policy Exchange, the Institute for Public Policy Research (IPPR) and the Social Market Foundation.

Of these reviews, two have had a specific relationship with planning and its delivery of infrastructure including housing. Led by Kate Barker, they have provided a means of examining the wider system of the land market and institutional investment

Table 2.1 Comprehensive spending review process

CSR 1	CSR 2
Year 1 Background research on new issues, assessment of previous programme effectiveness.	
Year 2 Bids and lobbying for resources from departments.	
Year 3 Finalisation of review and publication – generally in the autumn.	*Year 1* Background research on new issues, assessment of previous programme effectiveness.
Year 4 Preparation for implementation; pilot work.	*Year 2* Bids and lobbying for resources from departments.
Year 5 Implementation.	*Year 3* Finalisation of review and publication – generally in the autumn.

Source: the author

in the provision of housing. These reviews of the land-use planning system also considered the way in which developers' contributions are made available through the system to support infrastructure planning and delivery. However, although less associated with planning, the Varney Review (2006) looked at the distribution of land and buildings in public use and promoted a more systematic approach to the use of co-location and shared back offices. This approach has been translated directly into the development planning process (CLG 2008c).

The work on efficiency and the reform of local government is now being taken forward by Sir Michael Bichard in the Review of Operational Effectiveness (HM Treasury 2009a: 69). In this report, he has developed the work of the Lyons Report on the role of local government, place shaping and funding and the report provides a key background document to the Spending Review in 2010, which will be delivered in 2012 (see Table 2.1 for process). Bichard's recommendations build on and extend those of Lyons and Varney and include a number of recommendations, most of which have a significant potential role in the delivery of places:

- the introduction of Total Place, a full mapping of public expenditure and delivery by place;
- accelerated joint working in local areas between all public sector bodies, including central government departments;
- strengthening Local Strategic Partnerships;
- developing capacity across instructional boundaries;
- improving public service innovation and e-delivery.

In order to achieve this, Bichard states that it will be important for local leaders to continue to work together in a more integrated way, whilst central government departments will need to change the application of national delivery structures to make this difference (ibid.: 72). As stated, without any specific changes in incentives to extending joint working, these statements could be greater exhortation. However, the developing role of local expenditure programmes and delivery plans can make a significant contribution to changing behaviours and outcomes, and the role of spatial planning in local delivery is significant in achieving this. A pilot study *Counting Cumbria* (LGA 2009), undertaken to consider the Total Place approach, has demonstrated the range of public expenditure at the local level. This pilot focussed on revenue expenditure of services to support people but did not include any major review of capital spending. However, as seen above, the arrangements for the publication of local spending reports has now included capital expenditure as part of the process. Accompanying this and in order to facilitate delivery, Bichard has also recommended a further reduction in funding ring fences so that budgets can increasingly be part of a local pot to meet local needs (ibid.: 75). At the same time, he recommended extending the local performance framework, currently operating across local authorities, the police and health across the whole of the public sector, and this seems likely from 2012.

Asset management and property is also part of the re-engineering of the local state as they provide both the means and the delivery of much of what is required to join up at the local level. However, as the Carter Report has demonstrated, 'obtaining and compiling data about the size of the total estate owned and used by the public sector is challenging' (HM Treasury 2009b: 4). Of all the public sector property that is owned, Carter estimates that two-thirds is owned by local government, with a value of £240bn in 2008, although there may be a difference between book and disposal values in both directions, i.e. up and down. Reviewing and utilising the public estate is a key way of raising finance for other needed infrastructure but also to reduce running costs, which can also help to fund other services. In central government, it is estimated that one-third of current floor space for office workers could be reduced to bring them in line with private sector standards. This again would release assets and reduce running costs.

In order to reap these rewards, the Carter Report has proposed centralising the government's property policy and support to include all property in the public sector, including that in local government. This recommendation does not propose the direct management of property but that a more integrated approach to use of property assets and their potential release could be addressed. This approach creates a helpful tool in supporting local infrastructure planning and delivery by encouraging public sector partners to be active participants in this change process, although there would need to be clear incentives to all parties to the release of these assets and the applications of funds raised for services and new infrastructure. If applied in some ways, it could reduce the appetite for joint working and hold back significant infrastructure planning and delivery.

(VI) DELIVERY

The increasing focus on delivery through a joined-up approach at the local level has come through the development of the role of:

- LSP
- LAA
- LDF
- Performance management systems
- Homes and Communities Agency (HCA) Single Conversation
- Community Infrastructure Levy (CIL).

The local authority, together with its partners, is expected to demonstrate how it is delivering change and improvement through place shaping at the local level. The delivery of joined-up services, through the alignment and pooling of revenue budgets for staff and support, is already well developed between local authorities, health agencies and the third sector. The development of aligned and pooled capital budgets is not so well advanced. However, the 2007 Budget stated that each local authority would need to develop an Infrastructure Delivery Plan (IDP) (HM Treasury) and this has been reiterated in PPS 12 (CLG 2008c), HCA guidance (2009) and CIL regulations (CLG 2009g). This infrastructure delivery in effect will be under the auspices of the LSP, within the terms of their powers implemented from 2009 and will include:

- development of common evidence bases to identify deficits;
- increases in co-location;
- reviews of criteria for investment scheme selection;
- joint development schemes on released assets;
- more development partnership working;
- a proactive approach to meeting deficit requirements by all local partners through the executive councillor and the development management process.

(VII) SCRUTINY AND OVERVIEW

If the council is to be held to account over its policies, performance and delivery, the role of the new scrutiny function is critical. For many elected councillors, the role of scrutiny seemed second best to that of being involved with committees where decisions were made, albeit that they may not have had a leading role in making these decisions. The popular view was that a scrutiny role meant being sidelined and being taken out of the process. This view was further confirmed by the apparent openness of the process which could be determined locally. It was up to each local authority to determine how the scrutiny process would fit into its own constitution and a wide variation exists. In some local authorities, the scrutiny committee has the power to call in decisions made by the executive, whilst elsewhere they will concentrate on detailed reviews of existing or proposed policies. Another option that is used is that all decisions go to the scrutiny committee before they are taken for final decision. This range of practice is common in a newly emerging policy arena and whilst it provides the ability of each local authority to use scrutiny in the way it prefers, this local discretion has also served to undermine its central contribution of holding authorities to account (Ashworth 2003).

Apart from the decision-making processes within local authorities, the emphasis on performance through best value and through scrutiny processes provides professionalism with some of its greatest challenges. As Woodman states, professions developed by departmental hierarchies 'built up formidable bases of power' (1999: 211). Between 1976 and 1995, there was a 20 per cent increase in the regulators of local government and a 133 per cent increase in the regulators of quasi-public bodies (Hood *et al.* 1998: 62). Only councillors who are not part of the executive can be members of any scrutiny process.

The way in which scrutiny operates will vary in each local authority (Sweeting and Ball 2002). Scrutiny is more likely to be used for other purposes, including the quality of outcomes of earlier decisions, best value reviews or reviews cross cutting the council. A review of good practice in overview and scrutiny conducted by Snape and Leach (2002) found that there were several key elements of good practice at the local level which included:

- the challenge of breaking away from traditional committee systems;
- the value of 'in-depth' studies of significant issues;
- the value of more informal 'small group' (and individual) work;
- the value of (selective) studies of external (or cross-cutting) issues;
- opening up the scrutiny process to their organisations and the public;
- the value of pre-decision scrutiny of key decisions (via the forward plan);
- ensuring that scrutiny is effectively (and directly) supported;
- developing a supportive senior officer culture;
- involvement in best value and performance monitoring – but on a selective basis;
- ensuring that work of overview and scrutiny is properly coordinated;
- developing a channel of communication between executive and scrutiny;
- preparing properly for 'select committee' and 'expert witness' type of work.

In effect, the issues that surrounded the introduction of overview and scrutiny function remain in practice. It is often difficult to maintain the ability to consider issues without political party pressure and there can be a climate of distrust between the executive and scrutiny. Snape and Leach (2002) also describe this as the 'critical friend' dilemma. Leach et al. (2003) extend further their explanation of this issue:

> There are limits ... to the extent to which multi-party leadership of overview and scrutiny can take place. Apart from full council meetings, they provide the main opportunity for opposition members – especially in a majority controlled council with a one party cabinet – to express their opposition. It is unrealistic to expect members who are not on the executive [whether of opposition or controlling parties] to conveniently forget their party principles and priorities when they enter a scrutiny meeting. The important issue is how they express those principles and priorities. The legitimate language of overview and scrutiny is the language of reasoned debate. Thus the challenge for an opposition member [or indeed a discomforted majority party member] is to channel their 'opposition' into an evidence-based critique of executive policy or decisions or an evidence-based argument for the adoption or modification of a policy. The appropriateness of this kind of challenge is one of the key assumptions which lie behind the operation of Select Committees in Parliament.
>
> (37–8)

Although scrutiny is a new process within local authorities in England, it had a number of critics before it was introduced. Many councillors saw the process as one that was toothless (Sweeting and Ball 2002) and one that would have no real effect on executive decision making. As Snape and Taylor (2000) point out, one of the main purposes of scrutiny is to hold the executive to account both before and after decisions are taken. The scrutiny process can refer decisions to full council but this is likely to be confined to major issues of policy rather than numerous detailed decisions. This can be undertaken by requesting a decision to be 'called in', i.e. reconsidered in some way. However, the ability of scrutiny to work with decisions related to planning applications is more complex. The Local Government Act 2000 provides that only those elected members not serving on the local authority executive can determine planning applications. However, individual planning applications cannot be subject to scrutiny.

Scrutiny in local authorities is now developing to be increasingly like the functions of Select Committees in Parliament that also have a scrutiny role. These Select Committees were established in 1980 and have now evolved in style since their introduction. They are also under review to provide them with more power (Brown 2009). As Ashworth (2003) points out, the relationship between the two models can highlight some of the weaknesses in the local authority scrutiny model, such as the lack of centrally defined powers where scrutiny committees may exercise their ability to have influence over resources, and the dependence on the support provided to them at the local level. Ashworth also points out that in Parliament, MPs have considerable specialist support to undertake their work, where this is much less likely to be the norm at the local level. However, in her research, Ashworth found that councillors within scrutiny committees indeed did have confidence in their powers, which represents a change to the initial views reported by Snape and Leach (op. cit.).

One perceived weakness in the parliamentary system is the desire of those serving on Select Committees to be members of the administration and, therefore, not to be too critical of the executive through these means. Although they may have been true in the past, there are now some MPs who see their career to be in the chairmanship of such committees, e.g. Gwyneth Dunwoody in Transport and Dr Tony Wright in public administration. The chairmanships have also become places for former ministers to take a lead, although there is still some 'tooing and froing' with the executive. However, the profile of the parliamentary Select Committees has been high at times when the official opposition has been weaker and, to some extent, to be criticised by members of your own party can be more difficult to sweep aside that to be criticised by the opposition (Mullins 2009).

Scrutiny is a way of improving the 'user voice' in local government (Wright and Ngan 2004), although it is not the only mode available. Nevertheless, the routine inclusion of a scrutiny function into local government may take some time to mature as it has in Parliament, and much of the response to scrutiny still remains negative (Johnson and Hatter nd). The future for local government scrutiny seems secure, with a national scrutiny centre now established at the University of Greenwich. At this centre, copies of all scrutiny reports in local government are held, whilst training courses for those supporting scrutiny in local government and in Parliament are offered jointly.

Since scrutiny was introduced in 2000, its role has been extended. Local authorities are now able to scrutinise other local public bodies in addition to their own activities. Residents can now appeal to scrutiny committees if they are not satisfied with the council's response to a public petition and scrutiny reports can be used as part of the evidence in decision making. Proposals coming forward (CLG 2009d) suggest that the power of scrutiny will be extended to:

- broaden the number of bodies that can be subject to scrutiny committees;
- enhance the powers that scrutiny committees have;
- enable scrutiny committees to make reports and recommendations and make the bodies formally respond to the scrutiny committee.

All of these additional proposals will support spatial planning and its delivery. The findings of scrutiny panels and their reports form part of the evidence base that needs to be taken into account in the processes of spatial planning. Scrutiny panels can review approaches to spatial planning and the likely effectiveness of its outcomes. It can consider the methods and the likely time taken. The extension of scrutiny to the LSP may mean that more joined-up approaches to delivery of the IDP will be considered directly and public agencies may be held to account for their contributions and role in these processes.

CONCLUSIONS

The pattern and framework of local governance is changing. After initially standing outside these reforms, spatial planning is now at the heart of them and there are specific implications to consider. Local governance is changing to become more coherent and joined-up. Local partners are aware of the role they need to play with others in improving and delivering better places. The processes of governance, the mechanisms for bringing together resources, evidence and assessing the quality of outcomes in places are all changing. As a place-based activity, spatial planning relates to all of these.

The implications of local governance reform in England for spatial planning are considerable. Among these are that spatial planning has:

• a position at the heart of place shaping;
• a key and proactive role in delivering change in places;
• to work with a range of other organisations and processes in order to achieve effective delivery;
• to reply on the provision of evidence and consultation responses from other organisations rather than undertake its own evidence research, except where it has a specific requirement that then will be made available to others;
• a place at the nexus of vertical and horizontal integration.

CHAPTER 3

THE ENGLISH SPATIAL PLANNING SYSTEM

INTRODUCTION

In 2004, the spatial planning system in England was introduced through LDFs and Regional Spatial Strategies (RSSs). This change in approach from development or land-use planning to spatial planning was set out in the 2004 Planning and Compulsory Purchase Act. The LDF is a loose-leaf approach to the preparation of spatial plans for an area comprising of individual Development Plan Documents (DPDs). DPDs include the Core Strategy or overarching document, issue or thematic documents and Area Action Plans (AAPs). In addition to DPDs, Supplementary Planning Documents can be prepared and these do not follow the same process of examination but can be adopted locally. The programme of preparation for each of the LDF documents is contained in the Local Development Scheme (LDS) and the process has to be accompanied by a Statement of Community Involvement (SCI). Under the preceding approach, the Unitary Development Plan (UDP) was examined in an adversarial public process to determine whether it could be adopted as the development plan for the area. Under the post-2004 approach, each DPD is examined in an inquisitorial process by a planning inspector. This process commences from the time that any DPD is submitted and, although there may be a hearing as part of this examination, this only comprises one part of the process.

The introduction of a spatial planning approach has led to some significant differences in the practice of planning as might be expected. First, it is integrated within the local governance structures and takes its lead from the SCS. Second, rather than being a policy-based approach that characterises development planning, it has moved to a delivery role, integrating the investment requirements and the means of delivering them at the local level. Spatial planning also has a role in delivering other local objectives including the targets set out in the LAAs and the transformation of public service delivery locations. It also has responsibility for reviewing and identifying public sector assets for release. In development planning, the delivery of the plan proposals was undertaken by others. In spatial planning, the delivery is a proactive role for development management. In the former system, the regulatory approach was focussed on achieving contributions for infrastructure from those promoting development, primarily the private sector. Within the spatial planning approach, the LDF is responsible for integrating the investment from all sectors as far as possible and coordinating public sector investment as part of this. This integrated delivery role is undertaken within the local governance architecture, particularly under the leadership of the LSP.

LDFs are undertaken by district, unitary, metropolitan and London authorities. County councils are responsible for preparing waste and minerals LDFs. In two-tier local government areas, county councils have to cooperate with the district councils in the preparation of the LDF. At regional level, the RSS was prepared by the Regional Assembly and had an Examination in Public. The LDF had to be in general conformity with the RSS. This will be tested by the planning inspector. In 2010, Regional Strategies replaced RSS (CLG and BIS 2010).

This chapter sets out the way in which spatial planning is being delivered in England through the LDF. It identifies the key components of the LDF. In order to be successful, LDFs have to work in an integrated way at the local level in both practical and formal ways. The components of an LDF are set out and the ways in which they work together are discussed. There is a discussion on the way in which DPDs are examined by a planning inspector, defined as the independent person, to assess whether they are to be found 'sound'. There is no formal examination of the LDF as a whole.

WHAT ARE THE COMPONENTS OF THE LOCAL DEVELOPMENT FRAMEWORK?

Whilst the components of the LDF were set out in the 2004 Planning and Compulsory Purchase Act, the local governance architecture within which the LDF is constructed has been set out since. The fuller expression of this governance framework for LDFs is set out in *Planning Policy Statement 12, Local Development Frameworks*, June 2008 (CLG 2008c) and *Creating Strong Safe and Prosperous Communities*, July 2008 (CLG 2008d). The two sets of guidance are cross-referenced. The principal delivery role of the LDF within this framework is identified through combining the two sets of guidance into a single narrative and this can be found in the *Steps Approach to Infrastructure Planning and Delivery* (Morphet 2009a).

The LDF is structured as a loose-leaf document which contains a portfolio or folder of documents and components which are the most appropriate set for the area. These include DPDs and Supplementary Planning Documents (SPDs). As Cullingworth and Nadin point out (2006: 119), the term LDF is a non-statutory term and is not defined in the Act, but these documents together make up the planning policy and delivery plan for the area. The timetable for delivery of the components of the LDF and the order in which they were to be undertaken is contained in the LDS. The components of the LDF are set out in Box 3.1 and these are reviewed in turn next.

Box 3.1   Local Development Framework components

Local Development Framework (LDF) components

1   Development Plan Documents
2   Local Development Scheme
3   Statement of Community Involvement
4   Annual Monitoring Report
5   Supplementary Planning Documents
6   Local Development Orders and Simplified Planning Zones

LDF documents fall into two categories: required and optional.

1. Development Plan Documents (DPDs)

A LDF must include a Core Strategy and an Adopted Proposals Map. It may also contain additional optional development documents such as AAPs. These are classed as DPDs and outline the key development goals of the LDF.

DPDs are subject to rigorous procedures of community involvement, consultation and independent examination. Once adopted, development control decisions must be made in accordance with the DPDs unless material considerations indicate otherwise. DPDs are also subject to a Sustainability Appraisal to ensure the economic, environmental and social effects of the plan are in line with sustainable development targets.

1.1 Core Strategy (required)

The Core Strategy is the principal development plan document contained within the LDF. It sets out the general spatial vision and objectives for delivery of the LDF and can also include Strategic Site Allocations. It is a crucial part of the LDF in that it positions the council as both a strategy maker and a deliverer of outcomes.

The Core Strategy also plays a key part in the delivery of the council's SCS by setting out its spatial aspects and providing a long-term spatial vision. The Core Strategy must be kept up to date and all other development plan documents must be in conformity with it and the RSS (or the Spatial Development Strategy in London).

1.2 Adopted Proposals Map (required)

The Adopted Proposals Map should illustrate all site-specific policies in all the adopted development plan documents in map form.

The Adopted Proposals Map should also identify areas of protection such as nationally protected landscape and local nature conservation areas, green belt land and conservation areas.

Separate inset maps may be used to show policies for part of the authority's area, such as the policies for Area Action Plans. The Adopted Proposals Map must be revised as each new development plan document is adopted and should reflect the up-to-date spatial plan for the area.

1.3 Area Action Plans (AAPs) (optional)

An AAP is a development plan document focussed upon a specific location or an area subject to conservation or significant change. This could include a major regeneration project or a growth area.

The AAP should focus on implementation – providing an important mechanism for ensuring development of an appropriate scale, mix and quality for key areas of opportunity, change or conservation.

An AAP should outline protection for areas sensitive to change and aim to resolve conflicting objectives in areas subject to development pressures.

1.4 Other Development Plan Documents (optional)

These can include thematic documents concerned with housing, employment, retail development, etc.

However, additional DPDs (i.e. beyond the Core Strategy) should only be produced when truly necessary and where the Core Strategy can not guide and/or deliver.

2. Local Development Scheme (LDS) (required)

The LDS is a public 'project plan' identifying which local development documents will be produced, in what order and when.

The LDS acts as the starting point for the community and stakeholders to find out about the authority's planning policies in respect to a particular place or issue, and the status of those policies. It also outlines the details of and timetable for the production of all documents that make up the LDF over a three-year period.

All local authorities submitted their LDSs to the Secretary of State by the end of March 2005.

3. Statement of Community Involvement (SCI) (required)

The SCI shows how and when planning authorities intend to consult local communities and other stakeholders when preparing documents.

A key outcome of the SCI will be to encourage 'front loading' – meaning that consultation begins at the earliest stages of each document's development so that communities are given the fullest opportunity to participate in plan making and to make a difference.

Every SCI must provide open access to information, actively encourage the contribution of ideas and representations from the community and provide regular and timely feedback on progress.

4. Annual Monitoring Report (required)

A report submitted to the Government by a local planning authority to assess the progress and the effectiveness of a LDF.

The Annual Monitoring Report will assess if:

- policies are achieving their objectives and sustainable development is being delivered
- policies have had intended consequences
- the assumptions and objectives behind policies are still relevant
- the targets set in the LDF are being achieved.

To achieve this goal, the Annual Monitoring Report will include a range of local and standard (Core Output) indicators. It should also highlight if any adjustments to the LDS are required.

5. Supplementary Planning Documents (SPD) (optional)

SPDs expand or add details to policies laid out in DPDs, or a saved policy in an existing development plan. These may take the form of design guides, area development briefs, a master plan or issue-based documents.

These documents can use illustrations, text and practical examples to expand on how the authority's policies can be taken forward.

Local authorities must involve the community in the preparation of SPDs. They are also subject to a Sustainability Appraisal (SA) to ensure the economic, environmental and social effects of the plan are in line with sustainable development targets.

6. Local Development Orders and Simplified Planning Zones (optional)

The LDF may also contain Local Development Orders and Simplified Planning Zones.

A Local Development Order is made by a planning authority in order to extend permitted rights for certain forms of development, with regard to a relevant local development document.

A Simplified Planning Zone is an area in which a local planning authority wishes to stimulate development and encourage investment. It operates by granting a specified planning permission in the zone without the need for a formal application or the payment of planning fees.

Source: Planning Portal

(I) LOCAL DEVELOPMENT SCHEME (LDS)

The LDS has to be submitted to the regional government office for agreement. This is the only formal role that the government office plays in the progress of the LDF towards adoption and implementation. However, the government office will want to stay in touch with authorities and provide helpful advice, although it is up to individual local authorities to decide how much of this advice they intend to accept. The LDS also enables the local authority to set out which policies they wish to save from earlier plans and the evidence for this. This will then be tested by the planning inspector. Cuff and Smith (2009), writing for a right-of-centre think-tank, have suggested that the LDS could be scrapped in order to simplify the process.

(II) STATEMENT OF COMMUNITY INVOLVEMENT (SCI)

The LDS must include a SCI. The SCI sets out how public consultation is to be managed as part of the process of preparing each of the DPDs and SPDs. Until 2009, the SCI was examined by the planning inspector as part of the Tests of Soundness; after this, it will be considered as part of the local authority's overall approach to consultation by the Audit Commission. The LDF process has a strong emphasis on 'front loading' which means that people, communities, landowners and stakeholders need to be actively engaged from the outset. This marks a change in approach from the pre-2004 system, where much of the engagement with the community and other stakeholders was focussed on examining objections to the plan at the Examination in Public.

Since 2004, the emphasis has been on a far greater involvement for communities in visioning, including the use of evidence. There is also an expectation that the later stages of DPD preparation are more likely to be confirmatory rather than identifying new evidence that would then undermine the basis of the DPD. Since 2009, the SCI has been brought within a wider local authority *duty to involve* which was created in the 2007 Local Government and Public Involvement in Health Act.

(III) PREPARING DPDs

The process for the preparation and adoption of each DPD follows a common pathway, whether this is for the Core Strategy, other DPDs or AAPs. Preparation of DPDs will be set within the local governance context and are also likely to need to be programme managed to ensure that they are completed on time and can fit in with other processes where this is necessary. The preparation of any DPD includes:

1 Establishing the vision and objectives set out in the Sustainable Community Strategy and the Local Area Agreement.
2 Reviewing other relevant strategies and policy documents from the local authority and partners, including:
   a strategic housing policy
   b economic and regeneration strategy
   c Joint Strategic Needs Assessment (JSNA)
   d health profile
   e local transport plan

    f   environmental and landscape strategies

    g school organisation plan

    h business plans of police, fire and rescue, ambulance, PCT

    i   business plans of universities and FE colleges.

3   Evidence assessment using common demographic projections, health outcomes, energy consumption, travel patterns, education outcomes and reviewing all consultation evidence from all local public sector bodies that are part of the LSP. Commission specific studies such as:

    a flood risk assessment

    b Strategic Housing Market Assessment (SHMA)

    c Strategic Housing Land Availability Assessment (SHLAA)

    d open space review.

4   Review public sector services and assets to promote co-location and assets delivery in public services.

5   Review consistency and coherence of approach with neighbouring local authorities, particularly where there are joint housing markets, sub-regional working or use of local services.

6   Prepare infrastructure delivery strategy and schedules.

7   Development of issues and options.

8   Indicating the preferred strategy.

9   Submission (which now includes six weeks consultation prior to submission).

10   Inquisitorial examination by an independent person (i.e. a planning inspector) against the Tests of Soundness; this commences from the date of submission.

11   Plan found sound or unsound.

12   Inspector's binding report and plan adoption.

(IV) CORE STRATEGY

Each LDF must have a Core Strategy which has to include a Proposals Map and a delivery strategy. The Core Strategy sets out how it is delivering the spatial elements of the long-term vision of the area as set out in the SCS. Although the Core Strategy acts as the overarching document for the LDF, initially it was not required to be prepared first. This allowed some local authorities to progress DPDs on other issues that were locally important but it became increasingly clear that the Core Strategy was needed to set the context for other LDF documents so, in 2008, it was made a requirement to prepare the Core Strategy at the beginning of the process (CLG 2008c).

    The Core Strategy has to be based on evidence which has both data analysis and consultation components within it. The data analysis will include assessments of demographic changes, the economy, transport systems, health, quality of life indicators and environmental indicators. The majority of this evidence will be provided by other parts of the local authority or partners. Specific studies that may have been undertaken for these activities will be added to this evidence. The baseline information on population is now included in the JSNA which has been prepared for each area by the local authority and the health service. Also in this category is local evidence such as parish plans and surveys by single interest groups which may amplify other data. Analysis will also be contributed through qualitative reviews and scrutinies that often provide evidence of 'what works here'. Evidence will also be provided from studies which have been specifically undertaken for the LDF. These will include Strategic Flood Risk Assessments, SHMA and SHLAA studies. All the specific studies commissioned for the LDF can be put within the evidence repository for others to use.

A second major evidence source is that derived from consultation processes. Until 2009, the approach set out for consultation in the SCI has been the main consideration. Since 2009, all consultation undertaken in the area by the local authority and its stakeholders now has to be taken into account. Further, any consultation processes carried out after April 2009 need to be undertaken jointly with others where this is possible. Assessment of the adequacy of the consultation undertaken and the way in which it has been used at the local level will be examined by the Audit Commission as part of its regular review processes of local authorities including *One Place,* which is a comprehensive area assessment of the way in which public bodies are working together in the local authority area for its benefit.

The key role of the Core Strategy is to indentify what is required in the area to achieve the vision as set out in the SCS and the LAA. The Core Strategy has to be in general conformity with national planning policies as set out in PPSs and guidance from central government although, unlike Scotland and Wales, there is no national planning framework for England. The Core Strategy has had to be in general conformity with the RSS which provided an overarching policy framework for the region and set out its requirements for housing, transport, the environment and economy. This framework identified a number of requirements for the region such as the provision of new housing units which have had to be interpreted and delivered through the LDF unless the local authority could demonstrate, through the use of evidence, that these housing requirements are not appropriate to their area. The LAA establishes specific requirements for the provision of housing which have to be delivered in the area and this might be for either all housing or just affordable housing or the identification of housing sites. These housing requirements are generally interpreted in the Core Strategy through the identification of strategic sites.

The Core Strategy then identifies what is deficient and required for the needs of the current and future population of the area. This is generally termed as infrastructure and will range from energy supplies to play areas and universities to community centres. These infrastructure requirements are based on an assessment of the existing baseline provision and the future needs related to the changes in the current population, any likely locations of intensified population and then any strategic sites where new development is being identified to take place. The definition of infrastructure includes physical, green and social categories (CLG 2008c). This covers all types of provision including utilities, transport, community facilities, day nurseries and green spaces. (A list of infrastructure types is included at the end of Chapter 6).

Infrastructure is provided by the public, private and voluntary sectors through their capital programmes which have to be set out in their annual accounts. Some types of infrastructure, e.g. transport or early years provision may be available through all three sectors. Infrastructure can also be provided through specific funding such as that provided by the Homes and Communities Agency or the EU. Contributions to infrastructure costs may also be made through developers' contributions in association with planning applications. Some infrastructure may be provided in neighbouring local authorities. Conversely, communities and individuals from other local authority areas may use infrastructure in the area for which the DPD is being prepared. Neighbouring local authorities will also have overlapping relationships on issues such as housing markets, school catchment areas, transport, waste management and drainage.

The Core Strategy then has to set out a strategy to demonstrate how these requirements are expected to be delivered. This delivery strategy has two main components. The first is set within the Core Strategy and identifies the processes and methods through which infrastructure is planned and delivered. This includes a governance approach, usually through the Local Strategic Partnership, development management policies, Annual Monitoring Reports (AMR) and risk assessment. In addition, the Core Strategy also has to include a schedule of infrastructure that is identified as required with a good prospect of funding. It will also identify infrastructure that is required but is not yet funded. The infrastructure that has a good prospect of funding provides an evidence base that supports the Core Strategy but sits outside it. The infrastructure that is required but is not yet funded, sits elsewhere and is probably best located within the SCS. It is also part of the evidence base.

(V) JOINT CORE STRATEGIES

Some local authorities are undertaking Joint Core Strategies. This approach is being pursued in a variety of ways and for a range of reasons. In West Northamptonshire, four local authorities have set up a joint planning unit which reports to a joint planning committee. This committee has been given the responsibility for the preparation of the

Core Strategy as a means of supporting and delivering the growth objectives in the area. A different approach is being developed by the four authorities that comprise the West of England Partnership – Bristol, North Somerset, South Gloucestershire and Bath and North East Somerset. The West of England Partnership has an economic focus and is geared towards developing the sub-regional economy. The four local authorities are undertaking aligned Core Strategies which can be joined up in a single approach for delivery. The West of England Partnership has not combined planning or technical staff or the governance arrangements to manage this work.

The approach in Greater Nottingham is another variant on this. The Greater Nottingham Partnership was set up in 2006 with a view to developing a programme for sub-regional working. The leaders of the local authorities in the Greater Nottingham Partnership agreed to develop individual LDF Core Strategies that will be aligned. The process is progressed by each local authority taking common reports to their individual council executives for agreement. In other locations such as Cheltenham, Tewksbury and Gloucester, there has been development work undertaken on a joint approach to the Core Strategies. Housing growth will be based in Tewkesbury, although many of the services needed to support new housing will be provided within Cheltenham. There has also been a practical need to appoint shared staff to support the process. In addition, the county council has established a Strategic Infrastructure Partnership and an approach to a Strategic Infrastructure Delivery Plan. This also includes the three other Gloucestershire district councils which are at different stages in the development of their Core Strategies. Another example of joint working between three authorities is in Lancashire – South Ribble, Chorley and Preston. These authorities are also planning for growth and are also being supported by staff at Lancashire County Council and a joint planning team has been established in the county council.

In the East Midlands, a joint planning technical unit has been established for North Northamptonshire which includes four local authorities – Corby, East Northamptonshire, Wellingborough and Kettering. This technical unit has the first sound Core Strategy which covers more than one area and is continuing to work to develop other DPDs. Like the West of England and West Northamptonshire partnerships, there is as strong economic and regeneration thrust to this work and each has local delivery vehicles set up to deliver the identified housing growth.

The policy move to develop more sub-regional approaches in England would suggest that more Joint Core Strategies might be developed and these have been encouraged by central government (CLG 2008c). However, current progress is slow and there may be difficulties in resolving the issues concerning the location of growth and other facilities such as waste-to-energy centres which are always contentious at the local level.

Box 3.2   Reasons for preparing a DPD in addition to the Core Strategy

---

- The scope of and detail in the RSS or Core Strategy.
- Market conditions, including the scale of the development challenge (both absolute and relative), whether it be growth or managed change, that LPAs face.
- The approach to delivery, including the size and type of land available for new development and how to make the best use of existing buildings/housing stock.
- The needs for land assembly/CPOs.
- The requirements of utilities/infrastructure providers.
- The need to address environmental pressures, constraints and opportunities (for example flood risk or coastal erosion).
- Timing, particularly in terms of when other regional and local strategies are being brought forward.
- Resources and timetabling.

Source: PPS 12 (CLG 2008c: §5.1)

(VI) OTHER DPDs

Other DPDs can be included in the LDF where it can be shown that an issue or an area needs to be addressed and where it is not adequately covered in the Core Strategy and/or the RSS. PPS 12 (CLG 2008c) identifies the issues that need to be considered before a DPD is prepared and these are shown in Box 3.2. These DPDs might cover a range of issues including the provision of Open Space, development management policies or developers' contributions.

Where DPDs are being prepared, there is a requirement that they should comply with a range of principles set out in PPS 12, including:

- participation and stakeholders
- not reporting national and regional policy
- sustainability appraisal
- justification and effectiveness
- timely progress.

(ibid.: §5.2)

According to PPS 12, DPDs must also:

- be prepared in accordance with the LDS and are in compliance with the SCI and the regulations
- be subject to sustainability appraisal
- have regard to national policy
- conform generally with the RSS

- have regard to any sustainable community strategy for its area (i.e. county and district).

(ibid.)

Finally, DPDs have to meet the same Tests of Soundness as Core Strategies and should not be used to take the place of the Core Strategy. Some local authorities were seeking to delay the choice of strategic housing sites to a later stage in the process through housing site DPDs. The revised version of PPS 12 addressed this point: 'it is the Core Strategy which should make clear the spatial choices about where development should go' (ibid.). The Core Strategy has the role of allocating strategic sites but 'if it is necessary to allocate sites which have not already been allocated in the Core Strategy, a DPD must be used to allocate these sites' (ibid.: §5.3).

DPDs offer some flexibility to focus attention on issues that have some importance locally. DPDs that have been submitted and found sound by the planning inspectorate cover a wide range of issues, including:

- small-scale housing sites (Mid Sussex)
- development policies (Redcar and Cleveland, Hambleton)
- development land allocations (Tunbridge Wells)
- general development control policies (Horsham)
- employment (Hounslow)
- sustainable resources (Chorley)
- leisure and recreation (West Wiltshire)
- education sites (Barnsley)
- regeneration (Middlesbrough).

(VII) AREA ACTION PLANS (AAPS)

AAPs may be prepared for areas where there is a need for a more detailed approach because of pressure or other changes that are required. They may also be prepared where more careful approaches to enhancement are required. In PPS 12 (CLG 2008c), examples of the type of AAPs that might be prepared are included for growth areas. It also identifies that AAPs 'should be used when there is a need to provide the planning framework for areas where significant change or conservation is needed'. AAPs should:

- deliver planned growth areas
- stimulate regeneration
- protect areas particularly sensitive to change
- resolve conflicting objectives in areas subject to development pressures
- focus the delivery of area-based regeneration initiatives.

(ibid.: §5.4)

PPS 12 also suggests that AAPs are useful in supporting CPOs and the implementation of change in any area. It also suggests that the Core Strategy can identify the criteria by which AAPs can be selected (ibid.: §5.5). As with Core Strategies, the AAPs should have delivery plans and timetables for implementation and site allocations where this is appropriate. Where AAPs are being used to support conservation, they should be detailed enough to demonstrate where specific policies are to be used (ibid.: §5.6).

Between 2005 and March 2009, 41 AAPs have been submitted by local authorities to the planning inspectorate for examination. Some AAPs have specifically dealt with growth issues such as those for South Cambridgeshire through the Northstowe AAP (adopted in July 2007) and the Cambridgeshire East AAP (adopted in February 2008). The approach in the AAPs can be used to suggest the development of masterplans rather than to see the AAP as a masterplan process. In some cases, they have followed sound Core Strategies such as in Plymouth. In other cases, such as Swindon, Kingston upon Thames and Reading, they have preceded the submission of the overarching Core Strategy and all these three have been for town centre areas. Of these 41 AAPs, one has been found unsound, six have been withdrawn and eight are waiting to be determined. The remaining AAPs were found sound. In the revised version of PPS 12 (CLG 2008c), it was advised that the Core Strategy should be completed prior to other DPDs or AAPs being prepared, and since 1 September 2008, when PPS 12 came into effect, fewer AAPs have been submitted. Considering the approach to AAPs that have been taken, successful AAPs have set out to deal with specific spatial issues in areas that need major change, including:

- regeneration, e.g. Longbridge in Birmingham
- growth areas, e.g. Northstowe in South Cambridgeshire
- major land release sites from other uses, e.g. former Ministry of Defence barracks in the Mill Hill East AAP
- town centres, e.g. Reading, Swindon, Kingston, Romford, Ilford, Bedford.

As a tool, AAPs have returned to the mainstream planning system for the first time since the early 1970s when there were similar approaches through the use of Action Plans (Cullingworth and Nadin 2006: 119). The similarity in title and role may lead to confusion of their role. Some have suggested that AAPs represent the delivery focus of the LDF, 'bridging the gap' between the Core Strategy and local delivery (Gallent and Shaw 2007: 632), or that this type of plan acts as a 'transformative and integrative' part of the spatial planning process (Albrechts 2006, quoted in Gallent and Shaw op. cit.: 618). However, within the English approach to spatial planning (CLG 2008a), AAPs are a complementary tool to consider an area in more detail if this is required, rather than being a sole delivery mechanism. To take this approach suggests that delivery is partial and only focussed on areas where specific change is required whereas, as noted above, delivery for the whole area is the key task of the Core Strategy.

(VIII) SUPPLEMENTARY PLANNING DOCUMENTS (SPDs)

SPDs can be prepared to support the Core Strategy but they are not required to go through the same formal process of examination by an independent person. For this reason, they may be quicker and easier to prepare but, on the other hand, they do not carry so much weight in formal processes such as planning appeals on specific sites. Other bodies may prepare and publish SPDs in addition to the LDF authorities. These include:

- government agencies
- regional planning bodies
- county councils
- any other body, e.g. AONB committee.

(ibid.: §6.3)

Examples of SPDs being developed include:

- public art strategy
- residential design guidance
- street scene strategy
- nature conservation
- residential parking standards
- community safety
- area management plans
- tall buildings
- archaeology.

The 2007 Planning White Paper (CLG 2007j) suggested that the requirement to list all SPDs in the LDS may now be relaxed so that it will be possible for LDFs to be more flexible and responsive to changing needs. However, as PPS 12 states, 'SPDs should not be prepared with the aim of avoiding the need for the examination of policy which should be examined' (CLG 2008c: §6.1).

(IX) LOCAL DEVELOPMENT ORDERS (LDOs)

LDOs were introduced in the 2004 Planning and Compulsory Purchase Act by amending the 1990 Town and Country Planning Act. LDOs allow for local authorities 'to extend "national" permitted development rights for all or part of their area for specific developments or general classes of development' (Cullingworth and Nadin

2006: 156). LDOs were regarded as a means to speed up the planning system but this is an approach that has been greeted with some scepticism about the confusion that such an approach would cause (ibid.). LDOs, in effect, guarantee planning permission for certain types of development and remove the discretion from the planning process when any specific planning application is made. Cullingworth and Nadin suggest that this approach 'borrows from the approach to development regulation in continental countries where the "regulation plan" determines the grant of a permit' (ibid.: 156–7).

LDOs may also have further uses, and the powers in section 61 of the 1990 Planning Act were amended by the 2008 Planning Act. There is scope for planning authorities to use these to promote particular initiatives. These could include:

- broadening the application of 'permitted development' rights in some or all of their area, to cover a wider range of householder and micro-renewable installations;
- providing an overall framework permission for the installation of district heating networks based on an existing generating station to serve existing housing;
- providing framework permission for a decentralised area network for generating facilities to serve several development sites and/or existing housing (www.pas.gov.uk).

As yet, LDOs have not been extensively used, so it is unclear how well they would work in practice. It seems that now there are few demands for their introduction. The role of LDOs in the spatial planning process is a mechanism for supporting delivery and they could be indentified as such in the Core Strategy and AAPs.

The Planning Advisory Service have commissioned Entec to undertake further research on their role and has suggested that there may now be good reasons to examine the use of LDOs (2009) because:

- There has been a clear focus from Government to examine how the burden of making planning applications can be reduced through both process improvements and removal of the need for planning permission where this is appropriate and proportionate. While people have strong views about changes which have resulted from this, there has been greater acceptance of the principle of change in how we manage minor development.
- The Killian Pretty Review (2008) has reinforced the need to promote the potential role of LDOs as a tool for achieving a reduction in planning applications where this is both appropriate to the local environment and brings benefits to customers and local authorities.
- An important provision in the Planning Act 2008 makes it easier for local planning authorities to introduce LDOs. The 2008 Act makes provision for the removal of the

requirement that LDOs should be made to achieve policies set out in adopted local development documents. Any local planning authority will be able to make an LDO.

(X) WASTE AND MINERALS LDFS

Although not explicit about this, PPS 12 (CLG 2008c) applies to waste and minerals LDFs. In areas of two-tier local government, waste and minerals LDFs are undertaken by council councils; elsewhere they are undertaken by unitary authorities. The setting of waste and minerals Core Strategies sat within the framework of the RSS.

The context for planning for waste is set by PPS 10, *Planning for Sustainable Waste Management* (ODPM 2005a) and its companion guide (CLG 2006b). This policy statement set out the role of planning for waste of both the RSS and the LDF, and it is clear from the companion guide that central government saw the role of the RSS as being critical in the development of planning policy for waste. PPS 12 (CLG 2008c) sets out some key principles for waste, which include:

- addressing waste as a resource
- seeing disposal as the last option
- providing a framework within which communities can take more responsibility for their own waste
- delivering the national waste strategy
- delivering EU requirements for waste management and disposal
- enabling waste to be disposed of safely and locally
- ensuring the design and layout of new development supports sustainable waste management.

(ibid.: §3)

PPS 10 also sets out the role of the Core Strategy for waste as:

- setting out policies and proposals for waste management in line with the RSS and ensuring sufficient opportunities for the provision of waste management facilities in appropriate locations including waste disposal;
- both informing and in turn being informed 'by any relevant municipal waste management strategy';
- looking forward for a period of at least ten years from the date of adoption;
- should aim to look ahead to a longer term time horizon that is set out in the RSS.

(CLG 2008c: §16)

The Core Strategy is also required to identify and allocate sites to support the pattern of waste management as set out in the RSS and also review sites that are not taken up every five years and roll them forward. The selection of specific sites needs to be on environmental criteria and should take into account the movement of waste to sites. Although the general context of waste management is for reduction of waste disposal and generally supportive of waste as something that can generate energy, PPS 10 does not contain any practical approaches to the way in which this might be taken forward in the Core Strategy. Some obvious considerations would be in the use of:

- waste-to-energy facilities at the local level which are popular and frequently used on mainland Europe which could power district heating schemes;
- larger waste-to-energy facilities which could provide major contribution to sustainable energy policy;
- the development of management policies which would allow greater space for the collection of recyclables within and outside the dwelling;
- the potential requirement for composting bins to be supplied for each new dwelling with a garden;
- the design of space for recyclables in all economic and employment uses including schools, offices, business parks and retail areas;
- the determination of a measure of 'waste miles', that is how far waste is transported for disposal;
- the location of neighbourhood and community recycling points and provision of them;
- the consideration of issues related to the size of refuse and waste collection vehicles and street layouts in new developments.

In June 2007, *Local Development Frameworks Lessons: Learnt Examining Development Plan Document* published by the Planning Inspectorate (2007), specifically addressed the issue of Waste Core Strategies. As it states in PPS 10, spatial planning should be supporting the delivery of sustainable waste management:

- through the development of appropriate strategies for growth, regeneration and prudent use of resources;
- by providing sufficient opportunities for new waste management facilities of the right type, in the right place and at the right time.

The Planning Inspectorate states that a Core Strategy 'should set out policies and proposals for waste management which ensure sufficient opportunities for the provision of waste management facilities in appropriate locations including for waste disposal' (ibid.: §14). The Planning Inspectorate suggests that in practice this means that the Waste Core Strategy should consider that waste generation, including collection and disposal together:

- be based on evidence
- articulate the issues faced

- set out the criteria by which sites will be identified and allocated
- the broad locations where sites will be sought
- identify what the potential could be for delivering sustainable waste management
- consider all options
- be subject to sustainability appraisal
- make key decisions
- use the proposed solutions to build the strategy
- should have a delivery plan
- should have a monitoring framework.

The Planning Inspectorate also identified the characteristics of a 'good' Core Strategy for waste are:

- Places and areas that are distinctive and distinguishable, therefore strategies should be spatial and bespoke and not just an assembly of development control policies.
- Strategies that are evidence-based but concise through not repeating national or regional policy and by avoiding the inclusion of unnecessary detail when the Core Strategy can signpost to the supporting evidence base.
- Strategies that make good use of graphic material, including a key diagram, where this aids understanding and succinctness.
- Avoid unnecessary prescription on matters such as technology, except where this is integral to the choice and delivery of the sites in areas that together make up the land platform for new waste management capacity.
- Written positively; the core strategy is there to help to secure delivery. Planning is pivotal to the adequate and timely provision of facilities and needs to move waste management up the waste hierarchy.

(ibid.: §15)

Following the publication of the revised version of PPS 12 (CLG 2008c), the Planning Advisory Service (2008g) provided more advice on the content and process for developing Waste Core Strategies. It stated that:

> the shaping, development and presentation of the waste content of a Core Strategy is not dependent on whether the waste planning authority is, for example, preparing the waste component of the Core Strategy for an all purpose unitary authority or is a county council working within a minerals and waste development framework.

Whatever the circumstances, the waste planning authority should produce a Core Strategy that:

- Helps to secure delivery and ensure the adequate and timely provision of facilities needed to move waste management up the waste hierarchy.

- Ensures sufficient opportunities for the provision of waste management facilities in appropriate locations by setting how sites and areas suitable for new or advanced waste management facilities will be identified. This should include criteria that will guide actual allocations and the broad locations for waste management facilities.

- Allocates strategic sites and areas that are critical to the delivery of the strategy's vision. This includes allocating sites to support the location of waste management facilities set out in the regional spatial strategy in accordance with the broad locations identified in the regional spatial strategy.

- Avoids unnecessarily prescriptive policy on matters such as technology, except where this is integral to the choice and delivery of the sites that together make up the land platform for new waste management capacity.

- Makes good use of graphical material to identify sites/areas, including a key diagram, where this aids understanding and succinctness.

In some areas, groups of authorities have agreed to prepare joint waste DPDs, including Greater Manchester, West of England and Tees Valley. Greater Manchester is the largest partnership and is supported by the Association of Greater Manchester Authorities (AGMA). In a study undertaken by GMGU (2008), of all the areas where joint waste DPDs were being prepared, a number of key benefits emerged as a result of this joint working:

- it allowed appropriate waste planning across local authority borders;
- was a better and more efficient use of resources;
- enabled the industry and the community to engage in a single process;
- enabled a dedicated team to be established to develop the work.

At the same time, a number of risks were also identified, which included:

- potential delay to the process whilst political approval was gained, and all had to work within different committee cycles;
- this approach created a very large project which needed considerable coordination;
- technical difficulties, e.g. GIS;
- adverse public opinion;
- authorities dropping out of the process;
- having to keep in step with other LDF processes, e.g. on community involvement.

(ibid.)

In PPS 12 (CLG 2008c), the role of the LDF in delivering the LAA is also set out (§1.6) and a number of local authorities have targets in their LAAs which are relevant to waste management. The specific targets chosen by any local authority from the 198 National Indicators can be found on www.localpriorities.communities.gov.uk. The specific indicators which are likely to have an impact on the Core Strategy if they were included in the LAA are as follows (with the number of local authorities adopting these targets in their LAA shown in brackets):

*   NI 186 per capita reduction in CO_2 emissions in the local authority areas (100)
*   NI 188 planning to adapt to climate change (56)
*   NI 191 residual household waste per household (38)
*   NI 192 percentage of household waste sent for reuse, recycling or composting (68)
*   NI 193 percentage of municipal waste land filled (32).

In the selection of waste disposal sites, PPS 12 provided locational criteria which include:

*   protection of water resources
*   land instability
*   visual intrusion
*   nature conservation
*   historic environment and built heritage
*   traffic and access
*   air emissions including dust
*   odours
*   vermin and birds
*   noise and vibration
*   litter.

(ibid.: Appendix E)

In a number of cases, some of these potential issues can be managed through conditions on planning applications, including:

*   hours of working
*   wheel washing
*   vehicle size
*   access to site by employees
*   large-scale biodiversity planning.

Overall, the provision of advice on waste planning through DPDs concentrates almost entirely on the identification of sites for disposal and does not give much advice or leads on waste reduction or waste-to-energy strategies. This is contained in PPS 22 (ODPM 2004a), where small-scale local provision of waste-to-energy plants are considerate and should not be rejected 'simply because the output is small' (ibid.: §8). Local authorities are also encouraged to include policies in DPDs which require 'a percentage of the energy to be used in new residential, commercial or industrial developments where the installation of equipment is viable given the type of development proposed, its location and design' (ibid.: §10), although it should not be framed in such a way to be an undue burden on developers.

The companion guide to PPS 22 (ODPM 2004b) identified the kind of waste-to-energy schemes that could be considered as part of a renewable energy approach. In particular, it highlighted both biological and thermal processes. One of the main benefits of adopting a renewal energy approach for waste was the reduction of the use of landfill sites, which would be both more cost effective as landfill tax increases year-on-year and also create fewer problems of methane emissions and restitution in the longer run. As the companion guide points out, the location of waste-to-energy plants may not be best suited to urban environments but rather closer to current landfill operations, sewage works or farms, not least because they require large chimneys to dispose of waste products.

However, waste-to-energy schemes are now being developed in urban areas including two on the Olympic Sites in East London which will provide power for the Westfield Shopping Centre, Olympic Village and its subsequent use, and all the Olympic venues.

Waste can also be turned into energy through the means of biological processes including anaerobic digestion, landfill and sewage gas. In some cases, wood and paper by-products and off-cuts are used to generate energy through burning, and some 98 per cent of municipal solid waste has been identified as being capable of generating energy through this means (ODPM 2004b: 86). All of the processes available for the use of waste for the creation of energy suggest that this should be a much larger component of Waste Core Strategies than is currently the case, where the focus is on sites for disposal and this might be an issue to consider in the future.

In 2006, there were concerns that LDFs were not addressing the approach to renewable energy as set out in PPS 22 and a review was undertaken and this showed that some 26 of the post-2004 LDFs include the relevant policy from §1 of PPS 22. However, it should be noted that a number of plans were subsequently withdrawn so the number with the policy inclusion now may be smaller than originally expected.

The approach to preparing a minerals LDF is common to all others. The targets for the level of aggregates to be planned for are set out in national policy guidance (CLG 2009h) and this guidance spans both regions and LDFs. The guidance is based on a national model of the way in which aggregates are used for construction and it assumed that there will be an increased use of recycled materials as part of providing the total required. The provision of recycled materials will also need to be part of the minerals LDF. A number of local authorities have undertaken minerals LDFs in parallel with waste, e.g. Wiltshire and Swindon. Others such as Cumbria have combined them in one Core Strategy.

(XI) COMMUNITY INFRASTRUCTURE LEVY (CIL) AND DEVELOPERS' CONTRIBUTIONS

Developers' contributions have been used to generate resources to mitigate the impact of development and are negotiated through specific planning applications. In some local authority areas, this approach has been extended to create a tariff that can be applied for each house or square metre of employment floor space, e.g. Milton Keynes and Ashford. These contributions are applied to the provision of infrastructure and could be for a range of facilities including highways, schools, open spaces or health. The means of determining the type of facilities that can be requested to be funded through developers' agreements is set out in Circular 5/05 and is then secured by a legal agreement under s106 of the 1990 Town and Country Planning Act. These contributions are in addition to the provision of affordable housing as part of housing schemes.

The use of developers' contributions at the local level has been variable. In some local authorities where there may have been a number of new developments, local authorities may have been able to fund new infrastructure through the use of these contributions (Ennis 2003). However, some local authorities do not collect many, if any, developers' contributions, as Crook *et al.* (2008: 1) found:

> Planning authorities have discretion as to whether to seek planning agreements
> or not, and it appears that this discretion was being widely exercised so that
> neighbouring planning authorities operating under similar development pres-
> sures secured very different numbers of agreements worth very different values.

The Government's view is that infrastructure should be primarily funded through mainstream budgets but that developers should also make a contribution to infrastructure funding (CLG 2008e; 2009g). Rather than taking a site-by-site approach to identifying infrastructure requirements, the Government has proposed the introduction of the Community Infrastructure Levy (CIL) that will be related to the IDP that is prepared as part of the LDF and particularly the Core Strategy. However, the use of the CIL will be discretionary in each local authority and if the CIL is not used then the use of s106 agreements will continue. The CIL may only be used to fund infrastructure that is associated with the needs associated with development in the area and not with existing deficiencies that will need to be met through other means such as mainstream funding, and there is work being undertaken across Government to align specifying streams of government departments to localities. On the other hand, where pressure on existing facilities will be cre-ated due to new development, then there may be a case for contributions to be used to increase their capacity.

The process of setting the CIL will start with the LDF Infrastructure Plan and from this a charging schedule will be drafted and will go through the same process of Examination by an Independent Person as other DPDs. The amount charged in the CIL will be related to the Infrastructure Delivery Plan (IDP) and will be based on the likely costs of infrastructure coming forward. It will be charged on development by metre of floor space that will be index linked. The relationship between the CIL and the IDP will be linked so that where there are changes in the IDP then there can be changes in the CIL. The CIL regulations came into force in April 2010.

The connection between development and infrastructure provision through legal agreements has always been available but the introduction of the CIL provides a means through which the requirements for infrastructure can be iden-tified at the outset and then all the resources available for its provision can be used to meet the requirements. The CIL will be applied to a list of pre-identified requirements based on evidence as set out in the IDP and the whole approach to infrastructure funding will be integrated. The practice hitherto has been to view developers' contributions separately from other funding and also there has been little need to underpin requirements with an evidence base. The development of the CIL will further extend the delivery role of the LDF as the local capital pro-gramme for the area.

Box 3.3   Principles for a monitoring framework

The principles of data collection for the AMR are:

- making use of existing information
- being consistent with national and regional monitoring approaches
- setting objectives, policies, targets and indicators
- taking a forward looking approach.

Analytical principles for the AMR:

- transparency
- flexibility
- continuity
- simplicity
- relevance
- time series, i.e. appropriate time frames.

Source: ODPM 2005d

(XII) ANNUAL MONITORING REPORT (AMR)

Monitoring is an increasingly important component of the local evidence base (CLG 2008d). Local authorities are expected to review their evidence base regularly and ensure that it is up to date (Audit Commission 2008a; 2009b). Monitoring of the LDF is set within the principles of 'plan, monitor and manage' and the AMR needs to be flexible to monitor those issues that are changing or that are relating to delivery. The monitoring approach is also expected to be joined up with other agencies and integrated with the delivery of other objectives. This is set out in Box 3.3 on the previous page.

Within this context, the AMR is required to report on five key tasks as set out in the 2004 Planning and Compulsory Purchase Act (s35) and these are set out to:

- review actual progress in terms of local development document preparation against the timetable and milestones in the local development scheme;
- assess the extent to which policies in local development documents are being implemented;
- explain why policies are not being implemented and set out what steps are being taken to ensure that the policy is implemented; or whether the policy is to be amended or replaced;
- identify the significant effects of implementing policies in local development documents and whether they are as intended;
- set out whether policies are to be amended or replaced.

(ODPM 2005d: 9)

The development of indicators and their use in informing policy change remains a challenging one. In some ways, what can be measured is generally what is counted and this may not always be the information that is required to assess outcomes. In some cases, monitoring will be needed over time and there is a need to obtain results more quickly for wider political objectives (Davies 2004). This interplay between policy and methods is at the heart of Wong's work, who points out that the 'methodological and conceptual development of indicators is very much influenced by the emerging policy agenda' (Wong 2006: 184). Wong also suggests that monitoring can be a tool of more centralised control of policy delivery, although there is also a need to balance good conceptual indicators with a local consensus of what should be monitored.

AMRs need to be part of the wider evidence gathering process at the local level and the interplay of the outcomes of place-based policies will all feed into the monitoring process. In some cases, such as monitoring of spatial outcomes or physical activity rates, the consequences for spatial planning may be in the provision of an adequate supply of facilities if all those existing are in full use. Other monitoring of air quality and surface water collection may lead to changing planning policies and targeted intervention, such as retrofitting in support of mitigation or adaptation in specific locations. AMRs can also be used to advise communities of the scale of investment being achieved in their areas and also to identify where more active approaches from partners or through development management will be required.

TESTS OF SOUNDNESS (ToS)

One of the new features introduced as part of the implementation of the LDF system was the development of the ToS by the Planning Inspectorate. These tests were published in late 2005 and were designed to enable all local authorities to have a clear understanding of what the inspectors would be considering as part of their examination of DPDs. In this examination process, the inspector's report is binding, so having a clear understanding of what is required is important. In approaching the ToS, the inspectors expect that the DPD will be sound and are only investigating those areas which appear potentially to be unsound. This means that the process of examination may only focus on a few key areas if the inspector is satisfied that the rest of the plan is sound. The local authority is required to appoint a programme officer who is the link between the local authority and the planning inspector, who will organise any sessions required.

The inspector can use a range of methods to examine the soundness of a DPD. These include:

- desk-based reviews
- written representations
- round table discussions
- informal hearings
- formal hearings.

This approach to examining DPDs was a new one. First, although it is an 'examination by an independent person', this is an inquisitorial rather than adversarial process. This marks a clear break with the former system of an Examination in Public. With hindsight, the use of the word examination and the same set of initials for these processes, EIP, may not have adequately distinguished the two processes and their fundamentally different approaches. The use of the process of Examination in Public has continued for the RSS and, although this has adopted a less adversarial style through the use of round tables and wider discussion, the key issues are still examined in a way which has more in common with courtroom procedures. These include the use of barristers and the contestation of evidence through the use of expert witnesses. Also, inspectors can allow anyone to appear if they consider they have a point which is worth consideration.

As the examination is inquisitorial, the inspector begins the examination at the point when the DPD is submitted. For the public or other stakeholders, objections to the DPD have to be based on demonstrating that aspects of the DPD are unsound.

The inspector determines the ways in which any challenge to soundness is considered. The inspector applies the ToS to come to a view and will also consider any challenges to soundness made by others. The inspector can call for more detailed evidence to be prepared, to discuss specific elements of the plan and can test the validity of the evidence that has been used. Individual objectors to the soundness of the plan have no specific right to be heard. The whole process takes up to one year to complete, including the preparation and issue of the inspector's report.

Although the ToS are clearly set out, they are less understood in practice and regarded to be overly complex. This is due to an operational unfamiliarity with their contents. In particular, local planners preparing DPDs have become attuned to the strong top-down culture of the RSS and reinforced by Government Offices of the Regions (GOs) (Morphet 2007a). This has frequently led to an overemphasis on the RSS, particularly in the framework it provides for local housing numbers, whilst other parts of the ToS have been overlooked. In the ToS, the need to demonstrate conformity of a DPD with the RSS is one-third of one of three ToS. As a consequence, a number of DPDs have either been found unsound or withdrawn.

The ToS have been set out in two versions. In their first iteration, published in 2005, there were nine individual tests, and each test had up to three sub-parts. The second iteration of the ToS, published in 2008, comprises three tests; although the number of sub-parts for each tests has increased. In effect, both sets of the ToS include the same points although packaged different ways. These are set out in Table 3.1 and Box 3.4.

In the application of the 2005 version of the ToS, one of the key roles of the independent inspector was to ensure that the evidence on which the local authority has based its DPD is properly tested. The procedural tests were meant to be a minor part of the process and undertaken at an early screening stage. The tests of conformity were geared towards considering both the process and the content of the DPDs. In particular, there was a need to ensure that the DPD had been prepared within the context of the other policy documents of the local authority and its partners and in particular that it was set within the SCS.

The tests which consider coherence, consistency and effectiveness may be the most important of the three sets of tests and possibly the most misunderstood in practice. One important feature of coherence, consistency and effectiveness is that the DPD is consistent and coherent with the approaches being taken in neighbouring local authorities where there are cross-boundary issues to consider. This might relate to approaches taken in a common housing market area, in a national park or where a town outside the local authority area provides key services for residents. Transport and employment might also be cross-boundary considerations. Where local authorities undertake Joint Core Strategies, then the outer perimeter authorities of the combined Core Strategy area will need to be taken into account. A second major concern in this group of tests is the use of evidence to generate options upon which the plan proposals and policies are to be

Table 3.1 Tests of Soundness 2005

Tests		
Procedural	i	The DPD has been prepared in accordance with the LDS
	ii	The DPD has been prepared in compliance with the SCI, or the minimum requirements set out in the regulations where no SCI exists
	iii	The plan and its policies have been subject to SA
Conformity	iv	It is a spatial plan which is consistent with national planning policy and in general conformity with the RSS for the region or for the Spatial Development Strategy if in London, and it has properly had regard to any other relevant plans, policies and strategies relating to the area or to adjoining areas
	v	It has had regard to the authority's community strategy
Coherence, consistency and effectiveness	vi	The strategies/policies/allocations in the plan are coherent and consistent within and between development plan documents prepared by the authority and by neighbouring authorities, where cross-boundary issues are relevant
	vii	The strategies/policies/allocations represent the most appropriate in all the circumstances, having considered the relevant alternatives, and they are founded on a robust and credible evidence base
	viii	There are clear mechanisms for implementation and monitoring
	ix	It is reasonably flexible to enable it to deal with changing circumstances

Source: Planning Inspectorate National Service 2005

based. In some of the earlier Core Strategy submissions to the Planning Inspectorate, this lack of provision of an evidence base upon which alternatives where generated was one of the key weaknesses. Proposals from earlier plans were rolled forward without any underpinning justification; that they were still appropriate in the circumstances led to plans being found unsound.

However, perhaps the most misunderstood of the original Tests of Soundness was test viii which was concerned with the mechanisms for delivery and monitoring. This test was at the heart of the deliverability of the plan but many local authorities and some GOs took this to mean the number of staff engaged on the development of the plan within the local authority office not in delivery. It is this test which has had most clarity and attention paid to it in the second version of PPS 12 (CLG 2008c). The last part of these tests of coherence, consistency and effectiveness related to the robust nature of the proposals over time. This implied not only a risk assessment but some alternative scenarios which could be reviewed as part of the process of ensuring that the DPDs would be able to withstand potentially significant major changes.

Box 3.4 Tests of Soundness 2008

(i) Justified

- founded on a robust and credible evidence base
- evidence of participation from stakeholders and local communities
- the most appropriate strategy when considered against alternatives.

(ii) Effective (deliverable)

- sound infrastructure delivery planning
- having no regulatory or planning barriers to delivery
- delivery partners who are signed up
- coherence with strategies from neighbouring authorities
- flexible
- able to monitored.

(iii) Consistent with national policy

- where the plan departs from national policy there should be clear and consistent reasoning.

Source: Planning Inspectorate National Service 2008b

Following the publication of these ToS, a number of local authorities submitted their DPDs. In 2005, four Core Strategies were submitted for examination and only one was found to be sound (Horsham). In 2006, 38 local authorities submitted their Core Strategies for examination, of which nine were then withdrawn, six were found unsound and one has still yet to be determined. The remaining 22 were found sound. By this time, local authorities were also submitting other DPDs such as AAPs, development policies and waste and minerals.

This progress was not as had been expected. It was slower and there were a higher number of unsound and withdrawn Core Strategies than anticipated (Wood 2008). The Planning Inspectorate decided to issue another document to support local authorities through the process. *Local Development Frameworks: Lessons Learnt Examining Development Plan Documents* was published in June 2007. In this, the Planning Inspectorate reported that the Core Strategies that had been found sound were moving in the right direction but there were still issues of clarification required. *Lessons Learned* was divided into three key sections – pre-submission, post submission and the examination. At the pre-submission stage, the inspector expects to have available the full evidence base. New evidence cannot be produced once the DPD has been submitted. It was also suggested that the Core Strategy could most helpfully be submitted prior to the other DPDs and that it would not be helpful to examine all DPDs together. It was noted that the main considerations and the 'tough decisions' needed to be taken in the Core Strategy and not left to be taken in subsequent DPDs. It states, for example, that the allocation of housing sites cannot be left until a Site Allocation DPD has been completed, 'the strategy should be driving the allocation of sites not the other way round' (§5.2). Finally, the Planning Inspectorate confirmed that the DPD should be focussed on delivery and that a 'number of Core Strategies seen to date have been particularly weak on implementation and monitoring' (§5.9).

The following year, the number of Core Strategies submitted seemed to be reducing rather than growing despite the provision of this additional advice from the Planning Inspectorate. In 2007, 19 Core Strategies were submitted, of which five were withdrawn and none were found unsound. Action was needed if the progress towards achieving full coverage of LDF Core Strategies across England by 2011 was to be achieved. CLG issued a revised version of PPS 12 in June 2008 which sought to simplify the ToS but confirmed that the 'the standard needed to be sound remains the same' (CLG 2008c: 3). The Planning Inspectorate published more of its own advice to accompany the revised PPS 12 (also in June 2008), as *Local Development Frameworks Examining Development Plan Documents: Soundness Guidance.* The revised Tests of Soundness are set out in Table 3.1. The Planning Inspectorate confirmed that the 2008 version of the ToS contained all the content of the previous 2005 version. The main difference was to sharpen the focus on deliverability which had previously been hidden. This changed format rebalanced the tests and made the role of the LDF as a key delivery process for local infrastructure planning more apparent.

Alongside this guidance on the ToS, the Planning Inspectorate also published two new sets of procedural advice for the examination of DPDs. In 2009, *General Advisory Guidance* and *Examining Development Plan Documents Procedure Guidance* were published together with a *Brief Guide for Participants* (2009) was published. These documents emphasise the change in the approach to the examination of the DPDs in comparison with the former quasi-judicial system. The first, and shorter document, sets out the point that the examination will not necessarily be made on a point-by-point basis and that it takes place across the whole of the time that the inspector is considering the soundness of the DPD. In both documents, the 'inquisitorial' nature of the examination is emphasised. In the second and longer set of procedure guidance, the inspectorate sets out what is likely to be happening in each week of the examination process.

CONCLUSIONS

The introduction of local spatial planning in England has been slower than had been anticipated. In retrospect, this has been for a number of reasons that might have been anticipated in 2004 but are now clearer to understand with the benefit of hindsight. These were identified in Shaping and Delivering Tomorrow's Places Effective Practice in Spatial Planning (Morphet *et al.* 2007). In summary these are:

* a failure to explain the delivery role of spatial planning within the wider local governance architecture;
* a lack of understanding about the spatial, i.e. place-based approach to delivery;
* insufficient training and development on the new approach on the job;
* the slower implementation of some aspects of the wider local government architecture to complement the delivery role of the LDF;
* a failure to communicate the change in role within local authorities to chief executives, leaders and others;
* a lack of understanding about the changed nature of spatial planning by government offices.

On the other hand, the development of more recent initiatives and publications has clarified the role of the LDF and together with the infrastructure delivery support provided by the Planning Advisory Service, there has been greater understanding of this role. Other confirmation has been provided through the publication of other advice or policy documents, including:

* *Planning Together 2* (CLG 2009a)
* *Local Transport Plan Guidance* (DFT 2009)
* guidance on *s106* and *Single Conversation* (HCA 2010)
* consultation on *Community Infrastructure Levy* (CLG 2009g)
* consultation on *Regional Strategies* (CLG and BIS 2009).

All of these documents have reinforced the role of local IDPs. At regional levels, the RSS is going to be recast as a Regional Strategy (RS) with an economic focus and this is discussed in more detail in Chapter 9. However, like the LDF, the RS will have a delivery plan and this will be linked with the LDFs for delivery at the local level.

CHAPTER 4

THE EVIDENCE BASE OF SPATIAL PLANNING

INTRODUCTION

The role of evidence in underpinning spatial planning is critical and one that has been well understood in development planning. In this chapter, the role of evidence in spatial planning is considered within a wider context of evidence-based policy making which is now applied to public policy, including spatial planning. This chapter then moves on to review the role of the integrated evidence base that is now available at the local level in England and is forming the key basis for spatial planning. From 2009, consultation feedback is included in this locality-wide evidence base, and is now an evidence source to be taken into account with other data. This localised approach in the use and application of evidence makes a significant contribution to the underpinning evidence required for spatial planning. This evidence is also meant to be more transparent. Spatial planning processes will also contribute evidence to this pool and support wider spatial interpretation. This chapter focusses on the factual and data analysis contribution of evidence to spatial planning and the next chapter discusses consultation evidence.

After this discussion of the provision of the evidence base available across the locality, this chapter moves on to consider how evidence is taken into account in the spatial planning processes. It introduces some of the key studies that are required to be undertaken as part of the evidence base for spatial planning and the considerations that are needed in bringing them together. Finally, this chapter discusses the way in which spatial planning evidence is made more accessible to those who are interested in reviewing it or adding to it through the use of websites and local evidence repositories.

WHY IS EVIDENCE IMPORTANT?

The role of evidence has always been important in public policy and spatial planning. It can be described as a necessary underpinning to 'getting a grip on the problem' (Osborne and Hutchinson 2004) to create a results oriented approach, although there is always a tendency when dealing with challenges, issues or problems to consider the inputs rather than the outcomes (Osborne and Gaebler 1993). Evidence is not an end in itself. However, the increased focus on evidence-based policy making has, it is argued, engendered a new and vigorous debate about the role of evidence, and Boaz *et al.* argue that the use of evidence in organisations and policy making has started to produce a 'tangible shift' (2008: 247).

Evidence has a number of roles. First, it can help to identify how places work, how people live and what kinds of needs they have (CLG 2007i). Evidence can measure the effectiveness of public interventions such as campaigns to change modes of travel, improve literacy or enable more people to go back to work. Evidence can be viewed as single tests of data, measuring one issue or outcome or they can be combined to consider the effects of synergistic interrelationships for areas, organisations or people. All evidence is 'owned' or sponsored and this process of 'ownership' will mean that the questions that are addressed through this evidence or even the way that it has been collected are likely to reflect the main interests of its 'owners'.

In recent years, there has been a growing focus on evidence-based policy making. This approach, which is most prevalent in medicine, has increasingly been used in the development of public policy. Evidence-based policy making has been used in three main ways to identify:

- What needs to be done?
- What has worked here or elsewhere?
- Did this approach work to solve the problem or improve the outcome?

The identification of what needs to be tackled using an evidence-based approach has been a longstanding feature of public policy with its roots in Fabianism. In some cases, evidence has been used to identify issues where attention is required, e.g. if there is shorter life expectancy or poorer air quality. This approach may also be used to identify areas where there are multiple problems that may not be the responsibility of one agency and this approach has been pursued at neighbourhood levels and in 'joined-up Government' (6, P. *et al.* 2002). In some cases, evidence has been used to demonstrate the case for intervention or greater financial support for people and areas. The problems of people living in fuel poverty, upland farmers, and areas with higher levels of unemployment are all understood through relational evidence that shows a particular area in comparison with others at the national average and above. Wong has pointed out that there has been a strong shift to 'research-based, evidence-based policy making' in recent years and the challenge remains to find the way through 'scientific rationality and complex political reality' (2006: 38).

A second type of evidence has been to identify what has worked elsewhere. There has been a growing concern that public interventions need some evidence of their likely outcomes before major investment is made. Pilot projects are a means of testing approaches before wholesale commitment of funding, although frequently pilot projects are not then translated into general use. This may be because they did not fully achieve the outcome expected or because the underlying issues or conditions have changed (Davies 2004). There may also be political pressure to implement an initiative without waiting for results of pilots. Finding examples of what has worked is not confined to England. Experience and approaches from other countries are also considered (Cabinet Office 2009). As Collins comments, in central government 'rarely is a policy enacted … without an appeal to evidence of some kind. That said it is usually the policy that comes first. The idea tends to lead the search for evidence rather than the other way round' (2009: 15). Although there are fundamentally different cultures, and sometimes systems, between countries, international approaches to problem solving can stimulate wider consideration of issues. In Government, this horizon scanning for initiatives and approaches from other countries is part of a total approach. The introduction of the Community Infrastructure Levy, for example, is very similar to a longstanding approach used in Australia (McNeill and Dollery 1999; Morphet 2009b).

The final main use of evidence is an examination after the event to see if the interventions have worked and what can be learned for next time. This stage of evidence gathering is generally less developed but, through the role of audit and scrutiny, has increased. The changing role of the Audit Commission and the National Audit Office has moved from solely undertaking financial auditing to a much wider consideration of outcomes and their value for money (VfM) and has had a widespread influence on the delivery of public policy and the way it has been reviewed (Power 1997). Performance and outcome assessment are based on this approach. At the local level, the auditing process has included a plethora of individual service performance management approaches and some locality wide regimes including:

- Best Value (BV) (1997–2003, although still contributing in some areas)
- Comprehensive Performance Assessment (CPA) (2003–2009)
- Comprehensive Area Assessment (CAA) (2009)
- Local Area Agreements.

These reviews and individual studies of particular services, including planning (Audit Commission 2006a; 2006b) and property (HM Treasury 2009b) have taken evidence of what has been working at the local level and then published it as good practice advice. Both types of evidence, whether based on performance management or specific studies, are then used to evaluate future performance and this evidence is used to achieve improvement (Van de Walle and Bovaird 2007).

There has also been growth in the role and power of scrutiny approaches in outcome evaluation. In Parliament, the expanded role of Select Committees commenced in 1980 through the Stevas reforms and have grown to the point where, at times, the views of the chair of a Select Committee have been viewed to be more important than those of a cabinet minister (Mullins 2009). In the recent period, these roles have become more public and views of the chairs of Select Committees are regularly sought by the media. Their reports are increasingly influential and their power of scrutiny has influenced new legislation and the direction of government policy. Select Committees take evidence in public and then issue reports. In planning for example, the report by the Select Committees of the Department of Communities and Local Government (CLG) has investigated the shortage of planning skills and then spent time pursuing improvements through the government department (House of Commons 2009).

At the local level, scrutiny has been implemented since 2000 and has yet to develop to the same degree as that in Parliament. As in Parliament, scrutiny panels at the local level can consider any issues and although they can make recommendations, they have no power to implement them. The four principles of effective scrutiny are show in Box 4.1 and it is the final point – effective public scrutiny should be making an impact on public services – that identifies its role in the contribution to evidence.

Local scrutiny panels can invite people or organisations to give evidence and this can be taken in public, although the panels have no power to ensure that this evidence is given. Most scrutiny has concentrated on the way in which the local authority has performed, although there has always been the potential to consider cross-cutting issues, such as how public services are delivered in particular localities or to look at the lives of particular groups such as older people. Scrutiny can be effective in reviewing specific approaches to housing provision, regeneration, transport use and provision and services interventions.

The use of evidence in local decision making also has implications, particularly where there are moves to view individuals as consumers. People's views can be harvested through market research rather than democratic engagement. In reality, it is probably somewhere between the two. The 2009 Places Survey results for all local authorities in England has been used to demonstrate that local authorities have not improved the level of satisfaction of citizens and communities with their local leadership and services, although specific service satisfaction levels are high (CLG 2009c). Others have argued for a transition to the predominant role of citizens rather than consumers. Sandell (2009) states that treating people more as citizens than consumers will provide better understanding of the democratic engagement process. On the other hand, Bevir and Trentmann have argued that when using consumerist approaches,

Box 4.1   The principles of effective scrutiny

Effective public scrutineers:

*   provide a critical friend challenge to executives as well as external authorities and agencies
*   reflect the voice of concerns of the public and its communities
*   should take a lead and own the scrutiny process on behalf of the public
*   should make an impact on the delivery of public services.

Source: The Centre for Public Scrutiny 2007

local reasoning plays a part in making choices and providing evidence of what is most important to citizens and communities, and that this cannot be necessarily dismissed as self interest (2007: 174). Evidence for policy choice is an important factor and this inevitably leads to links with consumer culture. When being surveyed, people do not necessarily differentiate between types of service providers asking these questions. People can be surveyed using different formats, with a more qualitative and discursive approach being taken to improve the understanding of a citizen's role but this is unlikely to replace perceptions of service quality.

There are also issues in using evidence to make decisions. As the Audit Commission points out, 'the information available when a decision is made will never be as relevant, complete, accurate or timely as might be desired, and those who make decisions are often ill-equipped to draw appropriate conclusions from whatever is available' (2008a: 5). The role of evidence at the local level has been heightened through the provision of the 2007 Local Government and Public Involvement in Health Act and its accompanying guidance (CLG 2008d). The Act included a 'duty to involve' that has been placed on local authorities and this covers both the collection and publication of evidence. It also includes a single and more systematic approach to consultation at the local level. The Audit Commission has also highlighted the importance of evidence in the decisions that are made about service delivery and use of resources (2008a; 2009b). However, as Davies (2004) points out, there is always a tension between the role of political judgement and the application of evidence.

Inevitably, there are always problems in terms of which issues are researched and the selection processes at work in choosing them. Evidence gathering can be a political process and research can always be diverted in its course either through scope creep or in a wish to avoid likely outcomes (O'Brien et al. 2008). Although the evidence may be transparent, the selection of research issues may not be. Some studies have confirmed the power of evidence and the implications of its availability within the new information age. Mayo and Steinberg (2007) considered this within a national context. Their study found that the increased availability of data was now making citizens more interested in what is available and more capable in finding and using information. Further, they found that many citizens are now generating their own content (Brabham 2009) and expected to be interactive with information that it provides. This is particularly important as feedback on how services or policies work as well as prioritising issues. They also found that a policy to provide open access to publicly funded information, as exists in the United States, could be advantageous to the economy. It broadens the use of what is available, reduces duplication and provides a platform from which new services and businesses can be developed. This can also have implications for transparency of available information as demonstrated in 2009 as issues about MPs' expenses spilled over into other areas of public life.

David Cameron, the then opposition leader, has described this transition as turning everyone into 'armchair auditors' within the context of 'Google governance' (2009).

EVIDENCE COLLECTION AND QUALITY

The quality of evidence can be verified in a number of ways. First, there is a positivist test of 'replication', that is if the same method was used under the same conditions, the same results should be derived. Second, the methods of data collection to form an evidence base should be sound and reliable. When polls are published before elections, there is always a focus on the method used – telephone, internet, face to face, the sample size and the statistical margin of error in the results. All of these factors are controlled as far as possible. Collecting evidence is frequently undertaken by specialist companies such as Ipsos MORI, NOP and U-Gov. Using polling organisations is regarded as a means of guaranteeing independence. Some companies have been engaged in the collection of polling evidence at the local level for a number of years and are now able to provide comparisons and change data (e.g. Page 2009).

Evidence is available from a variety of sources and comes in many different formats, including those in Boxes 4.2 and 4.3, whilst the quality of data can be set against some measures, as shown in Box 4.4.

Studies where qualitative evidence is being collected also need to define their rules of engagement. Qualitative studies can be run through discursive means such as focus groups that provide people with an opportunity to express opinions on an identified issue or topic. They can also be important in drawing together views about specific places and what is important to communities (Goodsell *et al.* 2009). In qualitative research, it is important to ensure clarity on the issues being researched, and the objectives of the research process. Without this, more discursive approaches can run off course and dilute the quality of findings (Clark

Box 4.2   How evidence data is collected

Data is collected in a number of different ways, including:

- primary data collection through surveys, studies
- secondary analysis
- performance data measured against indicators
- outcome data
- user perception studies
- consultation
- longitudinal studies
- scrutiny and more reflective studies.

Source: The author

Box 4.3   Types of data

Data can be:

- quantitative
- qualitative
- measureable
- impressionistic
- real time or delayed
- raw
- interpretive
- isolated
- aggregated.

Box 4.4   Defining data quality

The quality of data can be defined by:

- *Accuracy* – data should be sufficiently accurate for the intended purposes.
- *Validity* – data should be recoded and used in compliance with relevant requirements.
- *Reliability* – data should reflect stable and consistent data collection processes across collection points and over time.
- *Timeliness* – data should be captured as quickly as possible after the event or activity and must be available for the intended use within a reasonable period of time. Data must be available quickly and frequently enough to support information needs and to influence service or management decision.
- *Relevance* – data captured should be relevant to the purposes for which they are used.
- *Completeness* – data requirements should be clearly based on the information needs of the body and data collection processes matched to these requirements.

and Hall 2008). In this approach, the selection of focus group members is important (French and Laver 2009) and frequently independent facilitators are used for focus groups to improve the confidence of the participants and the reliability of the results of the process. When any data is collected and used, then its quality and provenance needs to be made clear. Evidence that has been gathered in ways that are less independent may nevertheless be used if reliance on their findings is moderated by the extent of data quality.

INTEGRATED APPROACHES TO THE USE OF EVIDENCE FOR SPATIAL PLANNING

The development of an integrated approach to the use of evidence within a local governance framework is set out in *Creating Strong, Safe and Prosperous Communities* (CLG 2008d). In this, the LSP is given the responsibility for preparing the SCS 'based on evidence and data from the local area and population' (§2.4). 'The duty to involve' includes the provision of information to support communities in engaging in decision making. As part of this, the role of information in supporting consultation and involvement is defined so that local representatives should be aware of:

- the different options available, the pros and cons of each and any other relevant background information;
- the decision-making process (i.e. how decisions are made, who makes the final decisions and what evidence is taken into consideration).

(ibid.: 22)

In addition to this, there is also a requirement that activities to inform should not take place in isolation, 'but as part of an integrated approach across the area' (ibid.: 25). Finally, there are some key information tests that need to be considered as part of the spatial planning process which are that authorities should be able to demonstrate that:

- they understand the interests and requirements of the local community;
- they use their understanding to ensure information … (is) provided on the right issues, targeted at the right people, and accessible to those the authority is trying to reach;
- they have an appropriate corporate approach to providing information.

(ibid.: 25)

The establishment of the core principles of a common evidence base for the local partners, including those preparing spatial plans, is set out in *Planning*

Box 4.5   Efficiency in data collection: using the COUNT principle

The COUNT principle of data collection is:

Count
Once
Use
Numerous
Times.

Together (CLG 2009a). This sets out a series of ways in which spatial planning and local evidence gathering and use are intertwined, including:

*   taking a collaborative approach to evidence gathering and use (see Box 4.5);
*   telling the story of place which includes the uses of evidence as set out in spatial analysis;
*   evidence providing the interconnection and common basis for spatial planning and the SCS as shared inputs;
*   the consultation processes and outcomes of the evidence base;
*   taking a shared approach to performance management and monitoring;
*   using a common sustainability appraisal.

At the local level, a common base for demographic evidence is being developed in the Joint Strategic Needs Assessment (JSNA). This is an English system (DH 2007; 2008) and is the common basis for all service estimates of current and future need. This is an important departure from existing practices at the local level where services have frequently used different population data and projections in relation to their own services. However, there may be issues about how these join up in terms of the spatial scales and age groups used for definitional purposes. Having a single approach in the JSNA reflects the understanding that all services are working with the same community.

A further issue with demographic data is how it is projected forward and which methods are used. Each service is likely to use different approaches. Some will be based on birth rates, some occupation rates of dwellings and some mortality rates. For the needs of spatial planning, there will need to be a three-phased approach which is consistent with the JSNA. This is as follows:

Phase 1 Consider the existing population and its needs into the future.
Phase 2 To this add any additional population that may arise from intensification of the existing housing stock, for example:
*   moving from under-occupation to full use
*   sub-dividing existing stock
*   change of use
*   garden grabbing
*   windfall sites.
Phase 3 To this add likely population changes from the development of identified strategic sites and in-migration.

All of this evidence can be used at the local level to identify services deficiencies and needs both now and in the future if they are considered in the context of current facilities, access to them, their current capacity and quality.

CONSULTATION PROCESSES AS EVIDENCE

Consultation in planning is a central part of the process of preparing a vision or a plan and a means of confirming public acceptance of specific stages of the process. However, the position of consultation as a process to one which is part of evidence gathering is changing its nature. This switch has been promoted through the 2007 Local Government and Public Involvement in Health Act where consultation has been made part of the duty to involve; the consultation process is now included as part of the evidence base and included within decision making rather than as a separate process (CLG 2008d). Furthermore, the definition of evidence has been extended so that all relevant consultation, undertaken by the wider public sector and other organisations such as parish councils, developers and communities, should be taken into account.

This approach to consultation is more robust and systematic. Although planning has long engaged in systematic consultation, it has also been criticised for being tokenistic or shallow (Brownill and Carpenter 2007). There has been little evidence that consultation responses have been sought through the use of modern methods, with planners frequently relying on public meetings, exhibitions and newspapers. The inclusion of the processes and outcomes of consultation within the evidence base, and then to have this evaluated, increases its importance and may encourage more engagement. It also means that spatial planning processes will need to systematically include ways it can demonstrate that consultation has been used as evidence as part of the process of developing its plans. In PPS 12, the inclusion of consultation as part of the evidence base is underlined (CLG 2008c: §4.37), and the Statement of Community Involvement is no longer to be examined as part of the LDF but is being brought together with all the other local public sector consultation processes and reviewed by the Audit Commission as part of Comprehensive Area Assessment.

USING EVIDENCE IN SPATIAL PLANNING

The role of evidence is central to the process of spatial planning. As Davoudi and Strange (2009) point out, *Patrick Geddes' maxim*, 'survey analysis, and plan', within the more positivist tradition, has always formed the basis of planning. Over time, some of the debates in planning have been about differential access to evidence and whether evidence has been used to inform judgements or planning decisions. Healey might describe this as the 'policy or governance' considerations in planning processes, and sees planning as being more than 'the translation of knowledge into action' (2006: 219). The planning debate is frequently caught between the dilemma between what 'is' and what 'ought' to be. Much of planning practice deals with what is manifest in a place and developing strategies to manage or encourage change. This now extends to making this happen. Durning (2004) also found that as planning develops as an academic subject, its research findings and contributions to the literature have to be more like those of other subjects where practical applications of research are more distant. This could serve to reduce the confidence that planning practitioners have in the use of planning research over time or at least see it as being less relevant to their own needs.

However, the debate is necessarily more subtle than this. The focus on individuals as consumers rests on a wish to counterbalance 'producer-based' approaches to policy making and service delivery. Rather than being oppositional, consumerist and collaborative approaches represent an attempt to achieve the same ends that are both democratically based, but they represent different means to achieve them. All of this matters when considering the role of evidence in spatial planning. At the local level, parish plans are a significant contributor of evidence and are locally based. Nevertheless, community-based or parish plans may not have been developed collaboratively nor may they have achieved a consensual agreement on local priorities. All evidence will need analysis and then political choices are made. Any evidence base has wider currency once it is in the public domain and it is easier to challenge. As part of the process of developing the LDF, it is suggested that the evidence base required to underpin the plan is discussed with stakeholders to identify 'what the main components of the evidence base need to be' (CLG 2008c: §4.56). One of the key ToS in PPS 12 is that the core strategy has been developed on a robust and credible evidence base (ibid.: §4.52) and is a central feature both in plan preparation and deliverability.

The importance of evidence for spatial planning within the English system is identified in PPS 12 (ibid.: §2.1); it provides the spatial evidence to underpin the wider plans and strategies that the local authority is pursuing (ibid.: §2.2) and in this way is a net contributor to the evidence pool. This can be scoped at the beginning of the process (Atkins 2008) but will also need to be kept under review during the process as the evidence needs to be available at the beginning as far as possible but it will also become available as plans are prepared and implemented. Circumstances might change and these can require some immediate response. Major events such as the closure of a factory or land that has been flooded for the first time might require an immediate review. Other changes such as the increase in the birth rate after 2001 may have creeping implications for infrastructure and service delivery such as nursery and school places and housing with more bedrooms that may emerge over time. Other important demographic changes such as the age structure of the population from retired to young families can also significantly increase service pressure without creating a need for additional dwelling space.

LDFs also need to provide evidence of how they are to be delivered and, as part of the ToS, the evidence to demonstrate this needs to:

*   show that it is consistent with other plans and strategies for adjoining areas;
*   be based on infrastructure delivery planning;
*   demonstrate that there are no barriers to delivery;
*   demonstrate that all delivery partners are signed up.

                                                (After PPS 12 (CLG 2008c: §4.45))

SPECIFIC STUDIES FOR SPATIAL PLANNING

Spatial planning approaches draw from the wide sources of evidence discussed here. They will also need specific studies that can be used for developing the plan or testing it and these can also be contributed to the wider evidence pool. For example, studies on flooding will be useful for emergency planning, health and other emergency services. When preparing an LDF, 'each council must decide which information will be required for their own purposes' (Atkins 2008: 1.7). The development of evidence with other authorities as a part of Joint Core Strategies is also considered (CLG 2008c: §4.18). The development of a joint evidence base for both the SCS and the LDF is recommended (ibid.: §4.35) and has been implemented in some authorities, e.g. Lancaster (Planning Advisory Service 2009).

(I) WATER CYCLE STUDIES (WCS)

One of the key concerns in collecting the evidence that underpins the spatial planning process is to ensure that there is adequate information on the supply of services such as water, drainage and energy. Although utilities are required to supply services wherever required, they can also contribute evidence on existing supply and likely areas of shortage in the future. With water, there are two key areas to consider. The first is the supply of water for domestic and commercial use. The second is a concern about waste water and drainage which is related to heightened risks of flooding. Both issues are relevant when considering new development and the consequences of a more intensified use of existing land and buildings. WCS are now frequently being used at the local level to bring all these considerations together with those agencies and partners that are involved in water management. WCS have primarily been developed for areas of growth but are being used more commonly to review water issues elsewhere (see Box 4.6).

The methodology for a WCS has been set out by Defra (2007) and is in three stages – scoping, outline and detailed. The scoping study helps to define the area under consideration which may be part of the local authority or wider to cover more

Box 4.6   Using a water cycle study

A water cycle study will help to plan for water more sustainably by:

- bringing together all partners' and stakeholders' existing knowledge, under-standing and skills;
- bringing together all water and planning evidence under a single framework;
- understanding the environmental and physical constraints to development;
- working alongside green infrastructure planning to identify opportunities for more sustainable planning;
- identifying water cycle planning policies and a *water cycle strategy* to help all partners plan for a sustainable future water environment.

Source: Defra 2007

than one local authority. It also establishes the management of the study process in which stakeholders should be involved and assesses what information is already available. The environmental risks and constraints in the area are considered and whether the existing system can cope with future development needs. This will include an assessment of existing capacity. This may then continue on to a more detailed study which identifies the measures required for implementation if there are specific issues to be addressed.

Undertaking a WCS can be an important contribution to evidence in areas where new development is being planned or alternative development scenarios are being reviewed. There may also be existing water issues to be considered and these can also be reviewed in this way. Although privatised services, water providers, like other utilities, are subject to a strong regulatory regime and known as 'services of public interest' within EU law. The utility regulators, in this case Ofwat, have strict rules about investment and pricing and the terms of what can be funded and charged are reviewed every five years. As part of the competition regulation, utilities are not permitted to discuss their unpublicised plans beyond the current five-year period and this often creates dilemmas for planners who want to review the options over a longer period, although the water companies have now been asked to publish 25-year water resource management plans (Defra 2009).

In growth areas, WCS have been undertaken for Greater Norwich, Milton Keynes and Basingstoke.

(II) FLOOD RISK ASSESSMENT

The increase in areas that have flooded for the first time has been seen as evidence of the impact of climate change and has brought flood risk assessment to the fore in spatial planning evidence gathering. In many areas, the risk of flooding has been reduced from one in 100 years to one in ten years. The likely incidence of flooding can be seen on maps available on the Environment Agency website (www.environment-agency.gov.uk). The increased risk of flooding has also had a major effect on the assessment of sites for future development and has had the effect in many local authority areas of reducing the number of available sites for development. In some cases, the potential risk of flooding can be mitigated through design approaches, including only locating residential accommodation the first floor, for example – a technique that is also used in other countries.

The high level of first-time flooding which occurred in England in 2007 was considered by the Pitt Review (Cabinet Office 2008) and has also been accompanied by planning guidance (CLG 2010a). Through PPS 25, each local authority is required to prepare a Strategic Flood Risk Assessment as part of its evidence base. Guidance and advice on how to undertake a Strategic Flood Risk Assessment is given in the companion guidance to PPS 25 (CLG 2009j), which also provides flow charts, case studies and further information leads. The assumption is now that any development could be at risk of flooding during its lifetime (which is normally assumed to be minimally sixty years). The role of flood risk assessment is to appraise, manage and reduce the risk of flooding in these areas though systematic, evidence-based approaches. In most local authority areas, this process is being undertaken by specialist consultants rather than in-house and the Flood Risk Assessment is one of the major studies that are commissioned as part of the spatial planning process. It is also one of the key studies that will be used by all other partners in the area and may be an important determinant for their own service planning both for the emergency services but also the location of services and the back-up for the future.

There are two main ways in which flooding can occur at the local level.[1] The first is through rivers and other water courses overflowing their banks. This might be due to heavy rainfall on upland areas and may be seasonal. The second can be due to this together with high levels of precipitation in urban areas where the drainage system is unable to cope with the volume of water. This flooding may be caused by drainage design, capacity or lack of maintenance. In both cases, the application of Sustainable Urban Drainage Systems (SUDS) is a response which can be applied to new development (Defra 2007a), through development management policies for individual development. The implementation of SUDS may also be an initiative that could be identified as an infrastructure requirement for potential flood risk areas that are to be retrofitted.

(III) HOUSING

The role of evidence in underpinning the LDF requirements for housing have changed over time. The population-based approaches were frequently viewed as unsatisfactory by planners because they were not able to then translate these numbers into tenure. There could also be an overall adequate supply of housing, including planning consents, but this may not have matched specific housing demand. Other approaches identified the housing market in detail and then the land available to match the requirements, taking into account more detailed locations, tenure types and likely delivery from a more complete basis for identifying housing requirements. This approach also sets out links for the provision of housing with adequate community services and this can be a reason to intensify housing in some areas where the viability of services could be secured through increased community size.

The main issue in terms of the evidence base for housing in the LDF process is the derivation and use of targets for housing supply numbers. These have been placed in the system in three main ways that are all strongly influenced by Government:

- Regional Spatial Strategies (until 2010)
- Local Area Agreements (which may or may not be the same as RSS figures)
- National Housing and Planning Unit – whose figures are generally higher than all other requirements.

All of these approaches are based on *projection* methods of calculation related to population, past trends and indications of the likely mix required by tenure and household size. Other methods of calculating housing requirements for the future are based on a mix of information that includes:

- migration projections and forecasts
- past building rates
- assessment of current need
- provision of housing through intensification means.

Policy for the provision of housing was set out in the Housing Green Paper (CLG 2007f) and it is translated into a local strategic housing plan that covers all the issues in relation to housing needs for the future. However, when translated into the LDF, the only housing that is taken into account is that derived from government-based projections on planned and identified sites. Housing that is provided through other means including conversions and change of use, together with housing redevelopment sites – so-called 'windfall' sites are not and cannot be taken into account (CLG 2007b). Although the strategic housing role has been defined, there has been criticism that it has not been sufficiently developed or used at the local level (Audit Commission 2009c).

The continuing emphasis of the role of development planning in ensuring that enough housing is built to meet projected requirements remains a central focus in the spatial planning process. In the LDF and the LAA, the focus remains on the provision of new dwellings which need to be added to additional capacity created through demographic change (see section on older people Chapter 7) and the intensification of urban areas through:

- subdivision of existing properties and granny annexes
- conversion to housing of schools, churches, warehouses, pubs
- development of gardens
- use of small plots previously uneconomic to develop
- use of space above shops.

There are also estimated 500,000 vacant dwellings in England that would add to the useable stock to meet some of these needs (CLG 2008g). The focus on new housing development is part of the approach to maintaining and growing the economy as an indicator, a stimulus and as a support. If companies need to expand or grow, this can be impeded through a lack of provision of housing available in the areas and at the price required.

Within spatial planning, the role of housing is to ensure a range and mix of homes in localities taking into account the need for choice and to meet demand. The evidence base used to assess housing requirements at the local level has primarily consisted of population projections and demographic change and planning was not concerned with tenure but overall supply. The approach has now been overtaken through a more detailed approach to housing provision PPS 3 (CLG 2006c). This set out the key objectives of housing policy which are then to be delivered through local evidence collection and analysis. For housing, the 'specific outcomes that the planning system should deliver are:

- High-quality housing that is well designed and built to a high standard.
- A mix of housing, both market and affordable, particularly in terms of tenure and price, to support a wide variety of households in all areas, both urban and rural.
- A sufficient quantity of housing taking into account need and demand and seeking to improve choice.
- Housing developments in suitable locations, which offer a good range of community facilities and with good access to jobs, key services and infrastructure.
- A flexible, responsive supply of land – managed in a way that makes an efficient and effective use of land, including re-use of previously developed land where appropriate'.

(ibid.: §10)

The remainder of PPS 3 sets out how these objectives are met through the planning system and these requirements are underpinned at the local level through evidence generated through two specific studies. These are the SHMA and the SHLAA and are to be undertaken as part of LDF preparation.

The guidance on the preparation of SHMAs for the LDF identifies the standards to which the evidence provided on housing markets must conform if it is to be accepted. This includes both the process to be followed and the outputs to be delivered. These are shown in Boxes 4.7 and 4.8. The guidance outlines the specific evidence that needs to be collected in the SHMA. This supports the requirement for consistency of approach across a region, so that all the SHMAs can fit together and give an overarching picture.

Many housing market areas will include more than one local authority area. Housing markets around cities will reflect transport provision and commuting patterns. People will view the housing market as one which is understood by them as offering a range of housing that allows some upward mobility and downsizing within the same area. It will also offer the opportunity to move from social or intermediate housing into owner occupied homes. Housing market areas will include different types and sizes of houses. Housing markets may also be sub-regional and these may be identified by at least three features:

- house price levels and rates of change
- household migration and search pattern
- travel to work and other functional areas.

(CLG 2007g)

Once the SHMA has been undertaken, it can be brought together with the SHLAA, although in practice the evidence gathering for both may be undertaken simultaneously. The purpose of a SHLAA is to:

- identify sites with potential for housing
- assess their housing potential
- assess when they are likely to be developed.

(CLG 2007h: §6)

Box 4.7 SHMA core outputs

1	Estimate current dwellings in terms of size, type, condition, tenure.
2	Analyse past and current housing market tends, including balance between supply and demand in different housing sectors and price/affordability and description of key drivers underpinning the housing market.
3	Estimate total future numbers of households, broken down by age ad type where possible.
4	Estimate current numbers of households in housing need.
5	Estimate future households that will require affordable housing.
6	Estimate future households requiring market housing.
7	Estimate the size of affordable housing required.
8	Estimate household groups which have particular requirements, e.g. families, older people, key workers, black and ethnic minority groups, disabled people, young people, etc.

Source: CLG 2007d; e

Box 4.8   SHMA process checklist

The SHMA process should:

1   Ensure that the approach to identifying housing market areas is consistent with other approaches within the region.
2   Assess housing market conditions within the context of the housing market area.
3   Involve key stakeholders, including housebuilders.
4   Contain a full technical explanation of the methods employed with any limitations noted.
5   Justify assumptions, judgements and findings and present them in an open and transparent manner.
6   Use and report upon effective quality control mechanisms.
7   Explain how the assessment findings have been monitored and updated (where appropriate) since it was originally undertaken.

Source: CLG 2007 d; e

As part of this process, sites should lie in the sub-regional housing market area identified in the SHMA and it is this connection between the market requirements and sites which is at the heart of local spatial planning competency. Any assessment of the supply of housing sites will need to consider their locational suitability not only to market requirements but also to the existence of infrastructure including transport and community facilities. These provisions may not be in the same local authority area as many administrative boundaries do not reflect how people use their localities. If the SHMA traverses more than one local authority, then it will be important that the housing sites identified support the local authority's role in the housing market area. This will help to support the LDF Test of Soundness for consistency and coherence across boundaries. The minimum requirement is to identify enough sites for at least the first ten years of the plan, and ideally for the whole 15-year period of the LDF. The SHLAA is part of the evidence base for the LDF and as such should be kept up to date.

The methodology for the SHLAA is based on discussions with land owners, stakeholders, developers, social landlords and others (POS 2008). This is considered within the context of meeting overall housing numbers that have been set through the RSS or contracted through the LAA. The outputs of the SHLAA, i.e. the evidence that it is produced upon which decisions about housing locations will be made and the evidence base, are also expected to be kept up to date. It is expected to show:

*   a list of sites, cross-referenced to maps showing locations and boundaries of specific sites (and showing broad locations where necessary);
*   assessment of the deliverability/developability of each identified site (i.e. in term of its suitability, availability an achievability) to determine when an identified site is realistically expected to be developed;

- potential quantity of housing that could be delivered on each identified site or within each identified broad location (where necessary) or on windfall sites (where justified);
- constraints on the delivery of identified sites;
- recommendations on how these constraints could be overcome and when.

(CLG 2007h: §7)

Now that housing tenure is able to be taken into account in LDFs, one key concern may be that the lack of sound LDFs might hamper the provision of the affordable housing supply. The funding for affordable housing has been provided through a number of sources including the public purse and also through developers' contributions. The case for negotiating developer-provided affordable homes is based, to a large extent, on having an up-to-date evidence base of the housing market requirements and also the viability of the development to provide the affordable homes, within the financial downturn. Although there have been some concerns about the volume of affordable housing provided through developers' contributions and has depended on the skills of planning authorities as negotiators (Burgess and Monk 2007), the introduction of a Community Infrastructure Levy to streamline contributions has made it clear that affordable housing is taken separately and before other contributions are considered (CLG 2010b). On the other hand, the provision of affordable homes could be affected by the availability of a five-year supply of housing land so that a pipeline of development can be available. The provision of a five-year supply of housing land has been supported through the new Housing and Planning Delivery Grant to local authorities (CLG 2009k).

This places constraints and challenges to the spatial planning system at the local level. The provision of new housing is frequently not politically popular. If politicians can say that they are providing housing numbers that are required by Government, then they may find this to be a more acceptable argument to put locally. The switch to the LAA model, where local politicians have signed up to deliver specific housing numbers, makes this a more difficult argument to promote.

SUSTAINABILITY APPRAISAL (SA)

SA is an essential feature of the evidence base of spatial planning. SA provides a systematic way of reviewing the approaches to spatial planning in a way which seeks to make transparent and externalise the impacts of policies and proposals. It can also demonstrate the impacts of doing nothing, which can be significant in some cases. SA includes both types of evidence set out here – that derived from quantitative and qualitative data review and that derived from consultation. There may be an argument to consider SA as part of the external assessment of the spatial planning process rather than the evidence base and that by including it as evidence, this somehow reduces the external validation process. However, SA has an interactive relationship with policies and plans and it is the process within which alternatives can be considered and evaluated. SA is not compromised in its role as part of the evidence base but can have a stronger, more formal relationship with spatial planning and that the issues identified through the SA are taken within the spatial planning process.

Within a local area, spatial plans are among a range of plans and strategies that need SA. In some cases, there will be a good reason to bring the SA processes together because the plans interrelate with each other, the community can be confused by too many similar processes and it can be more efficient. At the local level, bringing together SA for DPDs and the SCS is likely to be beneficial and is recommended (CLG 2008c; 2009a). Application of the SA is required under the EU Directive 2001/42/EC on the 'assessment of the effects of certain plans and programmes on the environment'. As an EU Directive, this has to be transposed into UK legislation which, in England, is through the Environmental Assessment of Plans and Programmes Regulations 2004. For the DPD, then the SA is part of the evidence base and 'should form part of the integrated part of the plan preparation process' (CLG 2008c: §4.40). An SA is not a one-off process but needs to work in parallel with spatial planning processes. Guidance on SA has been provided for regional and LDF processes (ODPM 2005c), and this has identified the ways in which SA should be incorporated into the DPD preparation process from pre-production to adoption. This is shown in Table 4.3. For any DPD, having an SA is a necessary part of finding what it is sound and can be adopted.

There are different views about whether an SA should be undertaken by the spatial planning team or whether it is better conducted externally (Planning Advisory Service 2007c). In practice, whether this be undertaken internally or externally, it is likely to be influenced by the methodology of the SA and how the approach is conducted. What is most important is having a transparent methodology and an audit trail that can demonstrate the processes and the subsequent actions that have been taken to adjust any plans, policies or programmes. Other issues will concern the points of measurement or reference taken for the SA. As Cowell (2004) points out, there are debates within the sustainability field about weak or strong applications of SA. The approach that is taken will need to be open to examination and testing.

The role of SA has also been brought into greater relief given the fuller recognition of the implications of climate change at international, national and local levels

Table 4.1 Incorporating SA within the DPD process

DPD Stage 1	*Pre-production evidence gathering*

Stage A: setting the context and objectives, establishing the baseline and deciding on the scope

A1	Identifying other relevant policies, plans and programmes and sustainability objectives
A2	Collecting baseline information
A3	Identifying sustainability issues and problems
A4	Developing the SA framework
A5	Consulting on the scope of the SA

DPD Stage 2	*Production*

Stage B: developing and refining options and assessing effects

B1	Testing the DPD objectives against the SA framework
B2	Developing the DPD options
B3	Predicting the effects of the DPD
B4	Evaluating the effects of the DPD
B5	Considering ways of mitigating adverse effects and maximising beneficial effects
B6	Proposing measures to monitor the significant effects of implementing the DPDs

Stage C: preparing the Sustainability Appraisal report

C1	Preparing the SA report

Stage D: consulting on the preferred options of the DPD and SA report

D1	Public participation on the preferred options of the SA Report
D2(i)	Appraising the significant changes

DPD Stage 3	*Examination*

D2(ii)	Appraising significant changes resulting from representations

DPD Stage 4	*Adoption and monitoring*

D3	Making decisions and providing information

Stage E: monitoring the significant effects of implementing the DPD

E1	Finalising aims and methods for monitoring
E2	Responding to adverse effects

Source: ODPM 2005c: 39

(Stern 2009). In spatial planning, the need to consider the implications of climate change has been emphasised by the RTPI in the seven commitments set out in the *Planning to Live with Climate Change Action Plan* (RTPI 2009b). Whether in the assessment of flooding risk, energy generation or waste management, all form part of the SA, both individually and in a synergistic way. SA can learn from previous events and occurrences, but as the flooding episodes of 2005 and 2006 demonstrate, these can frequently occur in locations with no previous history of flooding. Climate change therefore suggests a more systematic approach to risk assessment, mitigation and adaptation.

INFRASTRUCTURE

The underpinning of what is required in infrastructure planning is 'evidence of what physical, social and green infrastructure is needed' and 'should cover who will provide the infrastructure and when it will be provided' (CLG 2008c: §4.8) and the outcome of the infrastructure process should be part of a 'sound evidence base' (ibid.: §4.10). This infrastructure evidence base will also underpin the Community Infrastructure Levy as part of the delivery strategy (ibid.: §4.12).

A key concern in using special studies as part of the LDF process is that their approach and methodology can be inward looking and silo-based. All of these issues require individual studies in depth, as do those included here, need a specific focus and attention, together with expertise on methodology and evidence collection and analysis. However, they also run the risk of being seen as ends in themselves, particularly where there are specialist inputs to the process. A key approach in spatial planning is taking the evidence into account and then coming to a judgement about how the balance of risk and outcomes can be placed. This is the same in the use of all evidence. However, it is true that the evidence collected as part of some of these studies, such as the Strategic Flood Risk Assessment, may override or generate a first assessment of options that may limit another alternative to be considered. When discussing the role of evidence-based policy making earlier in this chapter, we reviewed the extent to which the application of evidence is undertaken within a political context and this is part of the evidence process. Similarly, as noted above, consultation is part of the evidence base. In considering evidence on issues such as flooding, this may have a stronger role in a more undiluted form compared to other evidence that is considered and this needs to be taken into consideration within any sequential evidence processes.

PUTTING EVIDENCE IN THE PUBLIC DOMAIN

One of the key considerations of using evidence for spatial planning is that it should be publicly available and easy to obtain. Freedom of Information (FOI) legislation means that most information in the public sector is able to be accessed by any individual so this creates a new working approach to information availability (Mayo and Steinberg 2007). Information has to be available even where it is elsewhere on websites. This particular issue in planning has a high dissatisfaction rate recorded for the use of planning information on local authority websites where 52 per cent of people attempting to access planning information had difficulty finding the information they wanted (GovMetric 2009). One of the key problems encountered by those accessing information is the way that websites are designed to replicate departmental structures. This is a 'producer-focussed' approach. The information is set out in ways that make sense to the organisation or department and frequently has no user evaluation process associated with it. Many local authority websites locate planning information according to the legacy of planning systems, starting with UDPs as the landing page for planning policy and then moving on to LDFs. This is not user friendly.

Another issue is the language used to describe the evidence that underpins the spatial planning process. This is frequently jargonistic and relates how information and evidence is used in ways that most non-professionals will not understand. The evidence provided on the website is also frequently incomplete. It will list and frequently link to special studies that have been undertaken as part of the LDF process including Flood Risk Assessments or the SHMAA but the other evidence that has been used, such as reports on individual schools from Ofsted, health profiles, air quality maps and population data, are frequently held elsewhere on the website and not included as full evidence for the LDF. Indeed, there is frequently no framework for all the evidence that has been used in the process of spatial planning.

This may now be improved as the evidence for the local authority area is being collected into a single place so that it is easier to point people to this rather than special sections of the planning department's website. The use of FOI to obtain the information on which decisions have been taken has increased. This can include information about almost any issue unless there are contractual or security reasons why the information cannot be released. FOI applies to all public bodies and is most frequently used by the public to obtain information on decisions where they may be unhappy with the outcomes. It is also used by the private sector to obtain information on suppliers, size of budgets and other procedural matters. Given the scope and scale of the FOI, it is generally recommended that as much information as is reasonably possible is placed in the public domain and that it is set out in ways that make it accessible and legible for users. When preparing any document within a public organisation, including emails, it is reasonable to expect that it may be subject to a future FOI request and so needs to be drafted and considered accordingly.

CONCLUSIONS

The use of evidence in spatial planning is an important part of the process. Evidence can identify key issues and locations for action but these will always operate within a values-driven framework. Evidence has to be weighed against objectives and choices have to be made where there are competing claims for action. These choices are made by politicians based on advice from officers. Decisions will be based on local priorities, evidence and other considerations such as public consultation. Those who are able to participate and represent themselves will be served by consultation; those who may be less able to represent their own views may be served better by other kinds of evidence.

CHAPTER 5

COMMUNITY INVOLVEMENT IN SPATIAL PLANNING

INTRODUCTION

Community involvement is a central feature of spatial planning. It is a key source of evidence in the plan-making process and is a way that individuals, communities and businesses can see that their views have been sought and taken into account. The use of evidence in the spatial planning process needs to be transparent and collected in ways that are inclusive and appropriate. In this chapter, the purposes of community involvement, its relationship with spatial planning and the methods that can be used are discussed.

There has been much debate about the role of consultation and whether it can ever be more than a tokenistic approach. Parker (2008) identifies this scepticism and relates it to the quality of the processes that have been undertaken, whilst Doak and Parker describe the process of consultation in planning as potentially 'stillborn' despite a considerable push for more participative processes (2005: 30). Dickert and Sugarman (2005) have proposed that consultation should be based on ethical goals, where the processes and outcomes can also be evaluated by the community. Planning has a longer involvement in consultative and participative methods of engagement in its processes, and may have been on the first services to openly include participation as part of formal process (Morphet 2005). However, as Nadin (2007) points out, by the late 1990s it was struggling to keep up with the wider use of community-based approaches in local decision making.

The drive for more local engagement that was set out in *Modern Local Government: In Touch with the People* (DETR 1998) started the promotion of active engagement which has continued since. These approaches to involving people as communities, customers or individuals have not always been successful, but they do mark a change in focus. This has culminated in the 2007 Local Government and Public Involvement in Health Act which now requires a more formal and centralised approach to consultation through a 'duty to involve' by public bodies. It also sets a transparent approach to the use of evidence, so that those engaging in the decision-making process have a more equal access to the information available to political decision makers and can see if their views have been taken into account.

The interest in more deliberative democracy has been particularly developed over the last decade, and may draw its provenance from the private sector, where keeping close to customers is as important as managing the balance sheet (Mintrom 2003: 53).

Although the marketisation of the public sector has been regarded as an anathema to many, the return of a left-leaning government created a mixed public sector, which is drawing its tools from a variety of sources. More recently, the voluntary and community sectors have emerged as service providers (HM Treasury and Cabinet Office 2007). This means that the role and quality of public engagement through participative methods has to be more transparent. When all services were run directly by local authorities, elected councillors could claim a democratic mandate which did not replace a participative approach but at least could make some legitimate link between service user and provider. The evolution of the mixed economy has meant that the client or owner of the services has to take far more care of customer feedback and quality of delivery, not least where the provision of a service is out-sourced to another local authority, or the community or private sector. On the other hand, a mixed economy also enables services to be offered in new formats without lengthy negotiations about change and also allows segmentation of services to meet the needs of specific users.

The goal of increasing participation in the development and delivery of public services has many different and complex objectives. In some cases, participative democracy is a means of improving efficiency at all scales (Putnam 2000) whilst, in other cases, it engages people in hard decisions in a form of co-production. By finding ways of increasing ownership in decision making, then hard decisions may not seem so unpalatable. The recent shift to LAAs produces a quasi-voluntaristic model for housing where provision has previously been hierarchical. The LAA includes 'negotiation' and is described as a co-production approach to delivery although, in the case of housing, many local authorities would not have included any target in their LAA without extreme government pressure (Morphet 2009b). So participation 'in' and consultation 'on' issues do not guarantee a sense of ownership in the decision that is taken. In some cases, consultation can be politically inconvenient for organisations. It is sometimes much easier for organisational leaders to advise that targets, allocations of housing or other unsought developments such as prisons or hostels are imposed from a higher tier of government, as this exonerates them from the decision making process.

BUILDING SOCIAL AND INSTITUTIONAL CAPITAL

Although much consultation is conducted through single events for particular schemes or issues, there is now more consideration about building longer-term community structures and dialogue. In part, this derives from the notion of social capital as discussed in the work of Putnam, where In *Bowling Alone* (2000), he describes the way in which places benefit from sustained local relationships. These may come through neighbourliness but are extended through local organisations such as schools, places of worship, sports and social clubs and community organisations. Social capital is based on the notion of social reciprocity which, Putnam argues, 'is more efficient than a distrustful society ... trustworthiness lubricates social life. Frequent interaction between a diverse set of people tends to produce a norm of generalised reciprocity. Civic engagement and social capital entail mutual obligation and responsibility for action' (ibid.: 20).

The concept of social capital has been influential in the development of social change policy in England. Building on Putnam's notion that places with higher levels of social capital are more efficient, the approach suggests that the culture of work-lessness can only be dealt with through the development of social capital at the local level which influences this behaviour positively and this can build to more effective regional and national economies and less dependency on the state. In their assess-ment of the role of social capital, the Performance and Innovation Unit suggested that there were a number of ways of developing social capital at the local level which would have beneficial outcomes, including:

* promoting institutions that foster community
* community IT networks
* new approaches to the planning and design of the built environment
* dispersing social housing
* using personal networks to pull individuals and communities out of poverty.

(Aldridge *et al.* 2002: 7–8)

Although much of Putnam's research has been undertaken in Italy, social capi-tal seems to relate well to US society where there is a much higher affiliation with faith and neighbourhood groups than in England. It is also based on a fundamental principle of social control – where local organisations are exercising positive influ-ence and control over their members. This may not be either as acceptable or as effective in England where the ability to represent different views is a long held tenet of society. However, the notion of social capital has some positive features which can be considered and adapted to establish a longer-lasting approach to working with communities. More integrated local consultation by all local partners including local authorities, police and health could lead to more developed relationships with local groups, organisations, businesses and individuals. It may be possible to build a profile of key issues and interests which groups want to be consulted on or where they have identified some specific interest. These could be groups interested in neighbourhoods or villages but could also be special interest groups around age, specific health conditions or historic churches. Social capital can be translated into institutional capital. This represents the extent to which the community is engaged in managing its own affairs and can straddle formal and informal groups. Some local authorities have been developing institutional capital as a part of the process of engagement in spatial planning.

SERVICE USERS AS CUSTOMERS

A significant development in the delivery of public sector services in the past decade has been an interest in consumer or customer design of services. This approach is both drawn from the private sector where customer choice is one (but not the only) basis for markets. Some have described this as the 'marketisation' of public services (Clarke 2007: 98). This also implies a shift to a more diversified range of providers of services rather than single public bodies. However, the 'user' approach to the design of services is more than 'marketisation' arguments suggest. 'It also reflects a move away from a more monolithic approach to public service provision, where one size fits all' (Corry 2004: 7). Further, 'it is argued that people are who are used to being treated as consumers in the rest of life, exercising choices about money and services, are no longer content simply to be the passive recipients of whatever kinds of services that the state provides' (Wright and Ngan 2004: 18). A consumer approach has been most frequently found in the diversification of health care, through changing opening hours and availability of primary health care through walk-in centres, online and by phone. This represents a general move from a producer-driven approach to service delivery – i.e. services provided in ways that suit providers or which they consider to be appropriate to an approach which is consumer driven and where service users have the opportunity to access them at times and in ways that are convenient to them (HM Treasury 2007b).

The development of consumer-led design of services has incorporated a range of terms which each stand for part of this approach. These include 'contestability' and 'choice and voice' in public services (House of Commons 2004; OPSR 2005). The idea of 'voice' is that of listening and many local authorities indicate how they are responding to complaints, feedback and consultation through 'you say, we do' areas on their websites. However, this may reduce complex issues to levels which cannot easily be resolved. In this approach, the Government aims to be the citizen's champion for better services, rather than the service provider (Clarke 2005: 449). This presents some issues in practice, as the Government cannot disassociate itself from the responsibilities that it has for the services it provides. Even where services have been privatised, and it is potentially easier to make them more responsive, this does not absolve the Government or local authority from its ultimate responsibility. The notion of 'choice' is also about citizen engagement in the management of local services and also having their views considered in a more systematic way (Wright and Ngan 2004: 17). As Clarke points out, ministers have identified a number of reasons why choice must be a central feature of public service reform, including:

*   it is what users want
*   it provides incentives for driving up quality, responsiveness and efficiency

- it promotes equity
- it facilitates personalisation.

(2007: 104)

Different approaches to consultation may be needed at each point in the spatial planning process. When the local authority is developing its approach to the Core Strategy or an AAP, for example, it will be developing participative and inclusive methods, which may involve more visioning or engagement through externally facilitated approaches. However, the involvement of businesses, communities and individuals may change when the later versions of the Core Strategy are made available for consultation prior to its submission.

Part of the issue will always be the gap between those who are able to represent themselves or their organisations in an articulate and well informed way and those who do have easy access to the same kind of influence. Effective individuals and groups will know how to present arguments, evidence and where to apply pressure on politicians and other organisations. At the same time, there are still many communities, individuals and businesses that are struggling to survive rather than thinking about the future. Also, what local communities want may not suit the wider requirements of the area. However, full and comprehensive community engagement is a strong reason for local politicians to take an inclusive view.

A useful approach is to see consultation as part of corporate activity which can allow for a more professional and organised approach to all consultation events. This might allow longer-term relationships to develop and provide advice on how best to consult with different groups or in different areas at the same time as providing support on how the outcomes of this consultation can be used more systematically. What seems clear is that consultation benefits come from a more professional approach and it may no longer be something that planners can do as part of their skill set without seeking additional training or support from others with more expertise and experience.

THE ROLE OF CONSULTATION AS EVIDENCE

Although the role of consultation is embedded within the spatial planning, it is frequently regarded as a confirming process. Planners use consultation to assess how far the community is in favour of the proposals put forward or which choices are preferred. This is undertaken at different stages in the spatial planning process – when issues and options are considered and when the final draft of the Core Strategy has been prepared. Although consultation is an important step, it has not been given the same weight as evidence. The requirement to use consultation feedback as evidence will accord it a different status and role in plan making. Methods used for consultation will be evaluated in the same way as other evidence collection and, like more traditional evidence, the ways in which evidence has been incorporated into the plan-making process will need to be demonstrated. As with other evidence, an audit trail between collection and use has to be demonstrated. Spatial planning will also be expected to use consultation evidence gathered by other organisations and departments. As communities frequently become overburdened with consultations, joint consultation activities are likely to be preferred, where possible.

In a local authority, the overarching responsibility for consultation lies with the LSP and emerging indications of good practice include:

- a common consultation diary of all events in the area
- an online record of all consultation events
- an online commentary about each consultation point and how it has been addressed
- a variety of organisations can contribute consultation evidence including parishes and neighbourhoods, the private sector or community/interest groups.

CONSULTATION REQUIREMENTS IN PREPARING AN LDF: STATEMENT OF COMMUNITY INVOLVEMENT (SCI)

The role of consultation as an evidence source for spatial planning in the LDF was emphasised from the outset (ODPM 2004c). The case for community involvement in planning was set out as follows:

- involvement leads to outcomes that better reflect the views and aspirations and meet the needs of the wider community in all its diversity;
- public involvement is valuable as a key element of a vibrant, open and participatory democracy;
- involvement improves the quality and efficiency of decisions by drawing on local knowledge and minimising unnecessary and costly conflict;
- involvement educates all participants about the needs of communities, the business sector and how local government works;
- involvement helps promote social cohesion by making real connections with communities and offering them a tangible stake in decision making.

(ODPM 2004c: §1.4)

However, there are also barriers in the community engaging with spatial planning that need to be taken into account in the design, development and use of consultation methods:

- the costs of participation for local communities (and the planning authorities running community involvement exercise);
- the complexity of the issues;

- planning can seem a remote, bureaucratic process which does not encourage involvement;
- the difficulties of identifying and reaching different groups within a community;
- the language of planning with its reliance on technical expressions and jargon can be off-putting. Sometimes planners can inadvertently reinforce the barrier through the way they communicate;
- the perceptions that community involvement exercises will be captured by individuals or articulate groups which dominate proceedings. Community involvement is not about giving a free hand to unrepresentative vocal groups to block development irrespective of the case for it, nor is it about talking to a few, favoured organisations.

(ODPM 2004c: §1.5)

When preparing the LDF, it must be accompanied by a SCI. As Cullingworth and Nadin point out (2006: 437–8), this represents a major shift in what is required, and they see them as 'laudable intentions' (438). In PPS 12 (CLG 2008c), the Government's principles for community involvement in planning are based on the UNECE *Convention of Access to Information, Public Participation in Decision Making and Access to Justice in Environmental Matters* which states that:

> Each party shall make appropriate practical and/or other provision for the public to participate during the preparation of plans and programmes relating to the environment, within a transparent and fair framework, having provided the necessary information to the public.
>
> (Article 7)

Principles for community engagement for LDFs are:

- *Appropriate* to the level of planning.
- *From the outset* – leading to a sense of ownership of local policy decisions.
- *Continuous* – part of ongoing programme, not a one-off event, with clearly articulated opportunities for continuing involvement.
- *Transparent and accessible* – using methods appropriate to the communities concerned.
- *Planned* – as an integral part of the process for making plans.

(CLG 2008c: §4.20)

Consultation has to be continuous and proportionate to the issues being considered. The requirements for an SCI are shown in Box 5.1.

One of the key approaches to preparing the LDF is that of 'frontloading' which means that community engagement has to be from the outset. This should include the scoping and pre-production stages of the work and should contain:

1   Overall vision and common principles for community involvement.
2   The type of development plan documents you intend to produce and the stages in their production.
3   The individuals, groups and organisations that make up your community (including all the likely interests and any requirements for being involved).
4   When in the plan preparation process the community will have the opportunity to participate.
5   The approaches by which people can expect to be informed, consulted or involved.
6   How the outputs from engagement activities will be fed into the development documents.
7   How and when the community can receive information about progress or feed-back on outcomes.
8   How and when the community can expect to be involved in the determination on planning applications and the policy for pre-application advice.
9   When and how the engagement approaches will be evaluated and the SCI reviewed.
10   The resources that have been identified to enable delivery of the commitments in the SCI.

(Entec 2007)

Box 5.1   Statements of Community Involvement

A Statement of Community Involvement (SCI) should:

- Explain clearly the process and methods for community involvement for different types of local development documents and for different stages of plan preparation.
- Identify which umbrella organisations and community groups need be involved at different stages in the planning process, with special consideration given to those groups not normally involved.
- Explain the process and appropriate methods for effective community involve-ment in the determination of planning applications and where appropriate refer to Planning Performance Agreements.
- Include the local authority's approach to pre-application discussions.
- Include the local authority's approach to community involvement in planning obligations (s106 agreements).
- Include information on how the SCI will be monitored, evaluated and scrutinised at the local level.
- Include details of where community groups can get more information on the plan-ning process, for example, from Planning Aid and other voluntary organisations.
- Identify how landowner and developer interests will be engaged.

(CLG 2008c: §4.26)

The Entec report also identifies some key principles of what an SCI should include:

- A strategy that is neither too prescriptive nor too general which will ensure it is effective but retains an appropriate level of flexibility to be responsive to evolving local needs.
- A combination of engagement methods (involving different leaves of interaction) to ensure that activities will meet a broad range of individual's needs and expectations.
- Recognition of how greater effort or alternative approaches may be required to engage certain groups or individuals within your community (and how these will be delivered).
- A robust approach to managing information such as how stakeholder data bases will be managed, information shared with other departments and organisations and data protection commitments managed.
- Details of how the local authority intends to build the community's capacity (including raising awareness, building understanding, connecting people to the key issues and empowering certain communities who may not be traditionally involved). This could include a link to the local Planning Aid Office which provides support and planning advice to communities.
- Details of how the local authority intends to build trust and confidence in engagement processes generally; facilitating more meaningful relationships with stakeholders.

(Entec 2007: 8)

The 2007 Local Government and Public Involvement in Health Act includes a duty to involve which gives an overall duty to the Local Strategic Partnership for public sector consultation in a local authority area. In meeting these requirements, there is an implication that all the consultation undertaken within the local authority and by its LSP partners will need to be taken into account as part of the evidence base for the LDF. This specifically includes consultation on the Sustainable Community Strategy but will also include specific consultation activities, e.g. on library opening houses, town centre traffic improvements and consultations of changes in fire and rescue services. In the 2006 Local Government White Paper, it was proposed that the initial requirements for the SCI be examined by the independent person as a part of the Tests of Soundness (Planning Inspectorate National Service 2008b) and included in a wider approach to local community engagement at local authority level. This wider approach to consultation was included in the 2007 Local Government and Public Involvement in Health Act, where this examination will now be undertaken by the Audit Commission as part of the Comprehensive Area Assessment process also introduced by the 2007 Act and implemented from 2009.

CONSULTATION METHODS

There are many different methods of participation and consultation which can be used. The most popular approaches in planning have tended to be documents, exhibitions and public meetings (Sykes 2003). However, there has not been much evaluation of which approach is likely to be the most successful in different circumstances and on many occasions the use of consultation can seem to be more a box ticking requirement than a real process of engagement. When designing an approach to consultation, there are number of ways of choosing an appropriate method:

*   How many participants can the method involve effectively?
*   What type of participation does the method require?
*   How much does the process cost?
*   How much time does the method require to be deployed effectively?
*   Does the method match the outputs and outcomes required?
*   Where on the spectrum of participation does the method work best?

(1) COLLABORATIVE APPROACHES

One of the key theories that has been developed for planning has been through the work of Healey (2006). Collaboration has a focus on consensus building between groups and communities to achieve outcomes. This collaboration can also be between the community and organisations such as local authorities, the police, health organisations and economic partnerships. Consensus building may occur through the exchange of information, joint collection of information or the pursuit of joint policy outcomes (CLG 2008i). The approach to joint working has been developed in some areas of public policy such as health and social care. This has been through working on single outcomes and achieving these through budgets that have been aligned or pooled and staff have also been working in a more collaborative way. This approach to joint working is now extending to other activities including the provision of housing, reductions in CO_2 and improved estate management (CLG 2007c).

Collaborative working is operating across some sub-regions or in housing market areas, where groups of local authorities are working in ways that recognise functional urban areas rather than places that are confined within local authority administrative boundaries such as around Derby, Bristol and Nottingham. These approaches recognise the interdependency of places for the provision of employment and housing, transport systems or leisure and recreations facilities. Attempting to engage in consultation across boundaries may be more difficult than in single administrative areas as there may be less overall ownership of the process. In comparison, some stakeholders may find a cross-boundary approach easier to engage with as a larger area will represent places as they use them. Cross-boundary consultation requires particular attention in areas that do not have any formal democratic processes to support them. The development of informal sub-regions into those with formal governance structures may overcome this issue (CLG 2009d). Working across administrative boundaries also poses problems of accountability.

In areas of new population, it is difficult to find ways of consulting with people who have not yet arrived but will live in the growth area once it has been built. This poses particular problems of legitimacy and may lead some localities to assume that consultation is of less value. However, two different approaches to engaging potential residents can be used. The first is to assume that the new area will be much like existing areas as many of the new population might be already located nearby. As most house moves are over short distances, the views of nearby residents may well be pertinent and need to be taken into account. The second approach is to consider any research that has been undertaken in new communities elsewhere to determine what the key issues have been for new residents, business and service providers to see what can be learned in these circumstances.

Consensus building through collaboration can take time (Baker et al. 2006) and it may need a framework to be effective. Perhaps it is never possible to build a consensual outcome in some locations or communities or about specific development proposals. In some cases, decisions have to be taken which are locally unpopular but which meet the community's needs, and collaboration may be tested here. Those engaging in collaborative approaches may also have their own agendas, seeing this as a means of maximising their own position although even this collaboration may be beneficial (Rader Olsson 2009). Binding these difficult issues into the collaborative approach from the outset might work on specific sites as Bishop has shown from his work in Bristol (2007). However, this needs skill and patience and an external individual who can engage in shuttle diplomacy and bridge building as part of the process of indentifying successful outcomes. Any attempt at collaborative working implies a two-way process (Development Trusts Association 2006; CLG 2008g: 68).

(II) SURVEYS

Surveys can be undertaken in a variety of ways and the methods that are used will have an impact on the reliance that can be placed on the outcome. Surveys which are undertaken independently, using specialist survey providers, will always be regarded as being more reliable than other forms of survey. On the other hand, they may be expensive and outside the budget.

There are a variety of other survey formats. Some surveys are undertaken in the street. Here trained interviewers seeking out people that fit particular age, ethnicity or gender profiles that have been pre-selected to represent targets groups. Street surveys can also be on a first-come-first-serve basis such as those conducted at railway stations or on buses by the transport operating companies. Survey forms can be completed at exhibitions or following public meetings and can be about key issues or processes. Another popular form of survey is that undertaken by telephone. This might receive some negative responses as people make the assumption that it is a telesales call. However, someone who has received a service or attended a meeting and gave their details to be contacted later by phone, provides a good means of gathering information.

Some local authorities and other organisations are now conducting exit surveys after people have received a service – online or face to face. One way of collecting this information is through the use of a touchpad which can provide considerable information on service delivery immediately at the point where this has occurred. In some approaches such as GovMetric (www.govmetric.co.uk), it is possible to receive daily and weekly feedback on the responses that people have given on service delivery. This can be used in web delivery and again enables people to give feedback. Some local authorities undertake online surveys for users such as the annual Socitm survey which rates each local authority into different categories (www.egovregister.brent.gov.uk). In some cases, local authorities put feedback forms on their websites which allow users to comment if they have not been able to find the information they were seeking or the information was too shallow or confusing.

When using a survey approach, one of the key issues will always be the design of the questions, as these can have a significant role in the quality of any answers. It is usual to undertake a pilot survey from within the target group to see how they respond to questions, if they understand them and if the responses lie in the range of what was expected. Another consideration is how the questionnaire responses will be analysed. Is the address or postcode required, is the respondent's age, gender or working status relevant to the purpose of the survey? It might also be useful to know whether they are engaged in the process through membership of a group or association. All those administering the survey will need some kind of identification document so that those surveyed have some confidence in the confidentiality and credibility of the survey. Also it may be important to script all or part of the survey. This may be easier to do if the survey is undertaken by telephone but even having a clear introduction when stopping someone in the street can generate a better response even if the latter part of the survey is less scripted. In this approach, the questions need to be put in the form in which they are written and only pre-agreed prompts should be made otherwise there can be a concern about interviewer bias.

A final issue to consider in the methodology will be the survey sample selection and numbers of responses achieved. A higher response rate provides the opportunity to rely more on the data collected, although this can be moderated within statistical confidence levels. Response rates can be low and this needs to be taken into account.

If it is a small survey, then a minimum of 100 responses may be satisfactory. Also, late respondents are generally taken to be more representative of non-respondents and this might aid analysis and interpretation. If it is a larger or more professionally managed survey, then higher response rates would be expected. When reporting, it is expected that the method, survey numbers and responses are all part of the survey report and this should accompany the results. There may also be a commentary on the survey that may cover any specific relevant issues and a commentary on the results. The survey report can also indicate how the results are likely to be used and when.

(III) EXHIBITIONS

Holding exhibitions is a popular way of informing communities, individuals and businesses about change and can be used in connection with some of the other consultation methods set out here, including meetings, surveys and leaflets. Some exhibitions can be left in public areas such as in shopping centres or libraries. Where possible, it is also useful to have times when there are staff, councillors, community groups or scheme proposers attending the exhibition in order to give more information or encourage people to give their views and these times need to be well advertised. It may also be important to have people on hand who speak different languages. Exhibition material needs to be clear and well designed. They must give information and identify where choices are available about schemes or policy priorities. The exhibition might also show alternative sites for development and the reasons for them. Exhibitions need to be located in places that are relevant to the communities that are being targeted for their views and they need to be available in accessible locations and at times that meet local needs. In some cases, it might be useful to have a mobile exhibition that can move round neighbourhoods or rural areas. Holding an exhibition is not a robust method of consultation if used without any other method.

(IV) MEETINGS

Public meetings are frequently used for public consultation particularly in planning. These meetings can be held to discuss single planning applications, housing growth, changes within town centres or the future of an area as part of a spatial planning process. Public meetings can be organised in different ways and each will have an influence on the way in which the people who attend can participate.

The most common form of arrangements for public meetings is to arrange the meeting room in a 'theatre' style. This is where the seats are arranged in rows and there is a 'top table' from which people speak. Generally those on the platform will introduce the meeting and there may be contributions or presentations to the audience. Following this, there is generally an opportunity for the audience to ask questions of the panel. In this approach, there is little opportunity for interaction between members of the audience or between the audience and the speakers. Frequently, those who ask questions or make contributions are the most socially confident or who have come to make a specific point. In some meetings, local authority councillors may be sitting in the audience and may make a number of contributions from the floor. This style of consultation can be associated with others such as an exhibition and/or a survey. This type of consultation meeting may be useful to get across information but can be frustrating for both those who are seeking consultation responses and those who want to make them. It gives very few opportunities for people to speak and many people may feel after the event that their views have not been aired. The formal layout can also suggest that the decisions will be taken elsewhere and indeed options may already have been narrowed down.

A second form of a public consultation meeting is where the room is arranged in a 'cabaret' style – that is with a number of round tables, seating eight or ten people. In this approach people can be pre-allocated to a table to ensure a mix of participants or a grouping together of people with similar interests. Another approach is to randomly allocate people to tables as they arrive at the meeting. Once the meeting starts – this may involve a short introductory presentation but the major part of the session takes place in small group discussions around the individual tables – each table may discuss the same issues and questions, or individual or groups of tables can be given the same issues to discuss. A format for this approach that enables everyone to participate in discussion is as follows:

- Table members introduce themselves and say briefly why they have come to the consultation meeting – this allows everyone to make their point at an early stage of a session.
- A scribe or rapporteur is appointed to list out key points from discussion on a flip chart.
- Towards the end of the discussions, the group decides which of the key points they wish to report back to all the other groups (the number chosen can depend on the number of people attending and the number of tables).
- A report back is made of the key points.
- The flip chat sheets are collected and all participants receive a copy of all the points made; this can be accompanied by any presentations made and a simple analysis of the key points.
- This can be used to feed into setting priorities and can be used later to report back to groups on what has been done about the issues that were raised.

A cabaret-style consultation meeting provides everyone who attends with an opportunity to speak and enables a wide range of consultation responses to be collected. The reporting-back session allows each table to share its priority view that has been agreed through discussion. This approach reduces the dominance of individuals in consultation meeting processes and provides a richer range of consultation responses. This approach also encourages participants to remain in contact with the consultation process and they can continue to be updated.

A third approach to consultation is through a market place where there are different stalls or presentations around a room. Participants choose to take part in short presentation sessions which enable them to leave their views behind on notes or cards. Preferences can be voted on at the end of the session using paper or electronic voting methods. This approach can be useful in enabling a wide range of views to be put forward and it is an active approach. However, all participants may not attend all the presentations and the results for this process may be less rounded than those in the previous method. It is a useful approach for enabling a number of organisations to put forward their views and priorities.

Another approach to holding consultation meetings can be to appoint an external facilitator to run the meeting. In this, the facilitator can act as a 'compere' or 'master of ceremonies' and orchestrate the inputs between the participants. The facilitator can put questions to different organisations in the room and seek out their views or opinions. The facilitator can interview the representatives from different organisations using a broadcast media model. Another approach is to run a 'Question Time' approach modelled on the TV programme in which a panel responds to questions from the audience. These approaches can work when either places or issues are considered. It allows the independent facilitator to put questions to organisations on behalf of the consultees although not all consultees will have their specific questions answered. Another dimension to this is where all participants at meetings are enabled to vote on issues after discussion. The results of the votes can be seen on screen and this approach is generally run by a facilitator. Facilitators can also run visioning exercises which are helpful at the beginning of plan making and, like other approaches, these need a methodology and as Shipley and Michela (2006) advise, it is important not to rely on visioning events alone.

(v) NEWSPAPERS AND LEAFLETS

The use of leaflets and other written material such as articles in community newspapers allow people to spend time considering issues. Written material can also provide links to other tools such as online materials, and dates and places of meetings or exhibition. Written material can also be prepared in translation for those in the community who do not read English as their first language. Audio versions of leaflets can be made available on websites for those who are visually impaired or translated into other languages.

Any written material needs to be developed in ways that make it easily accessible. This means that consideration has to be given to elements of this approach from the outset, including:

- The key messages which are object of the consultation.
- The use of language – undertaking a plain English check is always a good idea, avoiding jargon and acronyms.
- Most people will have no idea what an LDF, DPD or Core Strategy means – it is helpful to use an approach that talks about the future of places and how decisions will be made about them.
- The form of the material – is a single A4 sheet best left flat or folded? It will depend on the issues to be considered – if you are using a map or diagram this may be better inside a leaflet.
- Quality of production – this needs to be fit for purpose. Something that is too glossy may appear as if all the issues have already been settled and so the consultation is viewed as a token process; a poor presentation may suggest that this is not viewed as an important process.
- Sponsorship and ownership – if the consultation is supported by a variety of organisations it is helpful to include their logos; however, although this may be important to the sponsors, it is not the main feature of the leaflet.
- Part of the leaflet can be a reply paid postcard or return sheet on which people can give their views.
- Where the leaflets will be available – they will need to be in places that people will go, e.g. schools, libraries, pubs (some local authorities have used beer mats to promote consultation), coffee bars, door to door, places of work, community centres.

(VI) ONLINE METHODS

The use of the web to obtain information and for social interaction continues to increase across all age groups. For younger people under 30, almost 100 per cent will have had some online communication in the previous week. Younger people also use social networking sites and integration between web and phone is increasing. Understanding the use of these media is part of any approach to consultation and a number of organisations have used these regularly to obtain views and opinions. The use of social networking sites for targeted surveys is also growing. In the UK, buying goods and services online is second only to the United States and this method of retailing is developing alongside more traditional methods. The development of online account systems, which track and use searches to build up profiles for advertising or to offer more services, are also an expanding area of the way in which the web is used. All these changes bring expectations about consultation methods for a growing part of the community and the more traditional methods may seem static and less user friendly to those populations being targeted through consultation. Murray and Greer (2002) found that the use of online methods was as successful as public meetings in the preparation of the RDS in Northern Ireland and that they also allowed a contributing relationship between participants and strategy development over time.

Although all local authority websites have details about spatial planning on them, the general ease of access to information about the LDF is very poor. Many local authority websites are structured to replicate the internal operation of the organisation rather than for the user. Engagement in spatial planning requires that the person seeking information already understands a good deal about the process and the jargon. Background studies and evidence used are hard to find as are the results from consultations and what is going to be done about them. The reform of local authority approaches to providing a combined evidence base including consultation should improve the situation but there is also much that can be undertaken which makes a difference to the role of the online channels as a means of consultation.

The issues that need to be considered for spatial planning web pages are:

- The 'landing' page needs to clear and unambiguous that this is about the planning and investment policies and programmes for the future; it should not be wrapped up in technical planning language.
- There should be regular independent user group testing of the layout and material on the website.
- It needs clear links to the evidence base of the local authority and other partners.
- It needs clear links to the consultation diary and how past consultation has been used.
- It needs to state clearly where the process is in its progress and how anyone can be involved at this stage.
- Documents should be clearly attached and easy to download.
- Where there is a specific consultation in current use, then this should be clearly signposted and possibly be set up as a pop-up when users view the web page.
- There should be opportunities for online feedback on the quality of the contact.
- People should be able to sign up to receive more information and be involved at later stages.
- Regular alerts should be used each time a new stage in the process is about to be started or is concluded; these can be by email and text.
- Organisations involved in different groups should be identified.
- Some information on the role and use of other policy documents should be given and links to these documents made.
- Parish and neighbourhood plans that are being considered as part of the process should be identified and web linked.

- General feedback forms should be available where users cannot find the information they are looking for and these should be used to improve the website layout and content on a weekly basis.
- Specific user groups for these pages should be formed so that the web content and layout can be improved, e.g. older people.
- There should be a link to the LSP web page.
- There should be a link to the SCS, the LAA and other performance management material.
- There should be a link to the scrutiny web pages and reports of any scrutinies undertaken for planning.
- All web comments should be logged in the same way as those received by other means – they can be kept in a web repository; telephone comments can also be turned into web files and any written comments can be added through the use of document imaging systems.

The role of websites in consultation is still being developed to its full potential. Many people use the web as their sole means of finding information. It could be difficult to attract attention to any consultation process but social networking and other alert approaches will encourage people to engage. Burrows *et al.* (2005) investigated the role of net-based approaches to establishing neighbourhood information systems where, in US examples, communities could prioritise actions within their area. This approach can be taken further through 'crowdsourcing' which enables people to collect information and provide content in a non-planned but collaborative way. Brabham (2009) has identified crowdsourcing as a good means of engaging people in areas that are geographically or socially remote within localities. Crowdsourcing is seen to be democratic. It is open to all and although it may be used by those who have a particular interest in any topic, it is moderated by the community of users.

(VII) INTERACTIVE DESIGN APPROACHES

Interactive consultation and design processes have become increasingly popular as a means of visioning and informing spatial decision making (Wates 2000). Planning for Real is a means of supporting community engagement in design and decision making. It involves building a three-dimensional model that represents the place and much of the discussion revolves around moving or adding elements to the place through new model representations. It is a method that allows a more realistic understanding and engagement by communities and individuals in potential changes in their areas (Gibson 1979; 1998; 2008). This approach is now led by the Neighbourhood Initiatives Foundation. Planning for Real was one of the first attempts to change the extent and style of community engagement in planning projects and a means of breaking out of more passive and formal methods such as meetings and exhibitions. It has also been an interactive and dynamic approach which has allowed those with differing views to explain and demonstrate the impact of their preferred approaches. It employs iterative processes where it can be possible to develop a consensus view.

Enquiry (or Inquiry) by Design has been developed in Western Australia and taken up by the Prince of Wales Trust in the UK. In Western Australia, the approach has been used to develop ideas for sustainable liveable neighbourhoods that take into account the natural environment (Jones 2001). A key feature is that when people come together to discuss a place, they are able to draw their designs in addition to talking about them and also to respond to the physical characteristics of the site. The outcome will be a set of design principles that can then be used as the development of the neighbourhood goes forward. The Department of Planning and Infrastructure in Western Australia has issued a Preparation Manual (2003) which provides a detailed approach to preparing for a workshop, advice for facilitators and room arrangements.

The Prince's Foundation for the Built Environment focusses the outcomes on a 'shared vision for the development site, which is illustrated in a series of plans including a master plan' (The Prince's Foundation nd). The Foundation has supported this approach in the development of a new settlement in Sherford, South Devon. This was conducted over three days in 2004 and resulted in an approach that is linked to deliverability and sustainability (The Prince's Foundation 2005). Carmona et al. describe this approach as being a means of engaging stakeholders in developing the vision and then this is being translated into more detailed design approaches as being a more technical issue (2006: 226). A similar activity took place in Birmingham, where they held a City Shapers Activity Day in March 2007 (CLG 2008g: 60) and this extended beyond planning into volunteering and getting involved in other ways.

These approaches are particularly useful when considering strategic sites and urban extensions. They can focus on place and can be the basis of further consultation as schemes develop.

(VIII) SCRUTINY, CITIZEN'S JURIES AND PANELS

Since 2000, every local authority in England has had powers of scrutiny although each local authority has chosen to develop them in different ways. The development of scrutiny skills and approaches has been supped through the establishment of the Centre for Public Scrutiny (www.cfps.org.uk) and this has enabled a variety of approaches to be shared between different local authorities and for those engaged in scrutiny to receive training. The Centre for Public Scrutiny has also undertaken a review of scrutinies into community engagement that provides examples from a range of local authorities including Worthing, Wakefield, Ealing, Essex and Bassetlaw (Centre for Public Scrutiny 2008). Scrutiny can review past policy and delivery current policies and forthcoming developments. Scrutiny can be document-based or scrutiny panels can receive evidence from individuals and organisations. Scrutiny reports have to be made to the full council, for the local authority and it is up to the executive of the council to decide how to respond.

Scrutiny can be a useful tool in developing the participative approaches to spatial planning. It can investigate the approaches taken and ask if the methods being used are appropriate to targeted groups and the issues to be discussed. Another approach which has been used since 2000 has been that of citizen's juries where a group of individuals act as a scrutiny team, as random representatives of the local community. In some local authorities, such as Lewisham, this approach has been used extensively and has included a range of subjects. In 2004, for example, the citizen's jury (2004) reported on 'to what extent should the car fit into Lewisham's future transport plan'. Citizen's juries can be a way of listening to the evidence put forward, having an interactive and inquisitorial approach to the evidence and then deliberating on what has been heard and how it might be usefully applied in the circumstances.

In Dublin, a randomly selected citizen's jury was established to consider waste management and incineration, which was a locally contested issue. In this case, the jury worked through a 'deliberation day', where the jury was briefed and then came to a conclusion at the end of the day. French and Laver (2009) discuss the issues associated with jury selection and conclude that success is in part related to the credibility of the process, where policy makers need to be committed to using the jury's deliberations from the outset in order to make this a credible exercise. However, these concerns may be more prevalent in single issue approaches rather than as part of more continuing processes. The development of all scrutiny depends on this engagement and recent proposals for local government suggest that scrutiny reports will require responses from those receiving them (CLG 2009d).

A citizen's jury may be effective in considering how best the process of developing community engagement or the development of a vision could work in the LDF process or they could look at the relative importance of issues within different circumstances or locations. Reports by citizen's juries do require those with the power of decision making to take account of what the jury has said and the jury can also enter into a process of deliberation with the politicians in addition to having a role of advising them (Barnes 2008: 475).

WHAT ARE THE MAIN BARRIERS TO ENGAGEMENT IN PARTICIPATORY AND CONSULTATIVE APPROACHES?

There are a number of barriers to active consultation and these need to be considered in the design of an effective approach because:

* the timing and location of meetings;
* the style of events – may be too formal or daunting;

- there are only to be for groups already engaged in the process;
- some groups may only be reached through their own community networks;
- there may be strong cultural or community pressures to stay silent;
- councillors may believe that active approaches to consultation reduce the validity of their own roles;
- expectations may have been raised too high before and failed to deliver;
- there may be consultation fatigue.

WHAT HAPPENS IF THE CONSULTATION METHOD CHOSEN DOES NOT EVOKE A RESPONSE?

One of the key issues when undertaking consultation is that people do not want to get involved. This may be because:

- the messages or the means of consultation are not clear enough
- people do not think that they can have an affect on any outcomes
- not enough or too much notice has been given
- people do not trust the process.

What can be done in these circumstances? A multiple approach to consultation spreads the risk so that there is no reliance on a single method. Where a survey has had a low response rate, follow-up reminders can help but it will depend on the type of survey being undertaken. A lack of response may also indicate the need to work more closely with the community and its leaders to build trust and confidence in the process. It may be sensible to work with locally established groups such as community sports and social clubs, or at school gates where parents gather before meeting their children. If confidence in the impartiality of the process is an issue, then inviting an external facilitator who can act as a broker between the local authority and the community might be helpful.

ENGAGING STAKEHOLDERS

Stakeholders are those who are effected by and can affect the outcome of any process. In practice, stakeholders are generally viewed as organised and formal interests and can include landowners, developers, local businesses, government departments, charities and faith and community groups. Increasingly, all key local stakeholders are likely to be represented on the LSP either on the main board or through thematic groups. For spatial planning, stakeholders include:

- the key sectoral interests within the local authority for which spatial planning provides a critical mechanism for delivering its objectives;
- critical stakeholders external to the local authority, e.g. the local strategic partnership and its members, parish councils and area committees;

- neighbouring authorities;
- the general public, which includes stakeholders such as local communities, comprising individual residents, residents associations and amenity or interest groups;
- statutory consultees, such as governmental agencies and utility providers;
- further stakeholders including other organisations/service providers – such as health trusts (or Primary Care Trusts), educational establishments, transport providers, emergency services and community development organisations;
- the development industry and landowners engaged in planning processes;
- the business sector including business representatives such as Chambers of Commerce.

(CLG 2008f: §3.3)

Stakeholders can become more engaged in the spatial planning process if local authorities:

- ensure early engagement in development plan preparation and provide as much information up front as they (the stakeholders) are able;
- are prepared to alter working practices in terms of allocating more resources to front-end activities such as site promotion and interactive engagement and ensure that members (councillors), managing directors and landowners are fully aware of the implications of change in their area;
- engage with local strategic partnerships to make them relevant and to ensure that they work with local planning authorities.

(ibid.: §6.3)

Some stakeholders, such as major landowners, will have specific and continuing interest in the spatial planning process. Establishing a forum of major landowners, including the public sector, can be a good means of engagement and also of fostering informal development and delivery conversations between these interests. This kind of forum is included as part of the LDF process (CLG 2008c). Other stakeholders may work in groups. Local businesses have different roles that they exercise in relationship to their involvement in the LDF process and may also be engaged through their own local organisations. Consulting through business breakfasts which are short and well planned could be the most successful approach. For other stakeholders including women, cultural communities and those with disabilities, all consultation activities should take them into account in their planning and design as part of an equalities and diversity assessment (Reeves 2005; Planning Advisory Service 2008f). Greed argues, in respect of women, that gender mainstreaming does have the potential to have an impact which is beneficial to men and women (2005).

THE ROLE OF PLANNING AID

Planning Aid was initially established to provide advice on planning applications for those who could not afford to employ a consultant. It has now been extended to help individuals and groups participate in preparing plans and in community planning approaches. Planning Aid is available to people who are:

- receiving any state means-tested benefits
- will not personally benefit from a development
- have not engaged any professional help on the matter.

Planning Aid can also help community groups and social enterprises. Planning Aid is run by the Royal Town Planning Institute (RTPI) and is funded by central government.

Similar support can be given to community groups by developers or development trusts which can be funded to provide community support. This approach is also used in master planning, although as Giddings and Hopwood (2006) point out, this needs consideration of the ways in which communities can be involved.

CONCLUSIONS

Consultation is a central element of spatial planning and it has a formal role in the preparation of LDFs as evidence that is embedded within the process as well as providing feedback on it. There are a variety of consultation methods that can be used and these are stronger when used in combinations. The use of web-based methods of consultation also emphasises that the approaches need to be appropriate to the target audience. Consultation is now more joined-up with other organisations and the use of its processes needs to be used in a systematic manner. Consultation is used as a means of informing decision making by politicians and can assist in demonstrating why decisions have been made.

Although planning has a long association with consultation and commitment to participative engagement, the development of a range of methods that are appropriate to circumstances and communities suggests that more professional guidance and support may be needed. Planners may need to undertake specific training in order to be able to identify the kind of consultation that needs to be commissioned or to undertake the processes directly. Different approaches to using the wider repository of consultation evidence and joint approaches also need to be used more actively in spatial planning to reflect the more joined-up approaches in its delivery outcomes.

CHAPTER 6

MAKING PLACES: DELIVERY THROUGH SPATIAL PLANNING

INTRODUCTION

The main objective of spatial planning is integrated delivery and this marks the major difference between land-use planning and spatial planning. Land-use planning has become synonymous with a regulatory, policy-based approach which is interpreted on each site as development comes forward. Land-use planning does allow more pro-active approaches but these have generally been pursued by developers and local delivery vehicles set up to promote regeneration or renewal. Spatial planning goes beyond this. The objective of spatial planning is achieving delivery which is rooted in an integrated approach to working between all sectors and agencies. It is also evidence based and programme managed. The legacy of nearly 20 years of Thatcherism had left land-use planning in a passive mode. Spatial planning is an active approach to places and one that is not fulfilled until the programme identified as being required for the people and places of the area is delivered.

Spatial planning in England sits within the governance structure of the LSP and has to deliver the vision for the place as set out in the SCS. It is possible to anticipate a convergence between the SCS and the Core Strategy over time, as the LDF becomes the capital delivery programme for the SCS. This might be a difficult position to take for more traditional land-use planners, where the primacy of the development plan and its processes, particularly the EiP, set it apart from other local strategy documents. The ability of the spatial plan to deliver is examined through the ToS and the transition from passive land use to proactive delivery approaches marks out the key differences and challenges of spatial planning. Spatial planning implies an active approach.

In this chapter, the way in which delivery can be developed through spatial planning is discussed and a more detailed approach to achieving the delivery strategy and outcomes through the LDF are set out. These may require planners to obtain some new knowledge and skills but spatial planning's effectiveness lies at the heart of this. In the past, the development plan was frequently the only plan available for the whole area and the quasi-legal processes associated with its adoption gave it an authority among users. It no longer retains that unique role (Prior 2005). The LDF clearly has a legal force but this cannot be exerted unless it is part of the local governance architecture. The LDF cannot stand alone.

THE INFRASTRUCTURE TURN

Although there is much speculation that planning's role in delivering infrastructure has emerged since the world economic crisis, it was always a key feature of spatial planning. However, the role of spatial planning in the delivery of infrastructure was not made explicit and is only now emerging as one of the key features of the new system. It is possible to speculate that this role of spatial planning was 'sleeping' inside the system to be brought forward when the rest of the local public governance system was ready to embrace and use it.

In England, the test of deliverability in spatial planning has been adopted in an indirect form since 2005 and from June 2008 explicitly (Morphet *et al.* 2007; Nadin 2007; CLG 2008c). The test of 'deliverability', as set out, requires that the Core Strategy of the LDF should be 'supported by evidence of what physical, social and green infrastructure is needed to enable the amount of development proposed for the area, taking account of its type and distribution. This evidence should cover who will provide the infrastructure and when it will be provided ... and draw on and influence any strategies and investment plans of the local authority and other organisations' and is primarily focussed at supporting housing growth and delivery (CLG 2008c: 8)

Most planners have focussed on developers' contributions as the main means of funding infrastructure as part of the planning process and assumed that this would remain their key role, not least when the potential for a CIL was added to the mix. However, the funding provided for infrastructure through developers' contributions, although on a significant scale in major developments such as Kings Cross or major retail developments, is small in comparison with the total value of public sector capital investment in any area and it is now on this agenda that spatial planning has been focussed. The evidence base required as part of the LDF Core Strategy has to consider the future infrastructure requirements in any area and is described as bringing 'together a very wide range of different services, since most require land to operate, so it can help support the coordination of services' (CLG 2008c: 4). The Core Strategy is also required to 'coordinate and deliver the public sector components of any area' (ibid.: 4). This is quite a different approach to one where planning has been the policy leader for land use. It is now the delivery engine.

Some planners regard this role as being too difficult, not least because they have poor experiences of working with some of their public sector partners within their organisations or outside. However, the other elements of new governance architecture such as the LSP, with its new role on the oversight of resources, the duty of public bodies to cooperate, the LAA as a local public service contract and CAA as a means of assessing delivery including the use of resources, all point to the role of the LDF, and the Core Strategy in particular, as representing any area's capital programme. The infrastructure requirements can be provided by other sectors and not all private sector development is large in scale. Privately provided nurseries, for example, are a key component in any community's infrastructure.

The role of the spatial planning in delivery of local infrastructure restores one of the early purposes of planning and one that would have been familiar 50 years ago. This role has been lost over time as the responsibilities for delivery have been taken over by separate departments and agencies. In the 1980s and 1990s, delivery was largely seen to be the responsibility of the private sector. In this model of delivery, public sector agencies managed their own projects and budgets whilst expecting developers' contributions to supplement these. Planning was the mechanism for generating additional resources through contributions from developer surplus. Decisions were made about the location of public sector investment which were uncoordinated and not always in sustainable locations. The planning system, with its ability to regulate on a site-by-site basis, frequently had no means of dealing with these projects in a more coordinated way. In the private sector, master planning has been used to develop proposals on larger sites but again these have frequently been disconnected from their immediate surroundings. This has left a position where the provision of infrastructure has become synonymous with developers' contributions.

The collection of developers' contributions has frequently been ad hoc, based on a combination of what is needed within the development site or the immediate area together with a viability test of what it is appropriate for any particular development to bear. The list of requirements may be identified by a service provider who requests a new school, swimming pool or clinic from their own service plans. They have not had to show how these requirements fit in with any evidence of service need and their own programmed investment. The 2004 Planning and Compulsory Act has shifted this position to one where the LDF is at the heart of local infrastructure planning and delivery. This marks a considerable change in the way that infrastructure delivery is planned and managed. The planning system has moved from one that is focussed on achieving developers' contributions to one where it works with all mainstream funders from all sectors in an integrated way to identify what infrastructure is needed for the next 15 years but also how it is to be provided and when. Many local authorities can identify the value of developers' contributions that have been raised through planning negotiation. Few can identity the value of current capital investment programmes, the projects that are in future programmes and how these relate to the infrastructure deficits in their area. Infrastructure is also frequently assumed to include only major items of investment such as roads or drainage. However, spatial planning is concerned with infrastructure that is needed to help places thrive and flourish. It can include locations for child care, cycle paths, informal green spaces and markets.

The transition from an ad hoc system of funding infrastructure, to one that is more integrated, lies at the heart of English spatial planning. It is why the LDF has to demonstrate that it has a delivery strategy that is operational and can be used to support the delivery of identified infrastructure over the life of the plan. When it is submitted, the Core Strategy or other DPD cannot identify in detail what is required and funded for a 15-year period. It can demonstrate this for a shorter period of five to seven years but, in the longer term, infrastructure requirements may change as services review their delivery patterns. Current approaches to health reflect a shift to an emphasis on primary care; in ten years, there may be a different model.

The shift to this focus on infrastructure delivery in spatial planning has not been immediately understood by planners and the wider community. For planners, when the initial requirements for the resources to deliver the LDF were to be identified, these were interpreted as staffing requirements for local planning teams within local authorities rather than as the resources to deliver the infrastructure requirements in the LDF (Morphet et al. 2007). When there was more understanding that this included infrastructure requirements, the next assumption was that this was related only to strategic development sites and that the infrastructure requirements would be funded through developers' contributions. Although the requirements were set out in more detail in the ToS (Planning Inspectorate National Service 2008b) and the revised PPS 12 (CLG 2008c) they were still not understood. In late 2008, the Planning Advisory Service ran 12 seminars and reproduced the seminar materials on its website (www.pas.gov.uk/infrastructure) in an effort to spread the message about the delivery role of the LDF. It then commissioned a *Steps Approach to Infrastructure Planning and Delivery for Local Strategic Partnerships and Local Authorities* (Morphet 2009a) that was then supported by further training and implementation materials.

The problems in understanding the infrastructure turn in spatial planning have started to attract analysis and debate. The problems in the misunderstanding of the delivery role of spatial planning have been identified by Morphet et al. (2007) and the approaches for addressing infrastructure delivery in a practical way have been studied by Baker and Hincks (2009: 178). Some have pointed to the difficulty in creating an integrated approach to delivery when central government departments are not joined up. Counsell et al. (2006) argue that it is the failure to have national planning statements or internal governmental integration that weakens the integrated approach at the local level. To some extent, these criticisms have been countered by the cross-government delivery agreement (HM Treasury 2007c) which has cut joined-up approaches for infrastructure planning as a high priority, together with the emergence of delivery plans for all local authorities (HM Treasury 2007d).

The difficulty in developing integrated approaches at the local level, given the disjointed national context, has also been identified. Haughton and Allmendinger state that as 'fragmentary' governance structures are increasing, this reduces the potential for more joined-up approaches which reflect local needs rather than being 'choreographed' within 'some fairly prescriptive rules' (2008: 141). What is interesting about the delivery role of the LDF is that it is able to develop its own operational approach at the local level and draw up its own priorities, which may be more subject to local politics than top down constraints. Local infrastructure decisions are already made within local priority sets. Comparison between any two local authorities implementing the same programme, such as Building Schools for the Future, demonstrates this. Many of the operational constraints are more apparent than real and can be used more flexibly than is generally expressed.

There are those who have focussed entirely on the role of the LDF's delivery through developers' contributions. Haughton and Allmendinger (2007) have reviewed the provision of social infrastructure in the Thames Gateway and suggested that the system will not deliver all that is required to meet the demands of the new population in this area. Taking a view of infrastructure being solely provided by developers without integrating it within existing investment programmes only establishes part of the approach. The early research that has been undertaken on the operation of English infrastructure planning and delivery has also tended to blur the lines between the use of developers' contributions and mainstream funding. In reviewing Ashford as a case study, Baker and Hincks (2009) go immediately to the provision of developers' contributions on growth area sites as the main issue. They remain silent on the wider application of public funds and infrastructure deficits in the rest of Ashford and how these are to be considered together.

Although the infrastructure delivery approach is only getting underway, some potential criticisms are being voiced. Baker and Hincks report planners' concerns of 'shopping lists' which are unattainable and that showing that the use of infrastructure was not funded was the 'easiest way to 'ruin' a plan' (2009: 188). They also reported concerns from planners that other organisations would not be able to work within their timescales. Much of the reported concerns about delivery come from a planner-centric viewpoint and the implementation of the wider governance model for integrated spatial planning will gradually see this being eroded. As Guy et al. (2001) have pointed out, developing social networks that support the provision of infrastructure can take time but it does need to be managed within a local context.

In Australia, where the focus of infrastructure delivery within spatial planning has been operating for more time, there is another potential criticism of this approach. Here, as Dodson (2009) reports, the focus on infrastructure planning as a means of generating funds from development and growth has led to the funding driving the planning agenda and being disconnected from wider planning objectives. In the Australian system, although the infrastructure delivered through developers' contributions is identified in a Priority Infrastructure Plan, the investment does not seem to be identified through an integrated process (Low Choy *et al.* 2007). This is not the approach being taken in the English system so together with the economic downturn, the LDF approach to infrastructure delivery is more robust and integrated although there are still priority decisions to be taken.

PREPARING FOR DELIVERY

In approaching the preparation of the LDF, and the Core Strategy in particular, the need to consider delivery from the outset is critical. There can be a temptation to view delivery as a follow-on activity after key decisions about locations and strategic sites have already been taken. Using the contextual material and guidance available from Government (CLG 2008b; 2008c; 2009a), it is possible to identify an approach to achieving delivery through the preparation of the Core Strategy which can be supported by the LSP and possibly a key infrastructure providers group underneath these governance arrangements.

A second consideration in preparing for delivery of the LDF is taking a programme management approach to the process. Programme management techniques are used less in planning but can nevertheless be applied and a number of local authorities are now appointing project managers to this role. The principle of project management that is important here, and discussed in more detail in Chapter 8, is that of viewing the whole process at the outset rather than considering each stage sequentially. This provides a good opportunity to identity key milestones, dependencies and where stakeholder engagement is required. It also identifies when it is important to communicate with others and obtain any key decisions. The delivery of spatial planning is dependent on this type of approach which will also enable LDFs to play a fuller part in wider organisational activities, both to inform them and to use their processes.

WORKING TOGETHER ON AN INFRASTRUCTURE DELIVERY PLAN (IDP)

An IDP needs to be undertaken by all the partners. It will be set out as evidence for an effective Core Strategy. To undertake this work, planners, working with others, will need to draw on and influence the investment strategies and infrastructure programmes within the local authority and other organisations in its area where possible. To achieve an integrated approach, authorities need to work with local investors from the public, private, voluntary and community sectors. From the public sector, this includes service providers within local authorities such as children's services, highways, housing, waste collection and disposal and regeneration. Externally, it includes health providers, the police, fire and rescue, universities, courts, prisons and government departments such as the Ministry of Defence, Job Centre Plus and the Her Majesty's Revenues and Customs. In the private sector, investment operates at all scales and some are essential services for any thriving community, such as leisure facilities and child care provision. The voluntary and community sector also invest in infrastructure through sports and social clubs, hospices and through the delivery of services. Producing an IDP also benefits partner service providers. It creates scope for greater efficiency and more beneficial outcomes in the planning and delivery of their individual service strategies and contributes to achieving their wider LAA targets and responsibilities.

The LSP is the place where all of these partners and stakeholders come together to establish working arrangements that consider future investment, planning and delivery decisions, as well as how local resources might be used effectively to achieve key targets, including those in the LAA. However, for both LSPs and local authority planners this requires some new understanding, knowledge and skills in working together. Many areas are already setting up shared evidence and consultation bases and this should be a critical component in managing and guiding the investment of all sectors at the local level.

Infrastructure can take many forms – it can be defined in physical, green and community terms (see list at the end of this chapter for examples) and is essential to support objectives of increased housing provision, economic growth and mitigating climate change, and of creating thriving and sustainable communities. In addition to housing and job opportunities, supporting infrastructure including green energy, utility services, transport, schools, open space, community, health and leisure services are all needed. All organisations must invest in their future if they can, in order to improve, expand or maintain their services. The integration of these individual processes and programmes will enable service providers to more effectively target areas of need with the potential to achieve greater efficiencies and savings. At the heart of this process is the development of land and buildings that provide the services for places and communities. Where investment for development can be identified, the capacity of existing services to accommodate new population growth should be captured and, where possible, quantified and any gaps in provision clearly set out.

If the plan is made with the involvement of all relevant parties, it will help to:

- identify and support the delivery of all infrastructure;
- direct the right level of growth and housing development in the right place;
- enable communities and investors to see what public sector investment is being made in the area;
- bid for funding from other infrastructure agencies;
- engage with infrastructure funding providers and deliver the right levels of infrastructure for growth.

Within a local authority, infrastructure planning will only be effective if it has corporate support as a cross-service approach as one of the requirements of deliverability. Coordination is key; this means that at least some of the following will need to be developed and put in place:

- chief executive engagement;
- engagement from senior councillors including the leader;
- a briefed and engaged corporate management team;
- common evidence base across authority services;
- ways of working with heads of service which can support evidence-based identification of infrastructure deficits;
- some working relationships with the LSP and LAA coordinator and SCS lead officer.

PPS 12 (CLG 2008c) identifies the Core Strategy as the means of 'orchestrating the necessary social, physical and green infrastructure required to ensure that sustainable communities are created'. To fulfil that role and to be found sound, the Core Strategy or evidence underpinning it must identify the infrastructure required to deliver the strategy, who will provide it, where and when.

Infrastructure planning forms an important part of a robust evidence base for DPDs and especially Core Strategies. The ToS assess whether the plan is deliverable so an understanding of what infrastructure is needed and how it will be delivered is key. PPS 12 advises that the process should identify as far as possible, infrastructure needs and costs, phasing, funding sources and responsibilities for delivery and, where necessary, contingency planning scenarios. However, the budgeting processes of different agencies may mean there is less information available when DPDs come forward than would be ideal. A proportionate approach to the level of evidence for different localities is expected.

The development of this infrastructure evidence base should be undertaken in a corporate way inside a local authority and in a coordinated way with partners and investors through the LSP. It should:

- take into account existing population and their needs, as well as new development and population growth;
- be based on evidence and undertaken in a systematic way;
- deliver through existing public sector and other investment budgets and take into account existing threshold-based public funding schemes;
- inform consideration of the location of growth and service provision;
- identify what is not yet funded, estimate costs and how it might be funded in future years, e.g. through capital bids, asset release, fees and charges, developers' contributions and CIL.

PUTTING IT ALL TOGETHER: A STEPS APPROACH

The vision for any local area is set out in the SCS. It sets the key objectives and how these are going to be delivered, driving the actions of the local public bodies to achieve these changes. It is based on evidence coupled with a narrative that identifies the aspirations for the place in the future. The SCS is owned by the LSP who give a lead to the delivery of the SCS. They may do this through thematic groups which represent the local key priorities. They now have a legal obligation to take an oversight of the use and alignment of resources in the area, performance management and consultation. They will be involved in how the SCS is being delivered in ways that meet local objectives and priorities for the area. The LSP is concerned with place.

The role of spatial planning in delivery means that it has to work within wider governance structures and in ways that work with meeting the ToS for the Core Strategy and any other DPDs. In this section, a Steps Approach to infrastructure planning and delivery is set out that creates a logical path through the process of infrastructure planning and delivery and the creation of an IDP. It can be adapted for use in any location and enables planners and others to view the whole process.

(I) WORKING WITH THE LOCAL STRATEGIC PARTNERSHIP (LSP)

LSPs have a leadership role in the preparation and delivery of the IDP. The LSP will provide a strategic lead through the executive group or a thematic sub-group and may have a key infrastructure providers group reporting to it on a regular basis. The delivery of the LAA is also the LSP's responsibility and a Core Strategy also has to demonstrate how it is delivering the targets set out in the LAA (CLG 2008c: §1.6). The development of the IDP within this cross-agency framework can provide:

- a strategic place-shaping tool to achieve community benefits and a means of delivering service efficiencies and improvements;
- a means of delivering strategic objectives for localities as set out in the SCS;
- a corporate process which must be undertaken in partnership between the local authority and other public service delivery organisations;
- an on-going process;
- a means of identifying current and future infrastructure deficits and needs;
- part of the evidence base for the preparation of local authority and partner strategy and service plans;
- a means of supporting the delivery of the LAA;

- a means of working with the private, voluntary and community sector on their investment proposals and delivery;
- a means of identifying infrastructure deficits that may only be met through sub-regional and regional approaches;
- embedded in the CAA process as part of the evidence base to demonstrate how partners are working together to improve both their communities and their use of resources, which will both be key parts of the assessment process.[1]

(II) DELIVERING THE SUSTAINABLE COMMUNITY STRATEGY (SCS)

As part of the development of the SCS and the Core Strategy, there may be visioning events which are an important part of the process. These need to be undertaken as the same event – there is no need for separate events which add to citizen and community confusion and costs. Where visioning may already have been undertaken, this can be used and may not need to be rerun for the LDF. Planners have frequently maintained separate approaches to visioning but as the LDF is now delivering for the wider purpose, the need for this has now gone. The SCS may identify the spatial interoperation of its objectives, but in most cases this has been left to be interpreted through the delivery plans that are associated with it. The LDF is the delivery plan for investment in place over a 15-year period. In order to deliver the SCS vision, the Core Strategy in the LDF will need to demonstrate that the LDF is delivering the Core Strategy. It will be able to demonstrate this by:

- working with the SCS to develop priorities and develop the roll of the vision;
- using SCS evidence;
- using SCS consultation events or running them jointly;
- establishing the Core Strategy's delivery role for the SCS on the local authority website;
- integrating the LDF into the main council website activity rather than managing separately;
- using plain English and/or the same terms of others for its activities – technical planning language needs to be used only when absolutely necessary;
- choosing the same thematic structure as the SCS for the Core Strategy;
- demonstrating on a table or some other graphical format how the LDF is delivering the SCS;
- identifying how the SCS is shaping priorities;
- showing how the SCS may lead to different approaches in different parts of the area;
- showing how the SCS outcomes are being measurably delivered through the Core Strategy through monitoring and reporting back to the LSP.

The LDF needs to be in general conformity with the Regional Strategy in order to be found sound. This is only one part of one of the ToS (CLG 2008c; Planning Inspectorate National Service 2008b) and does not override the rest. It also overlooks other parts of the process. The LDF has to deliver the LAA which also includes housing targets that form part of the contract between the locality and central government. These have been frequently overlooked but, like all other LAA targets, they need to be delivered through the LDF. A focus on the RSS process above the main role of spatial planning can also lead to planning being viewed as a highly emotive activity and, in some cases, a show stopper. In some localities where there may be highly charged political issues associated with development, uncertainty about national targets can be used as a mechanism for slowing down the LDF, which hampers the potential identification and delivery of investment for the wider locality.

In many ways, this perceived regional focus on strategic development sites and infrastructure provision through developers' contributions represents the approach of the former system. Seeing strategic sites as development islands has come about not through good planning but as an unintended consequence of the application of the legal context of developers' contributions. Here, any request for a developers' contribution has been required to be directly related to the mitigation of the development and almost always within the site under consideration. This has been expanded through a wider area-based approach in Circular 5/05 (ODPM 2005f) but this is only used by some local authorities. This approach does not take into account how new development might be able to utilise existing facilities and services and may have served to make new development inward-looking rather than being an integrated, albeit extended, part of existing communities.

This approach also affects the expectations of other stakeholders and partners. Mention of a discussion of planning and delivery with colleagues in other public services such as children's services or health immediately suggests a discussion about developers' contributions. Indeed, the Department of Education requires those in education to seek developers' contributions to support their services where a case can be made (DCSF nd). This approach has distracted the spatial planning consideration about the mainstream delivery of all services in the locality and the decisions that go with them that lie at the heart of spatial planning.

The Steps Approach that has been developed for the Planning Advisory Service is shown in Figure 6.1 and in the boxes that follow.

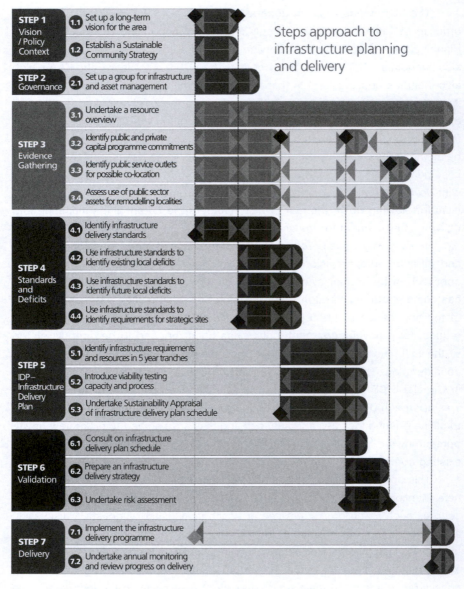

STEP 1
Vision / Policy Context

1.1 Set up a long-term vision for the area

1.2 Establish a Sustainable Community Strategy

STEP 2
Governance

2.1 Set up a group for infrastructure and asset management

STEP 3
Evidence Gathering

3.1 Undertake a resource overview

3.2 Identify public and private capital programme commitments

3.3 Identify public service outlets for possible co-location

3.4 Assess use of public sector assets for remodelling localities

STEP 4
Standards and Deficits

4.1 Identify infrastructure delivery standards

4.2 Use infrastructure standards to identify existing local deficits

4.3 Use infrastructure standards to identify future local deficits

4.4 Use infrastructure standards to identify requirements for strategic sites

STEP 5
IDP – Infrastructure Delivery Plan

5.1 Identify infrastructure requirements and resources in 5 year tranches

5.2 Introduce viability testing capacity and process

5.3 Undertake Sustainability Appraisal of infrastructure delivery plan schedule

STEP 6
Validation

6.1 Consult on infrastructure delivery plan schedule

6.2 Prepare an infrastructure delivery strategy

6.3 Undertake risk assessment

STEP 7
Delivery

7.1 Implement the infrastructure delivery programme

7.2 Undertake annual monitoring and review progress on delivery

Steps approach to infrastructure planning and delivery

Figure 6.1 The Steps Approach to infrastructure planning and delivery

Step 1 Vision and policy context

Any delivery plan will depend for its direction and priorities on current and future needs and the places' vision for the future. Without this sense of direction, the use of time and resources in improving any place will be dissipated and fail to meet the full potential of a more focussed approach. It is also important that the vision identifies and serves a common purpose so that all those engaged in working to improve the place and the lives of people who live and work there can see themselves as part of a team. Although individual organisations and departments have pride in their own work and want to promote their services or objectives, this is now set within an integrated context.

What:
- develop and use locality wide evidence base
- develop and use locality wide consultation base
- engage and integrate Core Strategy with SCS
- develop SCS delivery plan
- undertake combined SA across SCS and Core Strategy.

How:
- hold visioning events with a variety of stakeholders with (neutral) facilitators
- have focus groups with people who do not normally engage in luncheon clubs, at the school gates, at the job centre
- use parish planning processes
- have online polls
- engage schools in process
- have business breakfasts.

Risk: without this clarity, infrastructure investment may be duplicated, piecemeal and not be a sustainable use of resources.

Source: Morphet 2009a

Step 2 Governance

Working together to deliver the vision and governance approach will need a governance arrangement. This will ensure that the approach is set within the wider local context and that there is also a way of managing the process whilst enabling stakeholders and infrastructure delivery providers to fully participate. This group needs to be set within the LSP and may have an operational delivery group of infrastructure providers working to it. This infrastructure providers' group will be the key location where discussions about new investment, place-based remodelling, use of assets and co-location can be discussed. It is also the place for discussions about potential new infrastructure requirements for intensified or new population growth.

What:

- engage LSP in delivery process
- identify scale of current investment in the area from all sectors
- establish a (key) infrastructure providers' group (KISP) to work with the LSP and support LDF delivery process
- establish major landowners group to enable two information flows.

How:

- gather together existing capital programmes and put into single schedule
- hold workshops with infrastructure providers to identify their key programmes and budgets
- identity how each public sector capital programme is developed, how frequently it is updated and the criteria by which schemes are funded.

Risk: without this governance in place, infrastructure decisions could be taken in isolation and infrastructure planning could be less effective. It is also possible that the maximum benefit from resources will not be derived.

Source: Morphet 2009a

Step 3 Evidence gathering

The evidence used to support the delivery of the LDF needs to be used across the whole of the area and provided by the LSP partners and other sources. This will need to be supplemented by specialised planning studies such as that on housing markets or flood risk. All this evidence needs to be available in one place on the local authority or LSP website so that it can be easily and freely accessed.

Without gathering and using up-to-date evidence, the infrastructure schedule will not be able to deliver its requirements. It is also important that the evidence base is shared across all providers. Where different services are using different population projections, there will be differential views about local needs and priorities which may influence decisions about priorities for investment. The population estimates should be common to all bodies.

What:

- identify an infrastructure categories list for the area;
- establish a baseline of existing facilities from all sectors on a Geographic Information System (GIS) base;
- review the condition, capacity and use of each of the public facilities;
- establish a GIS database of all publicly owned land and buildings in the area
- identify all infrastructure schemes currently being built and committed to add to the baseline;

- collate a database of all funding streams that can contribute to the mainstream delivery programme;
- collate database of all other known sources of funding or work with those who have this information;
- identify potential opportunities for public sector co-location with organisations;
- identify opportunities for asset release from public sector property and service reviews;
- consider any relocations that might contribute to reductions in climate change.

How:
- use exemplar infrastructure categories list at the end of this chapter as a starting point for the development of a local schedule of categories;
- identify all public sector agencies with land and buildings in the area using a red/amber/green (RAG) assessment for ease of use;
- identify facilities that should be capable of dual use, e.g. swimming pools in schools and universities or the private sector;
- use existing information collected for National Indicators, e.g. NI 175;
- meet with other professionals in property and finance.

Risk: without this joined-up approach, infrastructure investment may be located in the wrong places or leave needs unmet.

Source: Morphet 2009a

Step 4 Standards and deficits

Standards represent what public sector organisations are attempting to achieve for their communities and users. To start infrastructure planning, these standards have to be indentified and underpinned through evidence. They can also be 'adopted' by the local authority through the duty to promote economic, social and environmental well being in the 2000 Local Government Act, s2.

The standard then has a veto applied to the existing facilities in the area taking into account the needs of the existing population, such as school places or ages. The implications of the intensified population needs to be added to this – where more people will be living as under occupied dwellings are used to their capacity and other buildings are turned into residential use.

What:
- identify all infrastructure delivery standards that are in operational use;
- identify gaps in standards;
- identify the trigger points for new service requirements, e.g. refuse collection rounds, libraries, health facilities;
- ensure that standards comply with changing legislation and are fit for purpose;

- review standards on a regular basis and confirm their use annually;
- apply the infrastructure standards to the locality for the needs of the existing population to identify deficits;
- repeat this process for intensified population and growth population cumulatively and over time to identify locations where there will be over provision or deficits of facilities;
- identify how service delivery patterns might be changing over time;
- identify whether there are needs for the revision of new or additional infrastructure based on wider governance processes, e.g. the delivery of the SCS or meeting LAA targets;
- identify which deficits can be met through existing funding sources, e.g. schools capital programmes, local health reviews;
- identify where developers might be asked to contribute for short-term revenue shortfalls of service provision.

How:

- over time, review the evidence base of standards to ensure that they are robust;
- publish standards on website;
- identify where standards might be amended to meet wider targets, e.g. sustainable construction of roads through whole life costing;
- identify where retrofitting policies need to be targeted to specific groups or vulnerable areas;
- review standards from an equalities and diversity standpoint – are they fit for purpose?
- identify if standards will inhibit co-location;
- identify which demographic data public services are using to assess their needs and attempt to bring these to a single set of projections;
- identify likely areas for intended population due to reduced under-occupancy, windfall site release rates, garden grabbing, conversion rates;
- identify areas where in-migration might occur.

Risk: without identifying standards that have some evidential basis, there is no firm basis for assessing infrastructure deficits. This might mean using funding inappropriately and not being able to support a case for a bid or seeking developers' contributions. If different demographic projections are being used, there could be disputes about priorities for investment.

Source: Morphet 2009a

Step 5 Infrastructure Delivery Plan (IDP)

The IDP identifies what needs to be delivered in the area through the Core Strategy for the 15-year period. It can be divided into five-year tranches and include what is required, why and where, who is to deliver it, who will run it and how it will be funded. In the LDF, only those projects that have a good prospect of funding can be included. For those projects where infrastructure is identified but not yet funded, these can sit within the SCS until such time as they can be delivered through mainstream funding, bids, regional delivery plans, private sector investment and developers' contributions.

The provision of an IDP, based on evidence and included within the SCS, provides a means of identifying forthcoming investment and opportunities for the private sector. Where bids are being made to the regional delivery plan or other bodies such as the HCA, the preparation of projects based on deficits will provide the evidence of the single conversation and should go some way towards making the business case fit any proposed investment. Publishing the list of needs but not yet funded infrastructure may provide the private sector with some indication of what is needed to prompt their investment.

What:

*   identify what infrastructure is required through previous steps;
*   prepare an IDP that includes projects with a good prospect of funding and those projects yet unfunded;
*   identify where services might need to be reconfigured to meet shortfalls;
*   place all requirements on an infrastructure evidence schedule;
*   put unfunded requirements within the SCS;
*   use unfunded requirements as a basis for mainstream funding, special funding opportunities, bids, private sector investment, developers' contributions;
*   establish delivery strategy through other DPDs including AAPs, development management and development contributions;
*   undertake a SA of the infrastructure delivery schedule.

How:

*   identify which infrastructure needs to be funded from mainstream programmes to meet current and future population needs in the next five to ten years;
*   review schedules annually to ensure that they are fit for purpose;
*   monitor rates of development and delivery of infrastructure from all sectors as part of the Annual Monitoring Review process;
*   identify a viability test to assess the rate of developers' contributions to be associated with planning applications;
*   can undertake SA as part of other SA activities on SCS and/or Core Strategy.

Risk: without this, there is a risk that the LDF may not meet the deliverability ToS and that investment that is needed in any area may not be fully coordinated to make the best use of scarce resources.

Source: Morphet 2009a

Step 6 Validation

The process of validation is a means of demonstrating that the partners, govern-ance and project management processes are all in place to support delivery of what has been identified and are working together to meet the delivery of forthcoming requirements. It is also an opportunity for the infrastructure providers to engage in the process and 'own' its outcomes; it may also result in infrastructure providers reviewing their priorities for investment and the criteria that are used to make funding decisions.

Pulling together all these components into an infrastructure delivery strategy is an important element of the process.

What:

- consult on standards and processes of infrastructure planning;
- include this as part of a wider consultation base in locality;
- include as part of wider CO_2 reduction strategy;
- validate with service providers;
- put to LSP for sign off;
- undertake risk assessment on the IDP and its implications for the delivery of the LDF.

How:

- hold with other consultation events;
- discuss as part of parish and neighbourhood plans;
- hold consultation as part of service reviews;
- hold service provider workshops through KISP;
- develop a risk assessment approach that will include mitigation measures;
- consider a plan 'B' approach in case circumstances for sites or requirements change;
- discuss potential loss of sites through first time flooding events;
- discuss how new major development sites will be handled if they become available.

Risk: without this validation process and contained engagement, the infrastructure delivery process will not be able to support any change in population or place or to meet any unexpected changes such as first time flooding, factory closures or sudden population changes.

Source: Morphet 2009a

Step 7 Delivery

The delivery of the LDF will primarily be through the development management process which will allow proactive engagement between the local authority, infrastructure providers and developers in seeking to deliver what has been identified. Where providers are offered funding through specific initiatives from central government or other agencies, the list of infrastructure requirements should act as a first 'pick' list for projects. Elsewhere, development management teams will be proactively seeking to deliver the infrastructure required through their own more proactive processes. Some infrastructure requirements will be able to be delivered through developers directly or through contributions which are negotiated as part the planning process.

An important part of delivery is monitoring and in this case the maxim 'if you can't measure it you can't manage it' is useful. Keeping the delivery of all infrastructure investment in the area will take time and will repay rewards as differential success rates for types of infrastructure or specific locations will identify which delivery funding is likely to achieve the required outcomes. The publication of forthcoming investment schemes and what has been delivered in the past year are important ways of informing local communities of what is being achieved in their name. Much of this information is in the public domain but is rarely pulled together in ways that inform people of success or progress.

What:

- implement the delivery programme;
- integrate delivery into development management processes;
- keep delivery news available to enable the community to follow delivery;
- demonstrate how completion is being used to promote other objectives, e.g. CO_2 reduction, improved access, place improvement;
- report back regularly on delivery progress.

How:

- publish a live delivery programme so that it can be followed and used;
- use project planning approach;
- appoint a delivery manager to promote implementation;
- ensure that development management processes are seeking delivery opportunities proactively through the development delivery process;
- put webcams on key delivery projects to promote public engagement;
- publicise scheme completions, have official openings with the mayor;
- include delivery reporting as part of the AMR;
- identify how much investment has been generated through the IDP.

Risk: without this approach, delivery may be piecemeal and uncoordinated; communities cannot see that there is investment going on in their areas and that the delivery plan is being fulfilled; the areas for more active interventions cannot be identified; the potential for the private sector to invest on the back of public sector investment is reduced.

Source: Morphet 2009a

FUNDING DELIVERY

The sources of funding that are brought together through the process of delivery of the IDP include all main sources of funding available for capital investment. These include:

- public sector funds for schools, health, transport, regeneration
- private sector investment
- community and voluntary sector investment
- funds for the housing, regeneration and regional bodies
- competitive schemes-based funding, e.g. from Heritage Lottery Funds
- charitable investment
- hybrid body funding, e.g. utilities, housing associations
- specific purpose vehicles set up to promote local investment
- developers' contributions.

Where funding is committed, this will provide a local prospectus or portfolio that might attract further investment. For much of the required infrastructure, it will be difficult to identify funding, and maintaining the schedule of what is needed but not yet provided will be equally important. It is suggested that this is located in the SCS and reviewed regularly as part of the Annual Monitoring Report (AMR) or other monitoring processes. The definition of standards that will support assessment of deficiencies will also need to be kept under regular review as part of this process.

INFRASTRUCTURE DELIVERY STRATEGY

When preparing the LDF Core Strategy for submission, each will need to be accompanied by the IDP that comprises two elements which support infrastructure planning and delivery. The first is the infrastructure delivery strategy that is within the Core Strategy and this sets out the arrangements for delivery. It will need to demonstrate the governance of the process, the evidence that it is based on and the need for it to be validated by the inclusion of the key infrastructure providers and major landowners.

The second component comprises of the infrastructure schedules of requirements and how they are to be delivered. This sits in the evidence base of the LDF Core Strategy. PPS 12 states that there should be an infrastructure delivery strategy for meeting objectives and it should include where, when and by what means the objectives will be delivered (CLG 2008c: §4.1). There should also be clear arrangements for managing and monitoring delivery.

The delivery strategy is expected to show:

- how much development and improvement is intended in the area;
- where and when the development is intended;
- where and when the improvement is intended;
- how the development will be delivered;
- locations for strategic development through diagrams;
- that delivery strategy is central;
- how objectives will be delivered either through the planning authority or through the council or other bodies;
- coordination of different actions to achieve the objectives and deliver the vision;
- when, where and who will be involved in delivery;
- that agencies/partners needed for delivery have been consulted and involved in preparation;
- the required resources have been given due consideration;
- realistic prospects of being delivered in the life of the strategy.

WHAT MIGHT THE INFRASTRUCTURE DELIVERY STRATEGY CONTAIN?

In order to demonstrate that processes have been put in place to deliver the Core Strategy, it is useful to consider what kind of arrangements have been set up. Table 6.1 provides some indication of the components of this strategy.

Table 6.1 Infrastructure delivery strategy

Element	Role
LSP delivery sub-group, e.g. terms of reference, minutes, diary of meetings	Can demonstrate cross-agency working, develop common approaches to infrastructure requirements and planning; demonstrate involvement of agencies and stakeholders
Common evidence base, e.g. website for all partners in the LSP	Can demonstrate that service planning requirements for localities are being undertaken on the same evidence base and framework
Major landowners forum, e.g. terms of reference, minutes, diary of meetings	To ensure that major and key landowners are part of the continuing process of infrastructure planning and delivery
Capital programme repository, e.g. website	Opportunity to keep capital commitments in focus by all parties
Common GIS of publicly owned land and buildings including their state, accessibility, catchment areas, capacity	Supports the evidence base and also provides means of more efficiently planning use of area
Common consultation evidence base for all partners in the LSP	Means of keeping the community's views in the process of infrastructure planning and delivery

Continued

Table 6.1 Infrastructure delivery strategy *continued*

Element	Role
Infrastructure providers group, e.g. terms of reference, minutes, diary of meetings, area reviews	Can demonstrate the ways in which infrastructure providers are being brought together to consider their requirements within a common approach
Infrastructure delivery manager – could be capital programme manager, part of the LSP, planner	Can be the focal point for this activity
SCS schedule of infrastructure deficits and requirement as yet only partially or not yet funded – need to demonstrate that this is an evidence-based list that supports the delivery of objectives – not a wish list	Can demonstrate a process through which infrastructure requirements are examined and supported through the LSP process
Development management policies and approaches	The role of development management in securing infrastructure delivery is central to their task and this may be set out in a development management DPD
Developers' contributions – can be shown as part of the infrastructure evidence base schedule or in as yet unfunded requirements	Developers' contributions either requested or offered are a significant contributor to infrastructure delivery at the local level and need to be included as one of the delivery means if it is possible to show that these contributions will be viable and result in the delivery of the infrastructure identified
Community Infrastructure Levy (CIL)	When CIL becomes available it will be based on infrastructure requirements identified through this process
Targets and measurable outcomes (PPS 12 (CLG 2008c: §4.47))	It is important to ensure that the process of infrastructure planning and delivery is being pursued and achieved; important for LSP, local politicians and the community to see what has been delivered in the area through all funding means
AMR timing, processes, interrelationships between components	Provides a means through which the infrastructure evidence base and unfunded projects can be reviewed annually

Source: The author

CONCLUSIONS

Spatial planning is primarily concerned with shaping places and the delivery of the broad range of social, economic and environmental infrastructures that is required by communities both now and in the future. Spatial planning has a role in identifying what is required by communities and how this can be delivered by multiple agencies working together in more joined-up ways through the LSP. Planners cannot undertake this task on their own and need to work in more integrated ways with others to achieve these outcomes. The development of a logical and structured process for delivery through the IDP as part of the Core Strategy will support investment in places and promote positive change. It will help to ensure investment in areas and facilities that need support to maintain at least minimal standards of delivery whilst populations may be changing in the area. If communities are accessing services across administrative boundaries, this also needs to be taken into account.

There are key differences between the post-2004 planning system and what went before, primarily in its shift from being a policy integrator to that of being integrated within the wider local governance architecture with a new key role of infrastructure planning and delivery. This represents a major shift from the planning practice that has been operating in England at least since 1991 and possibly before. However, it does have strong links with the origins of the planning system in 1947 and the PAG Group's Report on *The Future of Development Plans* (HMSO 1965) set out in the Development Plans Manual (HMSO 1970). As it stated:

> Major projects, whether by government departments, the planning authority,
> other local authorities, statutory undertakers or private enterprise will also have
> to be woven into the plan: and the plan as a whole must pay realistic regard to
> likely levels of future investment.

(1.7)

So this 'new' delivery role is one that is similar to the role of planning in the post-1947 and 1970 era, although many of the planning practitioners now in leading management roles have entered their careers at a later point when development planning was more policy focussed with the delivery elements being taken on through regeneration practitioners. Planners may now need to re-acquire delivery knowledge and skills and undertake this infrastructure planning and delivery role, both in its practical application but also through the need to engage in networks and the informal use of power and influence with other public sector colleagues earlier in the process of investment decision making.

INFRASTRUCTURE CATEGORIES

PHYSICAL INFRASTRUCTURE

Physical	Sub-categories	Indicative capital programmes and sources of standards	Tier of governance (assume all functions in London Borough, Metropolitain Borough and Unitary Authority)
Transport	Road	Highways Agency Local authorities	C, R CC, DC
	Rail	Network Rail	C
	Bus	Bus companies Local authority	 CC, DC
	Taxis	Ranks	DC, CC
	Travel management	Local authority	CC
	Airports	Airport authorities	C, R
	Port/harbours	Port/harbour authorities	C
	Cycle and pedestrian facilities	Local authorities Sustrans	CC, DC
	Car parking	Local authorities Private providers	DC
	Fuel connectors	Local authorities	CC, DC
	Vehicle testing stations	Department for Transport (DfT) Local authority	 DC
	Driving tests	DVLA	C
	Canals	British Waterways	C
Energy	Centralised power generation	Ofgen Individual companies	C
	Transmission and distribution systems for gas and electricity	Ofgen Individual companies	C
	Biomass processing	Local authorities	CC, DC
	District heating and cooling	Local authorities Strategic Health Authority	DC
	Wind power	Private sector	

Continued

Physical	Sub-categories	Indicative capital programmes and sources of standards	Tier of governance (assume all functions in London Borough, Metropolitain Borough and Unitary Authority)
Water and drainage	Water supply	Ofwat Individual water companies	C
	Waste water	Local authorities Water treatment companies	DC
	Drainage	Local authorities Environment Agency	CC, DC
	Flood defences	Local authorities Environment Agency	CC, DC
Waste	Collection Disposal	Local authorities Local authorities Private sector	DC CC
ITC	Broadband and wireless, public phones	BT Ofcom Individual telcos BT	C
Public realm	Footways Street furniture	Local authority	CC, DC
Historic legacy	Listed buildings	English Heritage Local authorities	C DC

C = Central Government; R = Regional tier; CC = County Council; DC = District Council

GREEN INFRASTRUCTURE

Green infrastructure	Sub-categories	Sources of capital programmes and standards	Tier of governance (assume all functions in London Borough, Metropolitain Borough and Unitary Authority
Open space	Parks	Local authorities	DC
	Children's play areas	Local authorities	DC
	Sports pitches and courts	Local authorities Private sector	DC
	Country parks	Local authorities	CC
	Green public realm	Local authorities	CC, DC
	National Parks and other Area management	National park Authorities	C
Rivers	River corridors	River catchment management authorities	C
Coast	Littoral	Natural England	C, R
Historic landscapes	Historic sites	English Heritage	C

C = Central Government; R = Regional tier; CC = County Council; DC = District Council

SOCIAL AND COMMUNITY INFRASTRUCTURE

Social and community	Sub-category	Sources of capital programmes and standards	Tier of governance (assume all functions in London Borough, Metropolitain Borough and Unitary Authority)
Affordable housing	100% affordable	RSLs, local authorities	DC
	Intermediate	RSLs, private sector/local authorities	DC
Education	Nursery and pre-school	Local authority Private sector	CC
	Primary	Local authority Private sector	CC
	Secondary	Local authority Private sector	CC
	FE	Local authority	CC
	HE	Universities	C, R
Employment	Job Centre Plus	DWP	C
Benefits/tax	Local offices	DWP/HMRC	C
Children's services	Children's centres Special needs and disability	Local authority	CC
Health	Hospitals	SHA	R
	Health centres/GP surgeries	SHA PCT	R R
	Public health and prevention	PCT Local authority	CC
Gypsies and travellers	Sites and facilities	Local authority	DC
Post Offices	Main Post Offices Sub-Post Offices Sorting offices Parcels	Post office DBERR Private sector Post Office Private sector	
Community services	Libraries	Local authority	CC
	Community centres	Local authority	DC

Continued

Social and community	Sub-category	Sources of capital programmes and standards	Tier of governance (assume all functions in London Borough, Metropolitain Borough and Unitary Authority)
Community services	Youth	Local authority	CC
	Social services/over 50s support	Local authority	CC
	Police	Police Authority	CC
Community services	Fire	Fire Authority	CC
	Ambulance	Ambulance Trust	R
	Cemeteries and crematoria	Local authorities	DC
	Courts	Ministry of Justice	C
	Prisons	Home Office	C
	Hostels	Home Office	C
	Places of worship	Individual organisations	DC
Culture	Museums/galleries	Local authorities Charities	CC, DC
	Theatres	Local authorities Private sector	CC, DC
	Cinemas	Private sector Local authorities	DC
Leisure	Sports centres	Local authorities Private sector	DC
	Swimming pools	Local authorities Private sector	DC, CC (schools)
	Festivals and town centre programmes	Local authorities	DC, CC
	Markets	Local authority	DC

C = Central Government; R = Regional tier; CC = County Council; DC = District Council

CHAPTER 7

TAKING AN INTEGRATED APPROACH TO LOCAL SPATIAL DELIVERY

INTRODUCTION

Place has had a growing role in public policy and delivery in England since 2000. Place is integrated within the system of local governance and spatial narratives are a means of identifying how places work and their needs in an integrated way; they are a means of overcoming institutional silos with conflicting priorities and targets. A contributor to this shift has been the many place-specific 'unexpected' events that have been attributed to climate change, such as an increase in locations that have been flooded for the first time, drought and other localised weather events at both ends of the temperature continuum. People use places in ways that suit them and place has become a metaphor for community-centred approaches which include:

* local decision making
* local budgets
* place-based outcomes
* removing centralised delivery targets.

Within this, spatial planning has an integrated delivery role to changing and improving places. Spatial planning has the tools and legislative framework to achieve localised, integrated improvement and it is now placed to perform this role. Spatial planning also has contributions to make in other areas such as the achievement of social objectives. There is a growing awareness of the ways in which health outcomes can be delivered through spatial planning approaches, including design and the provision of facilities. There are a number of other social issues that are now more firmly integrated into spatial planning, including addressing crime reduction and community safety, and a third area is older people, which is increasingly forming a larger proportion of the population. Of course, these issues are all interlinked and taking an issue-based approach also runs the risk of being one-dimensional or silo-focussed, but measuring outcomes against a variety of groups and locations provides a mechanism to assess the effectiveness of interventions.

Some particular issues which are now being considered in new and more localised ways are discussed in this chapter. These are grouped into social, economic and environmental issues and although they are discussed in this way, there are numerous cross-cutting issues between them. The choice of these three over-arching categories has been based on two determining factors:

*   it is a duty of local authorities to promote the social, environmental and eco-nomic well-being of their areas (Local Government Act 2000, s2);
*   local authorities have to define their infrastructure needs in social, green and physical categories (CLG 2008c: PPS 12).

In this chapter, an integrated approach to delivering different types of infrastruc-ture within each of the three categories is discussed in more detail. The main focus is on social infrastructure as this provides most support to communities and includes the largest amounts of public sector expenditure. Over 80 per cent of local public expenditure is on education, for example, and this is followed by health. Although public sector investment is due to reduce by 25 per cent or more between 2010 and 2015, there is still a major budget to be spent. The need to make public sector funding go further will also put more pressure on the use of assets and co-location of services. Some government organisations, such as the Homes and Communities Agency, have been investing funding into private sector schemes that have stalled in order to provide a kick start in some locations. Although private sector investment has slowed since 2008, there is some evidence that this might be returning in some sectors and locations and this investment will be seeking locations where it can have the greatest impact. All of this makes the role of infrastructure planning and delivery more important in the coming period to 2016.

DELIVERING SOCIAL OBJECTIVES

Social infrastructure provides a major contribution to the way people live their lives in communities and at home. It also has possibly the greatest range in terms of fund-ing and delivery of all three infrastructure types and a range of providers. Access to services is an important feature of well-being and can play a considerable role in improving a sustainable pattern of living. The delivery of social infrastructure through spatial planning has been primarily focussed towards the provision of school and health facilities through developers' contributions for strategic sites or major hous-ing developments. Infrastructure delivery has focussed on the integrated application of mainstream funding and this is an important consideration here. The focus on mainstream investment in social facilities, particularly for health and education, is important, not least as they are triggered by increases in population and, at the same time, have been operating under independent processes when considering their locations and types of investment.

The new, more integrated, approach suggests that this will need a change in order to deliver these outcomes. Haughton and Allmendinger (2007) suggest that there has been a loss of skills in pursuing these kinds of processes, although their work in the Thames Gateway focusses on the implication of new housing development rather than considering the more systematic approach that is now required to address investment deficits. Kidd (2007) and Harris and Hooper (2004) have considered the role of regional spatial planning in the delivery of health outcomes and their approaches have been primarily geared towards more strategic Health Impact Assessment approaches rather than local delivery through the LDF.

(1) HEALTH

The delivery of improved health outcomes through infrastructure improvements is one of the oldest roles of planning. Town planning was born, in part, to deliver an improved public health agenda, and over time that link has been weakened. Health delivery has been the role of specialist national agencies and at the local level through environmental health professionals who have concentrated on public health issues such as food hygiene, air quality and the management of risks through licensing.

The role of planning as a means of delivering better health outcomes is re-emerging in a variety of ways and spatial planning can act as one of the key delivery mechanisms for health. There are three key ways in which spatial planning can help to deliver better health outcomes. The first is in the design of communities and accessibility to facilities. In design, the ability to walk or cycle safely can make a significant contribution to healthier lifestyles (NICE 2008). The second contribution is through the location of health facilities and how they relate to other public services. The current trend to make primary health care the focal point of health delivery means that there is additional local investment. As part of the process of agreeing locations for new or expanded health care facilities, the LDF can use baseline assessments of existing facilities, their capacity and condition and work with the health trust to develop accessible approaches to health provision. All health facilities can have green travel plans which will identify where other investment might be used to improve access, e.g. in public transport or other supported transport schemes including those provided by volunteers. The health trust can also include transport and access criteria in the evaluation of different investment schemes as part of their business case appraisal.

The third way in which spatial planning can support improvements in health is through assessments of the Core Strategy and other LDF documents through the mechanisms of Health Impact Assessments (HIA) and a SA. These provide a good means of checking the relationship between spatial proposals and health outcomes in a systematic way. This can also be done through SA. HIAs have been used in the North-West (Kidd 2007) and in Liverpool, where they have particularly been used to examine the relationship between health and housing. This has included the provision of energy and water supplies as part of the assessment of health in specific locations.

There are a range of sources of advice and guidance on the delivery of health outcomes through spatial planning, many of which also include examples and case studies. The Planning Advisory Service note, *Prevention is still better than cure* (2008a) provides a good general introduction and includes case study examples from across England. The NHS has also produced two introductory guides on the relationship between health and planning, one written for health professionals (2007a) and the other written for planning professionals (2007b). The guide written for health staff introduces spatial planning to them, includes some case studies and strongly encourages them to work with planners to support health delivery. The guide for planners on health concentrates more on public health than the location of all health care facilities so this might not provide a fully developed approach and will need to be extended in practice. More recently, the RTPI has produced a Good Practice Note on *Delivering Healthy Communities* (2009a) which provides some pointers to ways in which spatial planning can be used to deliver health outcomes.

A more detailed set of guidance on ways that health outcomes can be delivered through Core Strategies has been prepared for health professionals through guides prepared by the NHS Healthy Urban Development Unit (HUDU) (HUDU 2007a and b; 2009a; 2009b) and the Mayor of London (2007). Initially set up for London, HUDU has a London focus but all of its publications have a wider application and use in spatial planning elsewhere. The HUDU Guide (2009b) encourages health professionals to become involved in the spatial planning process including being involved in developing a health infrastructure plan at the local level to secure the delivery of health outcomes. Although prepared for health professionals, this guide provides the most detailed and systematic approach to the delivery of health outcomes through the Core Strategy and includes a checklist. Although the guide has considerable useful features, in places its tone is prescriptive and this needs to be handled with care. Its major weakness is that it treats the Core Strategy through a health lens rather than considering how health outcomes will be delivered through more joined-up approaches at the local level.

Health Issues in Planning Best Practice Guidance (Mayor of London 2007) provides another comprehensive approach to considering the way in which health outcomes are delivered through spatial planning at the local level. Like the HUDU work, it inevitably has a London focus but it does provide the most comprehensive guide to all the likely health issues that will need to be considered in spatial planning together with further useful links and references. Unlike some of the guides mentioned here, it takes an issues-based approach and this can make it a useful cross-referencing tool when reviewing the health impacts of the LDF. It also includes a number of case studies and signposts that could be pursued to improve spatial health outcomes. In particular, it considers how spatial planning can deliver health outcomes through an examination of:

- the spatial determinants of health
- housing
- transport
- employment and skills
- education and early life
- access to services
- liveability, open space and public realm
- air, water and noise quality
- access to fresh food
- climate change.

All of these policy and delivery approaches that can be used in spatial planning are summarised in Tables 7.1 and 7.2.

Table 7.1 Using spatial planning processes to address health outcomes

	Process	*Sources/mechanisms*	*Outcomes delivered through spatial planning*
1	Using a common evidence base	Local health profiles, JSNA	Common approach to achieving healthier places
2	Identify specific locational issues such as lung disease, obesity	Evidence base as above	Specific emphasis on solutions
3	Develop a common understanding of language between health and spatial planning	Both planning and health have their own jargon which makes it difficult for both sides to understand each other and the public to understand neither	Glossary of terms which both health and planning will use
4	Audit of health outcomes from spatial planning proposals	Use Health Impact Assessment in Options Appraisal; review health outcomes as part of Sustainability Appraisal	Use spatial planning to address health challenges and problems

Source: the author

Table 7.2 Delivery of healthier places through spatial planning

	Health outcomes	Evidence	Spatial planning contribution
1	Reduce obesity and cardio vascular disease	Local health profile; JSNA; standard mortality rates (SMRs)	Improve walking and cycling facilities in areas of greatest need
2	Reduce lung disease	As above	Addressing air quality issues through locations of facilities
3	Reduce obesity in children	As above	In addition to other actions, review safe walking and cycling routes to schools through school travel plans and deliver improvements where needed
4	Help to reduce mental health problems which are related to safety	As above: Crime and Disorder Reduction Partnership evidence	Review evidence of safety audits, apply by design standards; consider locations of independent living housing
5	Reduce car travel to health facilities	Health facilities travel plans	Identify locations near to public transport and other public facilities; establish access standards with health trusts
6	Improve physical activity levels in all age groups	Baseline assessment of all sport and recreation facilities including those in schools, workplaces and private sector and identify potential gaps	Identify specific, evidence-based requirements on infrastructure delivery schedules
7	Maximising use of all recreation and leisure facilities	Use baseline assessment to encourage dual use; review facilities in other local authority areas which may serve communities within the local authority area	Work through the infrastructure providers group to develop dual use arrangements; secure these on facilities through s106 and other planning conditions

Source: the author

The evidence base that is required for delivering better health outcomes through spatial planning is now improving. In England, there are regional Public Health Observatories (www.apho.org.uk) which each provide considerable amounts of research and analysis of regional health needs within key themes such as avoidable injury, cancer and obesity. They also review health inequalities and consideration of the impact of these can be useful as part of the development of spatial planning documents. At the local level, there are public health profiles for all local authority areas and these can be accessed through the regional Public Health Observatories. The development of a joint approach to identifying health needs alongside other concerns has been driven through the establishment of JSNA which are now undertaken for every local authority area and are increasingly regarded as the main source of evidence about local needs. Each JSNA has a data set which allows local and national comparisons of health outcomes to be made (DH 2007; 2008). Another useful guide to identifying the evidence base required for spatial planning has been developed by HUDU (2007b) and this includes ways to find detailed evidence bases for mental health, obesity and other diseases that can be used as part of the spatial planning process.

Box 7.1   Health Impact Assessments

Why do a Health Impact Assessment (HIA)?

- Promote greater equity in health.
- Promote evidence and knowledge-based planning and decision making.
- Maximise health gain and minimise health loss by informing and influencing decision making in favour of health.
- Reduce inequalities by addressing health impacts on vulnerable populations.
- Encourage better coordination of action between sectors to improve and protect health.
- Identify the connections between health and developments in other policy areas.
- Increase awareness of health in the wider policy arena.

How to do an HIA

There are five stages to carrying out a HIA.

Screening – the process of deciding whether it is appropriate or necessary to carry out an HIA.
Scoping – how should we do the HIA? Determining the focus, methods and work plan.
Appraisal/assessment – identifying the health impacts.
Reporting and decision making – influencing the process.
Monitoring and evaluation – of the process, impact and outcomes.

Source: Association of Public Health Observatories: Health Impact Assessment Gateway

A further use of evidence is through the use of HIAs on spatial planning policies and proposals. The processes are similar to those used in SA and can be
incorporated within it. The key reasons for undertaking an HIA are shown in Box 7.1.
HUDU has also produced a checklist for assessing the health impact of planning
proposals (HUDU 2009c) which is more focussed towards London than the other
documents that they have produced. However, it does have a number of further links
and references which may be useful.

More detailed advice on the design of built and natural environments which
encourage healthier lifestyles are provided by NICE (2008) and CABE (2006). Both
of these concentrate on more detailed delivery issues, including design, access,
assessment of walking and cycling routes and how these should be planned into
development.

The final issue that needs to be considered in the role of spatial planning
in delivering health is through the infrastructure delivery strategy and schedules
which cover the use of mainstream health funding and the application of developers' contributions towards health. For health delivery planning, the role of the health
representative on the LSP will be the key entry point to the development and delivery
of health outcomes at the local level. The key areas that will need to be considered
in managing and delivering the mainstream health budgets are that:

- All health finance is triggered by population and this is reviewed following the
  publication of SMRs by the Office for National Statistics.
- The health service as a whole is one of the largest public sector landowners in
  the country and the use of the health estate for health and other purposes will
  play a considerable role in the development of the LDF.
- The evidence base used for health planning needs to be joined up with other
  services and population forecasts need to be agreed.
- The development of health care policy and delivery is important to keep under
  review as this changes over time. The current focus is on shifting delivery to
  primary health care provision which may mean hospital space becomes available or that new population growth can use the capacity created by transferring
  services to the local level.
- Public health activity is likely to be undertaken separately from primary health
  care planning within the health trust so it may be important to ensure that a full
  range of health interests are engaged in the process.
- The funding for new health facilities will be subject to business cases made
  by local health trusts to strategic health authorities. These business cases may
  become increasingly reliant on their ability to demonstrate that the planning of
  new provision can be demonstrably linked with other service provisions in the
  locality.

- Health care provision may need other investment such as specialist or whole life housing to enable people to live in their own homes rather than intuitional care. As a result, there may be some redundancy in residential care homes.

In considering the delivery of health care facilities through developers' contributions, the same principles apply as for all public services. First, there needs to be an assessment of existing provision, then the use of mainstream funds needs to be considered, and any additional needs must be soundly secured on the evidence base. In negotiating any developers' contributions towards funding health care facilities, it is important to ensure that as far as possible they are not tied to any specific type of delivery model prevailing at the time of negotiation but at the time of delivery. This will prevent the provision of health care facilities which no longer meet health authority requirements if they are delivered long after the developer's contribution agreement has been signed. If the contribution is expected to be in the delivery of a facility rather than a financial contribution, this may need to retain some flexibility about siting and size as far as this is possible in the process. The requirements for health care provision will also need to be identified in the infrastructure delivery schedule.

(II) BLUE LIGHT SERVICES

The role of spatial planning in delivering blue light services – fire and rescue, police and ambulance – have primarily been concerned with detailed locational issues, whether this is about service delivery or about design. The role of spatial planning in supporting the creation of safer places and reducing opportunities for crime has focussed more detailed approaches to delivery. Standards such as *Secured by Design* (www.securedbydesign.com) that have been developed by the Association of Chief Police Officers are now adopted by many local authorities who work closely with the local police and apply national guidance. Other policies for reducing crime, such as dealing with drug dependency and youth crime are also the subject of local interventions with health bodies and also through youth diversion activities with the youth service, fire and rescue services and other agencies. These are all important and need to be included within spatial planning approaches.

Other policies, such as that for town centre regeneration, which may have resulted in a drink-based night time or student economy, also need consideration and can sometimes lead to unintended consequences of change. In designating town centres, the assessment of their function and role throughout a 24-hour period is essential as part of the consideration of ways in which they function and can be successful. Many towns have large screen viewing facilities for major events, such as those in Manchester and Liverpool, but these can also encourage all-day drinking and partisan aggression in post-match periods. The ability of the blue light services to support this kind of mass town centre entertainment may need to be considered as part of overall design and emergency planning strategies for:

* ambulance access
* locations and drainage for portable urinals
* field hospitals
* places for lost and found people
* first aid locations
* spectator venues and crowd management.

In some cases, this may need an integrated approach with the issue of licences for drinking hours which are all within the local authority's control.

In addition to these more detailed considerations for design and delivery, there are also other issues to consider when working with the blue light services to deliver outcomes. These are based on their own operational requirements which are also changing over time. Each service is now considering where best to locate in relation to service provision, for fire and rescue, locations which are more accessible to major roads and motorways are now more important as this is where much of their rescue work is now located. Hence, relocations away from town centres to ring roads, with ease of access to urban and transport locations are now being implemented. Fire and rescue services are also considering co-locations with other services and this may be with the ambulance services and/or the police.

The ambulance service has a set of targets including an eight-minute response time and these are now frequently met through a range of vehicles and services rather than solely through ambulance provision, which may include motorcycles, cars and in built-up areas, through the use of bicycles. In more rural areas, the provision of ambulance services may be through a roaming service which provides a better opportunity to meet response times than provision from fixed facilities. The police services at the local level are also considering the best locations from which to deliver their services. In some cases, there is a preference for city centre locations, whereas elsewhere a more mobile or community-based delivery focus, sometimes using libraries or schools, is being pursued. All of these will need to be taken into account when considering the transformational role of spatial planning in improving public service access and the more effective use of public assets. The Surrey Improvement Partnership (SIP) has undertaken a study of baseline infrastructure requirements with the blue light and other strategic service providers which identifies the potential for co-location (SIP 2009a; 2009b).

Overall, it is important to remember that service delivery models are constantly changing as improved technology and evidence-based interventions are shaping practice. When using spatial planning to deliver the service requirements of the blue light services, it will be important to ensure engagement with those involved in service planning and delivery, including those which may be preparing business cases for future investment. Early joint discussions between these three services may identify potential for co-location or some back office services. They may also be able to provide docking points for more mobile services and create a better network of potential service provision, particularly in more isolated areas. A further considera-tion for service delivery may be population changes and areas of growth, whether for housing or economic uses. These proposed developments may have implications for blue light service delivery and as with all services that have delivery supported through spatial planning, it is essential to maintain a two-way dialogue, preferably through a local infrastructure planning and delivery group as part of the LSP.

(III) OLDER PEOPLE

There will be at least five million more people in the UK aged over 60 by 2026 (an increase of over 40 per cent in the next 20 years). The proportion of over 75s will increase even more sharply by 54 per cent (RTPI 2007). When considering the ways in which the needs of older people can be met through spatial planning, the most frequent expectation is that this is through care homes, special needs housing and increased health facilities. However, policy towards older people is changing and more effort at the local level is on keeping older people active. Thus, strategies for older people are likely to be focussed on fitness and activities, such as swim-ming, bowls and dancing. One of the key issues for the spatial planning process is to consider whether, as a greater proportion of older people become more active, there will be adequate facilities for the activity levels expected. There may be a need for more swimming pools than GPs. Policies for older people are geared to extend-ing activity levels, including participation in the work place, using free bus services to maintain social circles and in volunteering to support neighbours and family (Davis Smith and Gay 2005). Many local authorities now have specific teams supporting older people activities and healthy lifestyles and their contribution on likely require-ments for older people will be important.

When older people need more support and care, there is, increasingly, empha-sis on encouraging people to stay in their own homes. This might need specific aids and adaptations, including movement sensors, but for many older people, retrofitting insulation and energy management measures can be critical in their decision to stay at home. In many cases, older people may be in housing that is too large for them and need support to move to smaller and more manageable accommodation. This transition may increase the need for more specialist housing with warden support, but can release larger housing units for growing families. Older people can also be supported by their own families and there may be implications for extensions to exist-ing dwellings to provide separate accommodation.

Where the population profile of an area has a strong representation of older people, there may be other considerations for spatial planning. The first is whether the place is becoming a specialist location for retirement and the implications that this might have for the local economy. In this case, vacant housing is likely to be taken by the same age group. Where there is a more mixed population, death of older people may give rise to a release of the housing stock to the market and may see an upsurge of occupancy. Areas can move from low and under occupancy to much greater levels of occupation over fairly short periods and this can have significant implications for local services which could be greater than any newly built develop-ment. This can also happen where people decide to trade down their homes and release equity to supplement their pensions. As a large proportion of people have not made pension provision whilst working, it seems likely that equity release will become more popular in the future (Rowlandson and McKay 2005). Where people inherit property on the death of a family member, they are likely to release the prop-erty for other users. The pressure to take this route is frequently propelled through the payment of death duties but the changes in allowances in 2008, together with the downturn in the housing market, may delay some of the asset release sales.

All of these issues concerning older people, their needs and likely behaviours have a significant impact on spatial planning outcomes both in the use and require-ments for infrastructure. This might be direct or indirect, but its likely influence will have spatial concentrations and consequences that will need to be considered.

(IV) CHILDREN

The changes in the organisation of children's services at the local level have been considerable in the last decade. Children's services now embrace a range of activi-ties and all of these will need to be considered as part of the spatial delivery process and include:

- early years, e.g. nurseries
- SureStart and Children's Centres
- schools, including independent schools
- extended day schools which include a wider variety of facilities for breakfast, community activities, recreation and parent support
- Building Schools for the Future, which includes a wider range of community facilities
- children's play
- children's social services

- commissioned services
- post-16 provision
- further education
- youth services
- school transport
- green travel plans.

In development planning, there has been a focus on education rather than the wider role that children's services now play and they have a significant impact on local communities. In the past, the main interest has been in the provision of schools and frequently this has been confined to the provision of developers' contributions. However, spatial planning is concerned with the application of all public sector investment and this includes the full range of children's services. In some cases, such as early years' provision and children's centres, there will be strong links with other services such as health and housing. These are likely to be found in the relevant thematic group of the LSP. Services for youth might link with community and/ or safety themes. Although the children's services departments have been joined for some years now, it is possible that the parts of the service dealing with schools may still be separate from the rest and, to enable effective spatial planning, all parts of the service will need to be engaged.

The funding for children's services will be through a variety of mainstream budgets and is likely to be the largest portion of the local authority capital and revenue budgets. For school provision, all funding is triggered through the pupil census that takes place in January each year and all children in school on that date will be included in the financial settlement for the local authority. This occurs in the financial year commencing three months later, so that pupils included in the January 2010 pupil census will be funded from April 2010. This funding is based on capitation for revenue and capital and the allocations are in the public domain (www.teachernet. gov.uk). It is usual for the capital capitation allowance to be fixed across the country and for the revenue capitation allowance to be variable according to need and deprivation. The pupil census triggers the allocations for all the other school-based funding provided by central government. Much of this is capital funding which is allocated in three-year tranches by education phase – i.e. primary and secondary. The decisions on the use of this funding are local and will need to be brought into the wider consideration of school provision at the local level to take into account changing demographic trends and intensified/new development. Where local authorities have schools with vacant places, these will not be funded and local authorities will be expected to shift and shuffle places between schools to ensure that the capacity is available where it is required.

Most local authorities prepare a schools organisation plan which can be a useful starting point for discussion. However, these may need to be considered in detail, particularly when examining the school entry estimates. Some schools organisation plans predict long-term flat-line projections for entry and take no account of changing demography or new development. The population estimates used for school provision should be the same as those for all other public services and this may be an area where there is a 'double book' approach to the use of population projections, i.e. the population projections jointly agreed are not the ones used for service planning or bidding. It is useful to note that there can frequently be an optimism bias toward the client populations in projections used by services – that is to say they are likely to increase the numbers for the client group they serve. The same is likely to be true in older people's services. The starting point for population projections that are used for services is likely to be the local JSNA.

The role of spatial planning in supporting the delivery of children's services follows the same approach as other services, which is to:

- review evidence;
- review baseline of provision, its capacity and consolidation;
- review provision in neighbouring areas;
- identify current and future gaps based on expected change and incorporating any capacity in base line;
- identify locations where new provision is needed and review the application of current provision and investment, taking into account the threshold funding, i.e. the funding that will be released automatically as the children's population increases;
- identify potential dual use resources as an effective way to provide services and reduce running costs, particularly where there are sports and recreation facilities or where other services can deliver services from the same buildings.

Where there are likely to be new requirements for schools, the first step is to consider how existing provision can be remodelled. Using other initiatives, such as Building Schools for the Future, to relocate and amalgamate secondary provision is another means of supporting changing requirements for schools. For further education, now returned to the local authority sector, there may be incomplete capital investment programmes as many colleges move towards delivering foundation degrees.

There are other children's services that are not part of the direct local authority provision, although licensed and inspected by the authorities and Ofsted. Early year's day care can be provided by the private sector through day nurseries or childminders. Provision needs to be considered in new development, close to work places or new residential accommodation, possibly through the provision of some larger units. All provision of this kind will be registered and inspected locally within the children's services departments, so this can be a means of checking current provision and potential gaps. The independent school sector also will have investment plans over time and will need some engagement with the spatial planning process to deliver them. Finally, it is also important to consider universities and where these are located within the area. University expansion has fuelled new development and frequently universities have taken over major heritage buildings, e.g. in Buxton and Greenwich. In inner city areas, such as Liverpool and London, universities have also taken over large unused office buildings and hotels. The London School of Economics, for example, has taken over a significant amount of former office property in the vicinity of its buildings. In time, these can create mini-campuses inside the city. It is also important to remember that universities often wish to spawn business parks or incubator units nearby and are large property owners and developers in their own right.

DELIVERING ECONOMIC OBJECTIVES

Spatial planning has a role in delivering economic outcomes. This is at all spatial scales. At the regional level, a strategic view of the economy is taken by the Regional Development Agency (RDA) and the Regional Leaders' Board and expressed through the Regional Strategy (RS). The emergent RS from 2010 replaces the RSS, RES and other regional strategies and will provide an overarching economic strategy for the region that is accompanied by a delivery plan (CLG and BIS 2010). The RS will absorb the role of the RSS and be subject to an EiP. The role of the Regional Minister is to be enhanced and regional bodies to be co-located. It will be scrutinised by the new Parliamentary Select Committees for each region. Within each region, it is the sub-regional level which is now viewed as being the spatial scale where economic growth will be most effectively generated (HM Treasury 2004; 2007a). Sub-regional groupings of local authorities and other partners, including central government agencies, are being established and these are focussing on planning, transport, regeneration and housing (CLG 2007b). These sub-regional groupings do not cover the whole of England as yet but are present in all regions. The sub-regional arrangements vary within each partnership with some being more formalised than others. Sub-regional partnerships can be formalised as City Regions (CLG 2009d) or Multi Area Agreements (MAAs) or can have a looser arrangement. However, for each one there is an economic focus which may be on housing, transport, regeneration, skills or a mix of these issues.

At the local level, the provision of sufficient housing units is viewed as part of the economic agenda. The Barker Review (HM Treasury 2004) found that the country's economy is being hindered through a lack of supply of housing in places where businesses wish to expand or locate. Housing is also a key indicator of the national economy. Unlike other countries, new house building is identified as being a key factor in economic vibrancy and much of the country's financial infrastructure has been based on housing development (Morphet 2007a).

The world recession that took hold in 2008 has led the government to review the role of local authorities in supporting the economy. As a result, they have been given a duty to keep economic conditions under review. Local authorities have also been given incentives to promote the local economy in being able to retain a portion of the business rates generated by new business locations. Attention to supporting skill levels for individuals is also part of this localised approach. Some local authorities have taken a proactive approach to the recession through a range of activities. In Essex, the local authority has developed an approach to supporting the maintenance of a Post Office service through its own service outlets such as libraries. It is also considering establishing a local bank which can support the provision of mortgages and housing. In Gateshead, for example, a number of initiatives have been pursued, including:

- bringing forward capital expenditure
- supporting businesses with rent free periods in areas where the local authority owns property
- promote buy local policies
- promote green and environmental technology businesses.

(Henry 2009: 17–18)

As part of this shift towards giving the economy some priority, the Government has also reviewed its own guidance on the way in which the spatial planning system can deliver better economic outcomes. This had previously been set out in a range of different documents, including:

- PPG 4 *Industrial and Commercial Development and Small Firms* (1992)
- PPS 6 *Planning for Town Centres* (2005)
- PPS 7 *Sustainable Development in Rural Areas* (in part)
- PPG 17 *Transport* (in part).

In the introduction to the draft PPS 4, *Planning for Prosperous Economies* (CLG 2009b), the Planning and Housing Minister stresses the importance of planning in delivering economic outcomes:

In an increasingly competitive and knowledge-driven global economy, the Government's approach to ensuring the UK's long-term economic performance and resilience to economic shocks is based on maintaining macro-economic stability, ensuring employment opportunity for all, and using microeconomic reforms to tackle market failures around the drivers of productivity – investment, innovation, competition, skills and enterprise.

The planning system is a key lever the Government has to contribute towards improving economic performance. The planning system affects productivity and employment – the two drivers of economic growth – and helps to deliver wider economic and social objectives such as the regeneration of deprived areas and the provision of new housing.

(ibid.: 7)

In reviewing the role of planning in economic delivery, the Government has defined economic development, as shown in Box 7.2.

The role of spatial planning in the delivery of economic outcomes will depend on the integration of these approaches as well as their integration with other key policies. For example, all workplaces, regardless of their sector, will need green travel plans such as offices, schools, construction sites, factories and retail centres. All businesses will need energy supply, and some types of business will need additional capacity to allow their business to function. All businesses will generate waste and this will need disposal as well as waste management and reduction policies. Those who work in the area will also need places to live and enjoy other cultural and leisure pursuits.

Box 7.2   Government definition of economic development

What is economic development?

1   Provides employment opportunities.
2   Generates wealth.
3   Produces or generates an economic output or product.

What are the main economic uses?

1   Retail (including warehouse clubs and factory outlet centres).
2   Leisure, entertainment facilities and the more intensive sport and recreation uses (including cinemas, restaurants, drive-through restaurants, bars and pubs, nightclubs, casinos, health and fitness centres, indoor bowling centres and bingo halls).
3   Offices.
4   Arts, culture and tourism (theatres, museums, galleries and concert halls, hotels and conference facilities).

(after *Planning for Prosperous Communities* CLG 2009b: 14)

Delivering economic outcomes through spatial planning occurs in a number of ways. The development of a strategic approach to delivering economic outcomes through spatial planning is based on a series of factors. These include:

*   the regional economic context;
*   the sub-regional economic context;
*   existing local economic locations such as ports, airports, major retail or business centres;
*   evidence of local trends and pressures – are business sectors represented locally growing, declining or remaining static?
*   consideration of the relationship between local population, skill levels and future requirements;
*   the opportunities that may be available on strategic sites for generating regional or sub-regional opportunities to support the economy;
*   any overall considerations in relation to regeneration needs.

The consideration of strategic economic requirements has been the subject of considerable research and discussion about the economies of regions. This often stresses national debates about policy or the multiple effects of individual decisions. The strategic role of regional relocation policy, including the role of Lyons in reviewing potential relocation opportunities for government departments and agencies (2004) has been a long-standing approach to dealing with economic underperformance. The development of Manchester as the second city in England, in an attempt to create a more bipolar economic base, has been supported in a number of ways including its location for the Commonwealth Games, the transfer of a major part of the BBC and major investment in sustainable transport systems. It is also one of the first city region pilots.

Strategic approaches to economic policy are now set out in the RS. Regional economic spatial policy considers the priorities for sectors such as the concentration on local food production. The RS focusses on the transport and housing infrastructure which is needed to support the region's economy. The RS delivers through a variety of means including the RDA, the Homes and Communities Agency and other government bodies. However, their effect on decision making on mainstream public sector investment has not been so strong and this is an issue that is being addressed in the RS (CLG 2009d). Each region has identified its own priorities and these are to be delivered in a way that relies on a competitive approach with other regions. However, some regions have had more policy influence at the centre, partly due to evidence of need and this remains an issue to be resolved. The effort in helping to grow the economy in the North of England is always to be considered against the needs for infrastructure to support a generally more thriving economy in the South East and South West, which have much less influence than their northern counterparts. It is also important to remember that within each region as well as each local authority, there will always be a mix of those areas which are coping well and thriving and those communities that need extra support to help them achieve outcomes closer to the national average.

In considering the interpretation of what needs to be addressed in the LDF, the strategic context is important and now all local authorities have to undertake an economic assessment which will be a vital piece of evidence for this process. This will help to translate the regional context into local policy and delivery. It is likely that the SCS and other measures of success such as the LAA and the CAA will also be setting objectives for the local economy that will need to be taken into account.

Once an overall assessment of the economic outcomes has been made at strategic level, the LDF then needs to translate this into delivery at the local level through consideration of the pattern of development. There will be an assessment of several key factors, including:

- existing employment locations by type, e.g. offices, retail, tourism, industrial, distribution, health, education;
- the potential requirements for economic growth and existing capacity;
- consideration of energy, water and telecommunications requirements for economic activities now and in the future;
- the designation of town centres and other locations where economic activity will have priority;
- the identification of economic issues to meet growth and replacement gaps that will deliver the economic outcomes;
- the identification of locations where a masterplan for change may be required;
- the need to make some locations more sustainable through intensified or extended land uses, e.g. on urban peripheries, in areas only accessible by car;
- the consideration of economic activity in rural areas including market town strategies, rural industries, food and energy production;
- economic regeneration priorities across the whole area and ways in which these might be considered in more detail through AAPs;
- assessment of transport and other infrastructure requirements to support economic activity, e.g. day nurseries and identification of specific proposals in the infrastructure delivery schedule.

The delivery of the identified economic outcomes will depend on a range of tools, not all of which will be within the spatial planning process. However, working with those who are proposing economic activity on a site needs to be started at an early stage. A proactive approach on specific sites and locations will be led by those in development management and/or regeneration. In its shift from development control to development management, the delivery of the economic outcomes through the planning process is one of its key tasks. Spatial planning is focussed towards the delivery of earlier specified outcomes and infrastructure. In addition to this targeted approach, opportunity sites and changes of use will inevitably arise, whilst a more detailed approach to spatial policy should provide greater certainty for businesses in the development process.

There are also places where more strategic changes of land use away from those formerly used for jobs have been pursued as spatial planning approaches. In some cases, such as the former steel works outside Sheffield, sites have been redeveloped as retail centres. Elsewhere in South Yorkshire, coal mining areas are proposed to be redeveloped with housing (Audit Commission 2008c). These changes have a significant impact on local communities, particularly where there was a cultural relationship between communities and work places such as in coal mining areas. In areas where considerable regeneration is required, there have been research projects and action-centred initiatives to understand what might be the most successful way to approach these issues. Imrie and Raco (2003) suggest that this might be achieved by taking a wider social inclusion approach to regeneration rather than one that is only property led, whilst Taylor et al. (2002) recommend a larger role for neighbourhood regeneration organisations. Spatial planning allows a more integrated approach to these more strategic approaches where change is proposed.

In many cases, discussions on the role of community-based regeneration evolve into debates about community empowerment, both as part of the wider structuralist debates about the local economy (Amin et al. 2003; Kearns 2003; Wainwright 2003) and about democratic engagement and legitimacy. These are issues that need to be taken into account in spatial planning delivery approaches. Communities where people are not working, businesses are not thriving and communities are developing inward-looking cultures are all dependent on the state and not adding to productivity. Community-based approaches to regeneration are based on both moral and economic arguments, which the government has now incorporated into policies for third-sector engagement in social and economic regeneration (HM Treasury and Cabinet Office 2007). In an assessment of this debate, Raco (2003: 248) concludes that this community engagement in regeneration agenda is primarily about government efficiency, but there are also considerations for the communities that need jobs and other facilities. Areas with higher levels of worklessness have higher incidence of health problems, which can be a cause and an effect of people not working. Ways of tackling these issues now include health provision being focussed on areas of higher public health need rather than taking a common standard of provision of health care per head of population or within a certain distance. Spatial planning approaches to the economy need to consider what facilities are required in areas suffering decline and how they can be used together rather than representing separate policy streams on the ground.

There are also other types of development which might have an important influence on the local economy in specific locations. There may be the potential for live/work units which will reduce journeys to work and may support the development of start-up businesses. In many parts of the country, small businesses find it hard to make the transition from start-up to the next stage when they are employing more staff. This transition point is generally measured by the number of businesses registering for VAT for the first time each year, as smaller business do not require to pay this tax. Some analysis of VAT registrations over recent years, together with discussion with local business support organisations, can suggest that smaller business units are provided as part of larger development schemes. This is also a role of universities in the economy of the region and wider discussion about potential requirements for space, business parks and likely expansion need to be undertaken at an early stage in the development of the spatial planning process.

The final aspect in considering the delivery of economic outcomes through spatial planning is where developers might be expected to make contributions to mitigate the impact of their development through planning obligations or agreements. Any sizeable development is likely to have requirements for highways and transport contributions but there may be requirements beyond this which can have a considerable range and may include a variety of options as set out in Table 7.3.

Table 7.3 Examples of developers' contributions requested as part of the delivery of economic schemes

Type of development	Type of contribution	Possible mode of calculation
Retail, offices, other employment	Training and development of staff	Per square metre
Retail, offices, other employment	Selection of proportion of local staff	Probably a local assessment
Housing	Community facilities, e.g. nursery, place of workshop, school	Infrastructure requirements schedule and viability test
Retail, offices, other employment, housing	Public transport interchanges	Infrastructure requirements schedule and viability test
Housing	Library	Infrastructure requirements schedule and viability test
Tetail, offices, other employment, housing	Waste-to-energy plant	Infrastructure requirements schedule and viability test

Source: the author

DELIVERING ENVIRONMENTAL OBJECTIVES

Planning has always been concerned with the delivery of environmental objectives and the recent recognition of the implications of climate change for the use and availability of resources including energy and food have brought this to the top of all political agendas, internationally and locally. The understanding of the full role that spatial planning can play in the mitigation and adaptation to deal with climate change is only now being explored and understood and it is likely that over time this area of spatial planning delivery will be further developed. The RTPI has made seven commitments to climate change (2009b) together with an action plan that commits it to taking a series of actions over time. The commitments are:

1   Promote behavioural change.
2   Adapt existing places.
3   Deliver climate change responsive legislation and policies.
4   Improve current practice.
5   Celebrate best practice.
6   Develop a compendium of best practice.
7   Develop climate change education and skills.

In developing a practical approach to climate changes, a supplement to PPS 1 was published in 2007 (CLG 2007k) which discusses ways in which spatial planning can contribute. This is also complemented by the *UK Low Carbon Industrial Strategy* (HMG 2009b) that sets out a more developed approach to energy and construction that can be taken into account. The role of spatial planning in delivering environmental objectives can be identified as:

•   vision – having a picture of what a lower carbon economy will look like locally;
•   identifying the delivery strategy that will bring this into being;
•   working with partners to deliver the vision;
•   using development management, regulation and standards as means through which a low carbon economy can be progressed;
•   developing sustainable design standards to reduce carbon use and other embedded energy; promote rainwater harvesting in buildings and other locations;
•   preparing a landscape and biodiversity strategy that enhances any potential carbon capture; create locations for balancing ponds and flood meadows in urban parks;
•   monitoring carbon use and carbon reduction through the AMR.

In terms of the practical elements of delivery, these are likely to include:

•   using of locations within areas that have existing services, including brown field sites;

- ensuring that when choosing green field strategic sites, existing infrastructure capacity, including public transport are taken into account;
- seeking to intensify lower density areas to support the economic provision of local services and transport facilities;
- considering change of use or redevelopment of existing lower density edge of town retail locations;
- actively considering the redevelopment of car parks or the use of surface car parks as development sites to use existing infrastructure capacity and promote demand management;
- considering imposing a workplace parking charge and converting current workplace car parking space into other uses as part of green travel planning;
- assessing the greater potential for public service co-location to improve access to services and facilities;
- applying whole life costing standards to design and delivery;
- identifying priority locations for retrofitting for internal energy use, SUDS and other features that reduce carbon;
- promoting local energy sources through waste-to-energy or local generation means that promote self sufficiency;
- promoting the use of electric vehicles through the provision of charging points throughout an area;
- promoting the delivery of more services online to a deeper level to reduce the need of people to travel to service points;
- creating more allotments and locations where people can grow their own food;
- identifying locations for farmers markets to reduce food miles to promote the local economy.

Spatial planning can also promote environmental quality of life indicators and take action to deliver change where this is appropriate. These include:

- air quality
- water quality
- green spaces for activity, exercise and visual amenity
- children's play areas and pocket parks
- public realm and hard public spaces
- lighting strategies
- shop front design and the use of scale at street level
- streets as places and promoting active uses
- 24-hour drinking licence management
- promotion of on-street safety through design, management and other means.

The environmental components of spatial planning are fundamental and will grow over time as the community's consciousness grows. Major environmental as well as local issues are served by spatial planning and its delivery.

CONCLUSIONS

Spatial planning's role in the delivery of social, economic and environmental change in places is growing. This chapter has provided ways of understanding and responding to these issues from different perspectives and for different groups. Some of these needs may be difficult to reconcile spatially but dialogues between all parties at the local level are required as part of developing the solutions. Achieving change is sometimes dependent on influencing behaviour and sometimes requires more investment through the opportunity for more exercise, learning or entrepreneurial activity. Spatial planning can work to deliver these needs at the local level through more efficient and effective use of the scarce resources and investment that is available.

CHAPTER 8

MANAGING SPATIAL PLANNING

INTRODUCTION

The focus of this book is on spatial planning, its role, outcomes and the processes which are related to its delivery. In this chapter, this focus moves to the role of planners and others managing the activity of spatial planning. As is clear from the rest of this book, planners cannot achieve spatial planning outcomes on their own. The development planning process has moved from one that has been focussed on the development of policy to be interpreted by others to one where planning is at the heart of local integrated delivery.

The introduction of spatial planning has undoubtedly led to challenges for planners. The first has been the understanding that spatial planning requires a paradigm shift in planning practice as well as in the substance of the planning task. The second challenge has been to relocate spatial planning in the understanding of all those who are now engaged in it. This includes those within local authorities, in corporate and service delivery roles, councillors, stakeholders, public sector partners, the development industry, landowners, businesses and local communities. The extension of understanding the role of spatial planning for all of these groups is a significant task, and given the drive to join up bodies working at the local level, this may be easier for public and third-sector bodies to grasp than the development industry. Third, there is a challenge to insert spatial planning into the role and work of those developing integrated place-based approaches at the local level, including the LSP. All these issues are discussed in more detail in this chapter.

DOES SPATIAL PLANNING REQUIRE CULTURAL CHANGE FOR PLANNERS?

Spatial planning undoubtedly represents a cultural shift for planners and those who work with the planning system. There is considerable evidence that, since 2004 when spatial planning was introduced, planners have not fully understood the new approach, and this can be found in a number of places. First, the progress of spatial planning approaches particularly through LDFs has been slow (Wood 2008) and the progress then declined rather than speeding up (Morphet 2009b). Second, the role of spatial planning has not been widely understood by those working as part of the system, including government offices, and nor has their system of working

changed to one that reflects a more integrated approach to LDFs in their own working arrangements (Morphet *et al.* 2007). Third, the role of spatial planning as a
delivery mechanism for the wider local governance agenda has not been understood
by those delivering change through these means (CLG 2009a). Finally, planners
have felt uneasy about the changes and have not broadly accepted them (Planning
Advisory Service nd), despite revisions to advice and guidance and a range of specific and general support. Central government has also suggested that there is a
wider malaise among planners and argue for a more positive approach:

> Too often the culture of planning is reactive and defensive. We want a culture
> which promotes planning as a positive tool: a culture which gaps the opportuni-
> ties to improve the experience of planning, for those affected by its decision,
> whether business, community groups, and individual members of the community
> or planning professionals.
>
> (ODPM 2002 quoted in Shaw and Lord 2007: 63)

Although much institutional theory suggests that pressures for cultural change
come from outside the organisation, the development of culture is frequently from
within an organisation or a community (Anderson 2006; Kondra and Hurst 2009).
Cultural change can be generated in a variety of ways, including through establishing new rules, operating environments or leadership. Does the introduction of spatial
planning represent a paradigm shift that needs an accompanying change in culture
(Shaw and Lord 2007; Morphet 2009b)? What might constitute a good case for
the use of this term? The term *paradigm shift* was introduced by Kuhn in 1962, with
subsequent updating in 1969. Kuhn defined a paradigm in two ways. The first was
as an 'entire constellation of beliefs, values, techniques and so on shared by the
members of a given community' (1969: 174), which over time is challenged by a
different conceptual model. The community views these challenges to the paradigm
as anomalous and does not accept them, but further events demonstrate that the
anomalous changes constitute a new paradigm and this is then accepted. Kuhn's
second definition of a paradigm shift was more rigorous and scientific relating to
explicit rules in decision making.

There has been much debate on the extent to which paradigm shifts have
occurred in planning. Taylor has discussed the major changes since 1947 (1999)
and Galloway and Mahayuni (1977) have taken a longer-term view. Taylor's discussion tends to the use of the second and more scientific definition of paradigm
shift which, he argues, has not been applied in planning. Although there have been
major changes in the role of planning, he argues that these stem from the same family of interventions and that the apparently different approaches to planning since
1947 do not represent a paradigm shift. Galloway and Mahayuni argue a contrary
view and state that there have been shifts which have primarily been related to the

differentiation of approach in planning from 'is' to 'ought', that is from a regulatory approach to one that is more interventionist. Although Taylor rejects the notion that the strong version of paradigm shift has occurred in planning, he accepts that the 'generous' version could be sustained (1999: 329).

Is the concept of paradigm shift appropriate to describe the introduction of spatial planning in England? The introduction of spatial planning represents a shift in the role and function of planning which, it has already been shown, has not been readily accepted or understood. The planning community represents a strong and coherent body of those who understand its systems and processes, even if they do not all share the same values for its outcomes. Like any community, they have an understanding of the *essence* of planning, in which the plan has a central policy and de facto regulatory role. The outcomes of the process of planning are expected to be through the actions of others. Planning that involves physical change is primarily, although not exclusively, undertaken by others such as regeneration specialists or developers. The delivery and funding of development has not been included as a key element of planning since the 1950s (Morphet 1993).

The changing function and role of spatial planning was indicated in the definition provided when it was first introduced, as quoted earlier, but research found that this was being interpreted in different ways (Morphet *et al.* 2007). As shown in Table 8.1, these different perceptions of the definition of spatial planning demonstrates the cultural gap between planner's understanding of the pre- and post-2004 planning systems. The creation of a planning system, post-2004, which has a focus on delivery of infrastructure, involved in the management of public sector budgets and working to deliver agendas set by others, all seem anomalous in this context. The delays in the delivery of the LDF since 2005 have been due to uncertainty and then disbelief that this is the new role of the LDF.

Table 8.1 One or two definitions of spatial planning?

Key words in definition of spatial planning	Key words for planners in the definition of spatial planning
'Spatial planning goes **beyond** traditional land use planning to **bring together and integrate** policies for the development and use of land with **other policies and programmes** which **influence the nature of places** and **how they function**.'	'Spatial planning goes **beyond traditional land use planning** to bring together and integrate **policies for the development and use of land** with other policies and programmes which influence the nature of places and how they function.'

Source: Shaping and Delivering Tomorrow's Places: Effective Practice in Spatial Planning (Morphet *et al.* 2007: 48)

In order to reinforce the new delivery role of spatial planning, Government reissued the Planning Policy Statement on Local Development Frameworks in 2008, replacing one that had only been in existence since 2005 (CLG 2008c). It has issued guidance to LSPs and local authority chief executives on the corporate role in delivering infrastructure (CLG 2008d; 2009a) and supported the publication of *A Steps Approach to Infrastructure Planning and Delivery for Local Strategic Partnerships and Local Authorities* (Morphet 2009a) which has been widened from its initial audience of planners (Planning Advisory Service 2008b).

Does this new paradigm represent the need for a cultural shift for planners and their work? In many ways, the new paradigm for planning is closer to that which existed in the period 1947–1974, when post-war reconstruction was led by planning interventions through CPOs, CDAs and New Towns (Cullingworth and Nadin 2006: 22–3; Morphet 1993). In this case, is the paradigm shift confined to the role of planning rather than the skills and practices of planners? Is it possible for paradigms to switch back and forth? In the pure Kuhnian sense, the answer to this is likely to be in the negative, but taken as a change in a community's set of beliefs and understandings, then this is a possible consideration. This approach is also recognised by Masterman, who states that one definition of a paradigm is a set of habits (1970: 66) and that this approach to understanding the way that knowledge grows is Kuhn's sociological contribution.

If we take this view that planners hold paradigms about what they do and how they do it, which are reinforced by the mores of the community (Anderson 2006), this goes some way to explain why the post-2004 approach to spatial planning has become becalmed. Planners are trying to situate the present approach to spatial planning in the pre-2004 system and ignoring anomalies. For planners, these anomalies include the delivery of all infrastructure rather than that provided through developers' contributions, working within the leadership of the LSP and delivering the objectives of the SCS. Taking this approach provides an explanation to the slow progress of LDFs.

THE ROLE OF MANAGEMENT IN EFFECTIVE SPATIAL PLANNING

As planners develop through education and experience, the main focus is on their ability to be good 'professionals', which places an emphasis on the substantive and technical skills and knowledge which are required to practice planning. As planners progress in their careers and reach management roles, whether this means responsibility for a team, a department or a service, their promotion and progression is generally based on their professional abilities and experience. Few planners have any management training in the use of resources, how to manage processes or projects or how to work in complex environments with stakeholders. The management aspects of the planner's role are generally learned on the job. This approach may be satisfactory when planning develops through incremental changes over time. However, it is more thoroughly challenged when there is a step change in planning approaches, such as when spatial planning and development management were introduced in England in 2004. Then the major challenge for planners has been the acquisition of the knowledge of spatial planning and how it works. There was little consideration of the management of change in the introduction of spatial planning and, in cases, to see its operation within the preceding constructs of planning practice.

The role of management within professional areas has always been problematic and the source of continuing tensions. Management is frequently defined as a sub-professional activity, requiring little specific attention to training and a skill set which any professional can acquire as they gather more experience. For planners, the nature of the substance of planning makes this a particularly difficult issue. Planners have to deal with a range of stakeholders, recommend decisions based on a range of conflicting evidence and work with other professionals. The substance of their work is managing the planning process. However, this position can also be problematical. A reliance on strong professional expertise on substantive issues, which is set within its own legal framework and language, can protect planners from the management approaches used by other professionals. There is evidence that as planners have increasingly been focussed on the substantive content of their roles, recognition of their wider management skills and contributions has reduced. There have been concerns that planners have dropped off the management teams of large organisations including local authorities or have been subsumed into larger operational units under the control of another professional (CLG 2006a). Now professionals are developing their own management skills in order to practice their professions. They are taking MBA courses or in-house management development which is now frequently offered within organisations. This personal development often covers a range of activities, including:

- contingent leadership styles
- organisational literacy
- managing changes in the technical and organisational operating environment
- implementing change
- financial management
- people management – hard and soft skills
- business process engineering
- project and programme management
- business ethics
- communications

- working with stakeholders
- procurement.

The successful introduction of spatial planning and its delivery through a transition from development control to development management needed planners to acquire many of these management skills. The pre-2004 system of development planning, as a more policy focussed approach, was not so dependent on operational requirements to work directly with stakeholders for delivery rather than as part of the consultation process. The transition to spatial planning and ensuring that Local Development Schemes were delivered need project management. The leadership style required was less inward-looking, focussed on process rather than one that is more outward-facing and focussed on partnership working and delivery as part of a wider team. Leadership styles need to be contingent to the role rather than uni-purpose (Fiedler 1967).

Does leadership make a difference? In the past ten years, there has been a growing concern about the ability of the public sector to attract and retain planners in sufficient numbers in order to deliver an adequate planning service, when many planners have moved to work in the private sector. This issue has been seen to be primarily due to differing levels of pay, but as Durning (2007) has found, there are a number of other issues that impact on a planner's willingness to stay in a public sector post, including changing the way in which work is organised, improving staff morale through work/life balance packages, and improving IT. Beresford-Knox (2003) also cites the quality of management as having an impact on retention and performance. Page and Horton (2006) found although it is assumed that some issues were significant in terms of people's performance inside local authorities, this was not so and these include:

- whether they feel that they have interesting work
- feeling that they have accomplished something worthwhile
- access to training
- feelings about workload
- approachable line managers
- job security.

What matters more in high-performing organisations was how people felt that they were managed, including:

- telling people how they are doing
- making them feel listened to
- keeping staff better informed
- valuing and recognising staff
- finding ways to give staff greater input into decision making

* providing more room for individual creativity within a widely shared framework
* knowing what success looks like.

Does better management by planners improve the planning process? Enticott (2006) found that planners had been disadvantaged because 'planning has been largely protected from radical changes to internal management practices contained within previous reforms such as Compulsory Competitive Tendering'. So what can we learn from studies in management of public bodies that might support the delivery of effective spatial planning? Later in this chapter, there are sections on project and performance management and both of these have played a key role in improving all types of public service delivery, despite the unintended consequences of performance targetry. There is frequent disagreement on what is measured. This sits at the heart of the disillusion about the role of professionals, their judgement and accountability. New approaches to public management outcomes from the New Public Management and from Osborne and Gaebler (1993) and Osborne and Hutchinson (2004) have created a new platform for consideration. The funding of public services is, as a result, more related to outcomes that are being sought and delivered. The framework for setting outcomes may be driven from central government, although the detailed setting of standards and their choice within this framework is more likely to be local. Added to this, there has been a drive to switch the perspective of delivery from a producer focus to a user focus. As Turok and Taylor have pointed out, there is a 'challenge to the ethos of professionals ... and especially to any suggestion that specialists know what is best for local communities' (2006: 497).

Management is not an issue which is much considered in the training of planners, although it is increasingly becoming a more central role in practice, whether in the public or private sectors. As Kitchen reflects, planning became increasingly corporate over the period of his career (2007: 168) and that is a continuing trajectory. As Williams (2002) points out, to work successfully in public policy and delivery requires new types of collaborative working. This implies a more open working style and those successful in this new operating environment are likely to be 'competent boundary spanners' – delivering a joined-up government needs joined-up people. The introduction of performance management into development management has becoming increasingly important over the period since 1980, with more attention on the use of technology, the creation of teams focussed on specific types of development and outsourcing of aspects of the regulatory process such as planning appeals. This approach has not been so readily applied to development planning, although it does has formal stages in its process and deadlines to be met. The introduction of spatial planning in 2004 was accompanied by a requirement to improve project planning as part its preparation and delivery and the Planning Advisory Service has provided support generally and to a number of individual local authorities to improve their approaches to managing the process. However, management has remained a secondary consideration and, whilst this is the case, the potential for achieving up-to-date development plans which can support the achievement of better places can be undermined. The key components of management are shown in Box 8.1 and the risks in Box 8.2.

Spatial planning may seem to be less amenable to management than a more process-driven approach such as development control. Planners might argue that the problem-solving approach which spatial planning needs cannot be timetabled or that there is no singe owner for spatial planning, and the planner performs this ownership role as a proxy for others. There may also be little expected relationship with delivery so any management approaches would be wasteful and over engineered.

Box 8.1   Managing spatial planning: the key components

Managing spatial planning includes:

- identifying the key challenges – scoping;
- contributing towards and working within the overall vision for the area – framework;
- deciding objectives or being given them – deliverables;
- determining how to get there – the route map;
- organising to achieve – managing resources;
- telling everyone inside and outside the organisation – communication;
- management and maintenance – setting milestones and measureables;
- taking stock – monitoring and review;
- managing change – innovation, improvement, responding to external changes, e.g. credit crunch, globalisation, changing legislation and regulation;
- reviewing objectives.

Source: the author

Box 8.2   Identifying management risks

What risks may appear?

- organisational climate changes due to 'external' circumstances, e.g. credit crunch, climate change;
- operating framework changes in response to past mistakes, e.g. child abuse cases, major fires;
- conflict between organisational and employee goals and values emerges, e.g. strikes, resistance to change;
- organisation not performing and loses market share or role, e.g. failing schools, Woolworths.

Source: the author

Box 8.3   What makes services fail?

Public bodies are likely to fail when:

- there is uncertain accountability within the organisation;
- the organisation is more producer focussed than user focussed, i.e. strong internal culture;
- the organisation's main objective is as an employer rather than in providing local leadership and/or delivering services;
- political imperatives overcome practical considerations;
- people charged with delivery decisions have no direct experience of managing similar activities;
- practical delivery has lower status than policy.

Source: the author

Finally, how is quality assessed in spatial planning? Is this better assessed by competent professionals or by the users? There are also choices to be made about the use of resources and the methods to be undertaken. Should new evidence be commissioned or can existing evidence and surveys be reused? There also needs to be leadership in working with others and ensuring that the wider organisation and stakeholders are aware of the role of spatial planning in delivery. A management lead in the establishment of governance arrangements for the spatial planning process will also be required. Finally, spatial planning needs to be owned by the whole organisation and led from the top, both politically and operationally. This integration of spatial planning into governance is also occurring in Denmark (Sehested 2009), France (Booth 2009) and Norway (Amdam 2004). Box 8.3 sets out why some public organisations fail.

SKILLS

Management approaches that can be used to support the preparation and maintenance of development plans include softer and harder skills of management. The Egan Review (ODPM 2004b) was set up to review the skills required to deliver sustainable communities. This concentrated on the skills required across the property and construction professions and resulted in the establishment of the Academy for Sustainable Communities (which has now become part of the HCA). The review concentrated on development control as one of the main areas where planning skills needed to be improved. The review also recommended the development of generic skills across the professions and more training for local authority members. The skills that have been found to be most useful for regeneration have also been researched, with analytical, interpersonal and organisational skills identified as being the most important (NRU 2002). Turok and Taylor (2006) reviewed the skills needed for place-based working and these represent a mixture of softer skills such as leadership and communication with the harder skills of project management (see Box 8.4).

Although much of the focus on planning skills has been on those needed to work with other built environmental professionals, working within a partnership environment as required for spatial planning needs more focus on softer skills. Planners need to work in different ways that are less reliant on authority or procedures and more skilled in the use of networked and informal power styles. The role of spatial planning in delivering place-based outcomes also requires some new knowledge and skills. The knowledge required includes understanding the new local governance architecture, its drivers and language. This also includes developing a greater knowledge base of other services, how they function and how they deliver spatially. Spatial planning also requires the development of new skills which may include more on the ways in which specialists need to be commissioned and used in areas that planners may have felt competent in the past. Consultation is one key area where this may need to be reviewed. The operation of spatial planning within a difficult economic environment may require land and development expertise on issues such as viability, development value and evaluation.

In addition to these additional skills and knowledge, there is also a need for greater training and experience in managing the overarching approaches to the management of spatial planning and delivery. The first of these is project management which is an essential means of ensuring that deadline are met, work commissioned on time, dependencies are considered and risks assessed and managed. The final

Box 8.4   Skills needed for place-based working

Generic cross-cutting skills needed for place-based working:

- Strategic skills
  - leadership
  - lateral thinking
  - sound judgement.
- Process skills
  - communication
  - negotiation
  - adaptable
  - flexible
  - understanding.
- Practical skills
  - funding proposals
  - developing action plans
  - managing projects
  - managing food administrative systems.

Source: Turok and Taylor 2006

component of management is that of performance management, particularly in relation to achieving outcomes. Achieving outcomes needs clear management tools and approaches and these can be incorporated into the spatial planning process. Above all, spatial planning is a means of achieving change and all will need to understand if the methods chosen in any specific location have worked.

PROJECT MANAGEMENT

Project management delivers processes and outcomes. It is critical for all spatial planning activity where the spatial planning process has to be delivered within specified time frames and works through partners (see Box 8.5). Spatial planning can use project management to ensure that the spatial planning process such as individual DPDs or the LDS are completed on time, on budget and to the appropriate quality. Second, project management is needed into ensure that the infrastructure requirements identified through the process are delivered in a timely and coordinated way. Some elements of delivery may need to occur before others because there are dependencies. Each project will have critical success factors which are identified at the outset and that the project plan is set out to deliver. Finally, a project will need a project manager whose responsibility it is to take leadership and oversight of the project, whether it be the delivery of any DPD or the infrastructure elements that have been identified in its delivery schedule.

Project management is a tool to be used to support delivery and it is generally set within an agreed framework. The most commonly used approach to project

Box 8.5 Why have project management?

Project management provides:

- a common, consistent approach;
- a controlled and organised start, middle and end;
- regular reviews of progress against plan;
- assurance that the project continues to have a business justification;
- flexible decision points;
- management control of any deviations from the plan;
- the involvement of management and stakeholders at the right time and place during the project;
- good communication channels between the project, project management and the rest of the organisation;
- a means of capturing and sharing lessons learned;
- a route to increasing the project management skills and competences of the organisation's staff at all levels.

Source: the author

management is 'Projects in a Controlled Environment' (PRINCE) and it is possible to qualify as a PRINCE practitioner. There are versions of PRINCE that are used. The full version is PRINCE 2, although the approaches can be used without following the full approach in detail. This is generally known as PRINCE-lite. The PRINCE 2 system is supported by a range of templates that are available to download free on the Office of Government Commerce website (www.ogc.gov.uk).

PRINCE 2 contains some helpful features which can be used for all projects regardless of their scale. These include the identification of key users and stakeholders at an early stage, developing a communications plan and establishing a project board which provides a mechanism for reporting progress. The project board 'owns' the project and can be alerted if elements of the project are being delayed and decide on any remedial action. The project board will undertake a risk assessment prior to the project's start and identify any mitigation that could ameliorate problems. The project board considers all the necessary stages in completion of the whole project at the outset and sets key milestones. This ensures that those engaged in the delivery of the project and appropriate resources have been identified at the outset. The project also has a SRO, generally at board level, who will be responsible for the project's successful delivery and unblocking any strategic problems that occur. The processes of project management are shown in Box 8.6.

Box 8.6   The processes of project management

The processes of project management include:

- identifying the key objectives of the project;
- identifying the project activities and components that will contribute towards its delivery in a Project Initiation Document;
- putting these within a timetable;
- identifying dependencies within this or with other projects;
- identifying key milestones which may be legal, procedural or relate to a sense of progress being made with the resources available;
- identifying the resources required and available;
- setting a communications plan so that those involved and stakeholders can be kept informed as the project progresses;
- appointing a project manager to manage the whole process and ensuring that the project is run to the appropriate quality, in time and on budget;
- identifying a SRO who has oversight and accountability for the project;
- setting up a project board to oversee the process;
- undertaking a risk assessment which identifies the scale of any risk on a traffic light system and the mitigation measures that are appropriate for each risk.

Source: Office of Government Commerce 2009

Using project management to deliver DPDs and then implementing them provides an opportunity to plan time and resources. It can help to set SMART objectives as shown in Box 8.7. It also helps to anticipate problems and where likely pinch points are going to be. Major public consultation is generally best avoided in August unless the local authority has a major tourist destination, which could make it the right time. The project planning approach will also help to identify other issues that may be important in spatial planning preparation, such as the revision of the SCS or other policy reviews. Project management also helps if there is a sudden disaster that knocks the programme off course. For example, unexpected floods may delay spatial planning work in a practical way, but may also have deeper implications if some of the identified strategic housing sites have been flooded for the first time.

Using project management also helps to identify who is involved at the outset and when they need to be involved. In preparing an LDF, this can be undertaken partly through the SCI but there may be stakeholders (see Box 8.8) who are centrally involved in the delivery of any infrastructure or actions identified and it is helpful to involve them within the project planning process.

There are also a number of reasons why projects fail and these are also important to consider at the outset in order to avoid the pitfalls or to identify them as risks

Box 8.7   Setting SMART objectives

When objectives are set they need to be:

Specific
Measureable
Achievable
Realistic
Timely

Source: anon

Box 8.8   Identifying project stakeholders

A project's stakeholders can be any or all of these:

- project's customer;
- those who will be users of the deliverables;
- others in organisation who will be affected by the project's outcomes;
- people outside the organisation who will be affected by the project;
- managers and those who will have to implement;
- suppliers who will be delivering goods and services as part of the project or subsequently.

Source: Office of Government Commerce 2009

that need to be managed. These issues are set out in Boxes 8.9 and 8.10. Project management may be greeted with enthusiasm at the outset but its disciplines may be harder to meet in practice. If it is used as intended, there are likely to be conflicts with new issues that emerge which might seem to be more important, and there can be a tendency to 'stretch' project deliverables to incorporate further issues. This can result in 'scope creep'. This needs to be undertaken with care if it is not central to the project but rather an organisational 'fix'. Where legislation or practice demonstrates that the operating environment is changing, e.g. through an inspector's response to submitted DPDs, then this may require a review to ensure that the deliverables are fit for purpose. The potential for such changes can be included within the risk register which would allow necessary action to be taken within the project framework. In some projects, the project board or stakeholders group may start to ask some awkward questions about the process or its progress. There may be a strong temptation to remove this problem by changing the project board members but this needs to be done only in extreme cases as the benefits of a more acquiescent board will be outweighed by a lack of project continuity and a need to deal with the issues that have been identified.

Box 8.9   What challenges does project management face?

Project management can face challenges when:

- people find it hard to work together;
- there is a lack of common approach inside the organisation;
- it has to deal with unexpected crises that could have been foreseen;
- it is difficult to get people to focus on the project and not on their department or profession;
- the organisation does not understand the benefits of project management.

Source: Nokes and Kelly 2007

Box 8.10 Why do projects go wrong?

Projects can go wrong when:

- they are not thought through at the outset;
- the discipline of project management seems to get in the way of more informal ways of doing things;
- the project changed during process due to political pressure;
- the project board is changed during the project which reduces continuity;
- there is an 'optimism bias' that assumes that all will be 'ok' regardless of evidence to the contrary or unmanaged risks;
- projects are 'gold plated' – i.e. they acquire more deliverables as the project progresses.

Source: the author

Box 8.11   Project management requirements for LDFs

Local authorities are urged to ensure that effective programme management techniques are employed in progressing the Core Strategy and *orchestrating the production of the evidence base.* Various studies (on, for example, housing market assessments, housing land availability, flooding and transport) are necessary for the proper preparation of Core Strategies. Local authorities should seek to align the time-tables of these studies with the Core Strategy so that it is not unexpectedly held up. This will mean discussing the project timetabling with key stakeholders. It will also be helpful to reach agreement with the key stakeholders on what the main components of the evidence base need to be.

Source: PPS 12 (CLG 2008c): 4.56

The chair of the project board has an important role in ensuring that the project progresses. They will be working through the project manager and be in touch with the project on a daily basis. The project management will provide any early warning of problems or issues and these may be able to be averted or managed without calling a special board meeting. The chair of the project board also needs to call upon the SRO if there are major blockages or critical issues that emerge during the course of the project (see Box 8.9).

In preparing an LDF, PPS 12 (CLG 2008c) makes it clear that project manage-ment is a required approach as set out in Box 8.11. Using project management can be of considerable assistance in achieving spatial planning and delivery.

PERFORMANCE MANAGEMENT

The introduction of performance management approaches into the planning man-agement process have intensified over the past 20 years. The practice of planning in both the private and public sectors is now subject to performance management, although the outcome profiles for each may be different. In the public sector, the changing and layered approaches to performance management – Best Value (1999), Comprehensive Performance Assessment (2004) and Comprehensive Area Assessment/One Place (2009) have been set within the context of outcome targets for improvement and change in local authorities and organisations. In local govern-ment, there are now 198 targets against which performance is measured and many of these have a place-based and planning relevance. In central government and in other agencies, there are performance targets set through PSAs as part of the three-year CSR process. This approach to targets was initially silo based and focussed on vertical integration from the centre to a specific service (Bevan and Hood 2006; Hood 2007). Targets are now set as horizontal integrators linked to places such as those used in LAAs (CLG 2008d).

In the private sector, performance targets may relate to the volume of activity and business that a consultancy has or to the successful outcomes for clients on any particular project. These targets can be team, individual or branch office based and are likely to have some impact on the standing of the company, potentially its share price and its ability to satisfy professional indemnity insurance requirements in some cases. Performance management in spatial planning is set within the many targets that are set for places in both sectors and it is important to remember this.

Performance management may seem to be an activity which is more easily applied to development management, with its process-based approach and end point when development is completed. Spatial planning activities may seem less amenable to performance management approaches, although in considering the elements of spatial planning as set out in this book, there is the potential for performance managing many parts of the constituent processes and outcomes of spatial planning. Without performance management, it will be difficult to assess how far the objectives and processes have been met. Before considering this in more detail, the role of performance management is discussed.

WHY PERFORMANCE MANAGEMENT?

Performance management is a means through which organisations are held to account for the achievement of their objectives. They are used by managers to ensure that the resources under their control are being deployed to achieve what is required and are also used to ensure that staff and systems are undertaking their work at the pace and to the quality required. Some critics argue that performance management is geared towards quantitative outputs alone but all performance management has qualitative components. It is of no use identifying the stages required to complete tasks if the tasks are undertaken in a sloppy way and have to be undertaken again. Performance management is therefore associated with principles of quality management and assurance. Performance management is also concerned with outcomes. If drinking licences are given within the specified period of days but have not taken account of the cumulative impact of the number of licences in a city centre, the quality of the decision making will be at fault. Performance management is a key way for any organisation to achieve its strategic goals (Lawrie *et al.* 2003).

There are a number of reasons why organisations do not perform and these represent the barriers to improving performance that need to be tackled. They include:

- inertia
- perpetual change in systems
- no ownership of the problem
- investment in change not properly embedded, e.g. IT systems

- lack of direction
- unawareness of need to change or turnaround
- varied cultures of departments and sections
- assumed performance better than reality
- unawareness of users views of service
- inward looking and isolationist in style.

Performance management systems have been identified as an effective tool in improving performance (Hughes *et al.* 2004) and need to be developed to suit the needs of particular organisations or accountabilities for activity. They need to be incorporated into the 'day job' and not something additional; that is they need to underpin new ways of organising the tasks required (Audit Commission 2002). Performance management approaches can be focussed on one type of measure or can be a mixture of quantitative and qualitative outcomes brought together in a balanced scorecard method (Lawrie *et al.* 2003) as shown in Box 8.12.

There is evidence that the application of performance management systems has had considerable positive impact in some organisations. In a case study of the Environment Agency (Lawrie *et al.* 2003), for example, a number of organisations had been brought together in 1996 and needed improved means of ensuring that the whole organisation was working in a joined-up way to achieve the goals that it had set.

Box 8.12 The role of performance indicators

Performance indicators need to:

- be linked to corporate, team and task objectives;
- enable elected politicians to be able to assess progress;
- provide enough operational information for managers to assess progress;
- be able to be collected through regular day-to-day activities rather than as a specific one-off process;
- be collected and available in real time;
- be presented as a 'dashboard' or in specific reports available on a daily basis;
- be capable of alerting everyone when processes are not being completed on time and where this might have effects on other parts of the process;
- be seen in a red/amber/green traffic light summary format;
- be capable of being used for action-based interventions, i.e. to 'act on facts' (Audit Commission/IDeA 2002);
- be reviewed on a regular basis.

Source: the author

Box 8.13 Linking the performance framework to the LDF

The local government performance framework makes it clear that delivery (i.e. completion) of a sufficient number of houses overall and of affordable homes and the supply of housing land are among the 198 indicators for which information will be collected. Where completions or housing supply are falling behind housing provision figures, local areas may find that improvements in this indicator form part of a revised Local Area Agreement so directed by the Secretary of State. Prompt preparation and adoption of sound Core Strategies is a key means whereby performance against this indicator can be improved.

Source: PPS 12 (CLG 2008c): §4.57

In this case study, the use of a 'destination statement' was found to be a helpful tool. This brought focus and clearer outcome definition for the strategic plans and goals that the agency had and aligning different units in an essentially devolved organisation.

In implementing performance management systems, a number of key outcomes can be expected:

- clarity of direction for the organisation as a whole;
- greater understanding and alignment of the people in the organisation with its goals;
- greater sense of achievement of goals;
- greater focus on those areas that are not performing well;
- a feedback loop to ensure that the outcomes of performance management are informing better practice in the future.

PERFORMANCE MANAGEMENT IN SPATIAL PLANNING

The application of performance management in spatial planning has implications in the public and private sector. In the public sector, local authorities are bound to 'secure continuous improvement ... (through) ... a combination of economy, efficiency and effectiveness' (Local Government Act 1999: s3). In the use of performance approaches in local government, there is now evidence that the application of performance management has had a significant role in the improvement of services and organisations primarily for their users and the places that they serve (Hughes *et al.* 2004).

A national approach to the local performance framework for housing and planning has been set out by central government and the Local Government Act (CLG and Local Government Association 2008). This demonstrates the extent to which housing and planning delivery is embedded within both local governance processes such as LAAs and CAAs (see Box 8.13) as well as the interlinkages with other targets, such as:

- NI 141 percentage of vulnerable people achieving independent living
- NI 145 adults with learning difficulties in settled accommodation.

These are also accompanied by three specific housing targets to be delivered through planning:

- NI 154 net additional homes provided
- NI 155 number of affordable homes delivered (gross)
- NI 159 supply of ready to develop housing sites.

The application of these targets have been set out and then incentivised through the reward of planning and housing delivery grants. To these can also be added the targets that relate to:

- NI 8 adult participation in sport
- NI 171 VAT registration rate
- NI 185 CO_2 reduction from local authority operations.

In addition to these national targets, local authorities will be setting local performance management targets to ensure that spatial planning DPDs are completed in accordance with the LDS as submitted and approved by GOs. It is also important for local residents, businesses and landowners that they have adopted DPDs in order that they can be assured that the infrastructure requirements of the area are being progressed through the partners involved from all sectors. The key performance measures for DPDs can be managed through programme and project management approaches and increasingly local authorities are appointing trained project managers to support planners to improve performance through project management.

Finally, there is increasing evidence of the role of reporting performance information to the public, although there is no agreed practice on this. To some extent, the performance reporting of local authorities, and now wider to local partners by the Audit Commission, provides the public with an informed assessment of local performance and progress. In spatial planning, where the future of places is at the heart of the task together with their delivery, there is a need for accountability to citizens and communities as well as their role in setting the vision and priorities. This engagement with communities and people is more frequently overlooked in planning with its emphasis on the input components of consultation. Citizens also have a right to be informed in ways that are easy to understand, up to date and make sense to their concerns. Devising ways of reporting back performance can be discussed and developed using citizen's panels or focus groups (CLG 2008h). It is important to consider the different audiences for feedback on performance management information.

DEVELOPMENT MANAGEMENT

The transition from development control to development management is still in progress, but it represents an important turn from the reactive, regulatory approach of development control to one that is more proactive and similar to regeneration in its operational style. The focus of development management is on delivery and is part of the spatial planning system introduced in 2004 as LDFs. Development management needs to be managed differently to achieve these delivery outcomes.

The management of development control was never really considered until the late 1980s when there was concern expressed by the development industry at the delays in the time taken to deal with planning applications. The government supported their view and considered that such delays were hampering investment which was against the national interest. Much of the initial discussion about the relative merits of the speed of determining planning applications were set against the quality of the outcomes of the process, with many planners arguing that beneficial outcomes for local areas would take longer to negotiate. They argued that although there was an eight-week target for determining planning applications, there were few complaints to or by local councillors on the time taken to deal with applications and also frequently, the system was slowed down by developers delaying the submission of requested information and using the system to suit their own timescales. Whatever time it took though, the application process was initiated by the developer or agent and the local authority responded when the application was received or through discussion at a pre-application stage.

However, an earlier tradition in planning took a more proactive approach to development control. Between 1947 and the economic crises of the late 1970s, planners led a more interventionist approach to local change and development using a variety of tools such as CDAs and CPOs. There was a variety of initiatives and these involved the process of identifying development plots and proposals. The development control system, through the use of the site or 'planning unit', took a proactive approach to local land assembly and development. In some cases, this might have been to create sites for public sector development but this approach was just as likely to have been used to generate potential development sites for the private sector.

By the late 1970s, this role had started to fall out of practice due to two key reasons. First, the use of CDAs and CPOs had become too mechanistic and leading to breakdowns in communities. Although there was a chronic housing need in the post-war period, there was also a sense in which more land was being cleared for development than was ever likely to be used. There were campaigns led by public figures such as John Betjeman which, combined with the Skeffington report (1969), led to a more 'hands-off' approach. The second reason was that there was less funding available for new development and many once prosperous industrial areas such as inner London and Birmingham were experiencing high levels of unemployment and economic change. In response to these concerns, local authorities and government set up more specialist regeneration approaches to dealing with the downturn at the local level. These activities were also supported through EU structural funds, available from the 1970s and other funding through the urban programme which followed the inner area studies (Lawless 1989).

In the face of these criticisms, overzealous application of planning tools and a new agenda led by an emerging professional group, planners retreated into a responsive rather than a proactive mode, although all the powers available to them remained and have been strengthened over time. Inevitably, regeneration activities concentrated on those areas where change was underway or where new investment was needed. Other areas were more frequently left within a developer-led approach to planning based on individual planning applications submitted within development plan framework. The main focus remained on the speed of determination of planning applications. Central government provided some financial support to speed up planning applications and other approaches were used to improve the performance of the system.

As a response, the number of planning applications determined by planning officers increased through the use of delegation agreements. The potential for taking development out of detailed control through the use of LDOs and reduced requirements for types of householder consents were also introduced (Killian and Pretty 2008). The Planning Inspectorate introduced a common applications form, OneApp, which could work with more IT-based systems to manage the process. The advent of local authority one-stop shops and business process reengineering (BPR) also allowed there to be greater speed and efficiency in using resources. The 'fast track' system was introduced in some authorities to enable agents a speedier determination of their applications in return from greater quality control. Development control teams were set up to deal with the size of applications that were more efficient than the area-based teams which had been the norm before.

Yet in all this change, the development control process remained a responsive system rather than one where planning would take a proactive approach to delivery. This was not taken up until the role of development management was established. The introduction of development management as a delivery tool of spatial planning represents a significant shift in the role of those previously responsible only for determining submitted planning applications. It also has implications for the way in which the process is managed. It has been described as an 'end to end' process (Planning Advisory Service 2008c: 5), which extends from the encouragement of panning applications through proactive relationships with developers to following through delivery of the planning consents once granted. The shift to development management requires both a different approach to managing the process but also, it is suggested, a different culture. In practising development control, planners have to respond to planning applications once submitted, although there is also the role of providing pre-application advice if requested, and in some local authorities this advice carries a charge for certain types of development. However, this is very different from planners proactively seeking to deliver development requirements as indentified in the LDF. This implies an engagement in discussions with developers, landowners and potential users of land and buildings and then seeking to achieve the required development through negotiation and other tools such as CPOs in order to support land assembly. In summary, the role of development management has been described as a 'seeker and shaper of development opportunities' (Planning Advisory Service 2008c: 7).

Although development management is not new for planning professionals, those who have had their career in local authority development control may have less experience of this type of approach. In practice, it extends the experience and practice of planners who have had primarily local government development control experience into the experience of planners in the private sector who may be assembling land for development. Development management draws together the experience of public and private sector regulatory planners into the same activities. However, in practice, this may not be an easy transition for all planning professionals to make. In some cases, planners may feel uncomfortable about both promoting development and being involved in its regulation. Where development management is concerned with larger schemes, then the planning application is more likely to be determined by local authority councillors and this may not be an issue.

Moving from development control to development management approaches will need a managed programme of change which has a clear focus on the new activity and a transition programme which is likely to include:

- shifting the corporate role of development management by chief executives and executive councillors;
- training of planners and councillors to undertake this more proactive role;
- full use of programme and project management tools in the use of planner resources;
- close working with planners delivering the LDF;
- closer working relationships with other corporate professionals inside the local authority, e.g. capital finance, property, regeneration;
- closer working relationships with public service providers, e.g. internal service departments such as housing, leisure, transport and external bodes including those responsible for health, police, courts, universities, housing;
- skill development for technical skills for planners including negotiation, development appraisals;

- skill development of softer skills for planners including working with partners, networking, information sharing, facilitation and building consensus;
- revised procedures and processes;
- a programmed approach to proactively promoting the development required to be delivered;
- a revised set of performance indicators;
- regular reporting on the achievement of outcomes.

CONCLUSIONS

The management of spatial planning requires some new ways of working and patterns of organisation. For the LDF and the Core Strategy, having a project and performance managed approach should make a significant difference in ensuring that processes can integrate with those of others and they are achieved on time. For development management, the focus on the number of planning applications being determined within a set time period will still remain but for larger applications or those where the LDF determined infrastructure needs are to be delivered, then a new series of management approaches will be needed.

Some new business processes will be needed which support development management's delivery role (Planning Advisory Service 2008d). This could include the following range of specialists although not all roles will be necessary and may not be located in the planning department:

- Fund Managers – who have the possibility for negotiating funding required across all sectors and ensuring that development that is required has a good proposal of funding as far as possible.
- Business analysts – who make business cases for funding for the required infrastructure and will work with fund managers.
- Project sponsors – who have the lead and overview of development within specific areas or types of development; project sponsors may also commission development teams and act as the 'client' for internal services such as consultation processes, communication plans; they may also hold the budget.
- Client managers – who have responsibility for liaison with specific developers, landowners and/or public services.
- Development teams – made up of a range of skills to manage a range of projects in one area, e.g. a town centre or the development of a strategic site.
- Programme and project managers – who are managing resources and relating them to delivery requirements; programme and project managers will also manage dependencies between projects and the delivery of development and infrastructure within the timescales required.

- Partnership manager – who has the role of working with the managers and users of the proposed infrastructure to ensure that the specified development is fit for purpose and meets the criteria as set out.
- SROs – who may be executive councillors or local authority directors who sit above the process and take responsibility for promoting the scheme and overcoming instructional hurdles.
- Quality managers – who may provide a quality assurance process to ensure all that is undertaken is achieved efficiently and effectively.

Some of these roles in development management are set out in case studies developed by the Planning Advisory Service (2007b; 2008b).

CHAPTER 9

REGIONAL AND SUB-REGIONAL SPATIAL PLANNING

INTRODUCTION

Regional spatial planning in England is still in development and will probably not see its fullest expression until beyond 2012. It has been through a number of iterations and false starts, where spatial planning intentions have been diverted or subverted by other agendas. In this chapter, the approaches to regional spatial planning will be examined in their wider context as this provides a greater understanding of the processes at work in the development of regional spatial policy and its role in delivery. The regional scale has also been one of the areas of greater development in other parts of the UK. National plans that have been prepared in Scotland and Wales have a considerable bearing and influence on regional planning in England and in many ways begin to show the way things might develop in the coming years. In Northern Ireland, the RDS published in 2001 created much of the framework that is still being used today.

For regional planning in England, there have been a variety of tensions, pressures and challenges which have served to divert spatial planning to represent different interests rather than creating a coordinated framework for spatial policy. One of the key concerns of regional activity within England is that it has no democratic accountability. The proposals for English regional governance were dropped following the failed referendum in 2004. If the experience and history of Scotland and Wales is to be taken into account, following the failed referenda on devolution in 1979, it took 20 years of developing distinctive Scottish and Welsh policies and governance structures before the referenda were held again. It could be that this will occur in England in the early 2020s. Meanwhile, the development of regionally distinct approaches with some decision making about priorities for expenditure could be supporting an underlying pathway to directly elected regional governance structures in due course. In the meantime, indirect regional governance structures are developing quickly and sub-regional governance may be emerging more rapidly as part of this constitutional agenda (HMG 2008; HM Treasury 2009c; CLG 2009d). Turok (2008a: 15) has also questioned how far the development of sub-regional, local and neighbourhood approaches that are emerging are substitutes for each other or are complementary.

THE EUROPEAN CONTEXT FOR ENGLISH REGIONAL PLANNING

The development of regional spatial planning in England also has to be set within a wider policy context. The first is that which has emerged for mega regions – both in England and the EU. The publication of Europe 2000+ in 1994 (CEC) identified a spatial geography for Europe based on economic and physical geography. These mega regions, such as the Atlantic Arc, the Baltic Sea and North-West Europe, now have their own commissions with direct links to the European Commission. Each of these mega regions has started to develop in different ways and some with more developed approaches to spatial policy then others. From the outset, mega regions bisected nation states and were in part a way of recognising the different inter-ests and connections within and between European member states. In time, these boundaries have been extended and blurred so that greater proportions of mem-ber states have been set within each grouping. Support for these European mega regions has been given through INTERREG programmes set up to promote joint activity. A similar approach has also been developed in the United States where, by 2003, defined Megapolitan areas accounted for 20 per cent of the land area and 66 per cent of the population (Lang and Dhavale 2005).

This change in approach at regional level within the EU represents a more fundamental approach to the development of regional spatial planning and its asso-ciation with wider policy development and delivery. When the EU was founded in 1957, it had a concern for the wider territory, which was within the French and German traditions but one of the key points of the negotiation of the UK's entry in 1973 was the inclusion of its more location specific approaches to regional policy which had been in effect since the Barlow Report (1940). A range of measures to support areas that were lagging and those that were growing too fast was devel-oped such as selective assistance and new towns. The introduction of structural funds within the EU and their application to specific areas which had economic and social problems was introduced in the early 1970s and the first regional commis-sioner was from the UK.

By the early 1990s, this approach was being re-examined. The extension of the Single European Market for trade and then EU expansion to include more Eastern European countries introduced a debate about change. The Maastricht Treaty in 1992 included the last structural funds packages for Spain, Portugal, Greece and Ireland. After this, the EU started to move to work with localities in new ways. Part of this process involved the establishment of the Committee of the Regions (Morphet 1994) and the gradual transfer of funding from structural funds for meeting specific needs to funding being used to support development of cross border working and wider territorial initiatives.

The introduction of integration and the development of the ESDP from 1991 onwards were part of this longer-term process. In time, the proportion of funds spent on declining areas will be overtaken by that spent on the new approach through INTERREG. The policy also had a new name – territorial cohesion – and this applies not only to ensuring that areas work together to improve the integration and understanding in Europe but also to make Europe more economically successful within a local market place. Countries such as the BRIC nations (Brazil, Russia, India and China) all have the potential for growth and development which could far outstrip even a wider EU of 25 or more nations. The opening up of Eastern Europe had a positive role in this campaign. It provided both the opportunity for a cheaper and expanded labour force to improve competition. At the same time, this labour force was well educated and could be expected to spend their greater earning power on goods and services. Thus, this would benefit the economy of Europe as a whole if goods could be made and supplied locally within its territory.

As the role of the ESDP has increased, including the development of the mega regional arrangements (Hague and Jenkins 2005; Duhr et al. 2010), the approach to economic development and growth has been widened out. This has had implications for regional spatial planning in England and demonstrated through a number of key developments. First, the application of the approach to territorial cohesion policy means that there is a greater assessment of the application of all policies within their localities. At the same time, there is a greater emphasis on subsidiarity and its application. In the past decade, this interest has been seen at the other end of the spatial scale through *new localism* (Corry 2004) This has developed into a cross party interest in localisation (Conservative Party 2009; Bogdanor 2009; HMG 2009a). Hope and Leslie have translated this into an increased focus on spatial awareness within the central state in England, which they argue means that Government should be taking a much stronger interest in the implications of its policies at different spatial scales and between them. They argue that this increased spatial awareness has three key dimensions (2009: 37):

1   Variation and difference between and within localities.
2   Across Whitehall and interdepartmentally.
3   Local and regional delivery apparatus and advancing the sub-national machinery of Government.

Finally, Hope and Leslie make a series of recommendations including the creation of 'a duty to devolve' placed on central civil servants (2009: 45–6) that would be exercised through a 'devolutionary test' on all policy and legislation. At present, the distribution of actions and delivery mechanism for any central government policy is random.

The third consideration is the direct domestic management and oversight of public funding, particularly that provided by the EU. Since 1973, the funding provided for localities from the EU has been directed through a range of bodies that have been run by arms of central government, primarily through GOs and RDAs. Funds are managed by programme boards which include a variety of local stakeholders including democratically accountable politicians. However, in other member states, this funding has been put under direct democratic control. In Scotland, Wales and Northern Ireland, this issue has been solved to some extent through devolved governance, but no such system is yet in place in England. The proposed establishment of a directly elected regional assembly in England following the referendum in 2004 would have been one means of closing this gap but this failed and the Government has been left considering alternative means of achieving this.

The *Review of Sub-National Economic Development and Regeneration* (HM Treasury 2007a) has provided some initiatives that, if implemented, will make a significant step forward to more direct control of EU funding at the local level. At the regional level, new strategies are to be developed in the form of economic plans and delivery programmes (CLG 2009e). These are expected to be developed by regional leaders' boards which, although not directly elected, come closer to a local democratic control of priorities and delivery. These leaders' boards will report to special committees in Parliament. At the same time, there are to be enhanced roles and offices for regional ministers. Regional ministers have been established on previous occasions, but the development of a regional ministers group that meets regularly and proposals for an extended office are significant. Currently, regional ministers have also combined their role with another as a minister of state but there are proposals that these should be dropped and that the regional minister role becomes the main activity (Hope and Leslie 2009).

MEGA REGIONS IN ENGLAND

There has also been another development in regional spatial planning which has had some EU influence. This is in the development of the role of the English mega region. In 1994, there was a discussion that each EU member state should have a set number of regions within which their existing regions would fit. Larger states such as the UK, France and Italy might have eight regions, whilst Germany with the largest population could have ten. This approach has never re-emerged in any significant way, but in the UK, if applied, this could be defined as being Scotland, Wales, Northern Ireland, Northern England (North-East, North-West and Yorkshire and Humberside), Midlands (East Midlands, West Midlands and East Anglia), the South-West and the South-East. This makes seven regions and the issue of the eighth remains. Initially, Gibraltar was the eighth region but subsequent action through the

Council of Europe has now placed Gibraltar as part of the South-West. The eighth region could be London.

The mega regions of England have been developing at different speeds and have yet to really emerge as entities for spatial planning and delivery. Each mega region has its own key concerns and have been developed in different ways.

(1) THE NORTHERN WAY

The Northern Way has been evolving through a Treasury-led approach to addres key concerns of continuing economic underperformance in the North over more than 75 years. Although leading the country during the period of the industrial revolution when empire and manufacturing enabled England to lead world production in steel, coal, ship-building and energy, the 1930s depression left a legacy of economic dependency which successive waves of regional policy have failed to shift. Through various initiatives, public jobs have been moved to various Northern regions – health and income tax to Yorkshire and Humberside; pensions savings, BBC and education to the North-West; and education, pensions and agricultural payments to the North-East, but these moves have led to a greater dependency on government funding in these economies than before. These regions also have lower firm start-up rates and fewer women entrepreneurs (HM Treasury 2004).

In 2004, the Treasury embarked on a different approach to undertaking and ultimately attempting to shift these long standing challenges to the Northern economy. Not only did the Treasury want to see dependency reduced but also the potential of these areas to be positive contributors to the national economy. The evidence of why people are unemployed, or in prison, unable to read or sleeping on the streets shows a high correlation with their early upbringing, particularly for those children in care. This is a universal issue across England and not particularly confined to one region. However, often reasons why some people and communities had high degrees of crime, lower educational outcomes and lower life expectancy pointed to cultural issues within micro locations, such as parts of former mining villages, seaside towns, and some housing estates with a strong sense of local culture and mores were proving to be impervious to public policy interventions. These locations could be run by gangs or families where local people felt helpless to break out and their only ambition was to move away (Taylor 2008). Children were strongly socialised into an anti-school and anti-authority culture and parents, who frequently had never worked, were passing on their own experience as role models.

In 2004, a coalition of Government, local government and other public and private sector interests was established in order to respond to these challenges through the *Northern Way Growth Strategy*. They set up the Northern Way as a new organisation to take a culturally driven approach to economic growth within the region. This was a move away from seeing the North as a place that is dependent on government investment for its economic base. It placed private sector in the lead. It was also concerned to reduce inter-regional competition with an approach that was more joined-up, creating more value for the mega region, which it argues could make a stronger case together (http://www.thenorthernway.co.uk).

The main thrust of the approach in the *Northern Way Growth Strategy* is to concentrate on the mega region's strengths and the weaknesses. Its strengths were perceived as being its cities, interconnectedness, its universities and as a good place to live, outside the pressures of the South-East, whilst its weaknesses are low skills, high levels of inactivity and unemployment and underinvestment in transport (Balls 2003). The approach, developed in the *Northern Way Growth Strategy*, depended on the RESs as a means of delivering change. There was also an emphasis on city regions and establishing a new investment programme for them. The growth strategy included a number of key proposals for delivery but did not identify how and where they would be delivered or the necessary funding. MacLeod and Jones argue that the Northern Way is 'audacious' in its claims (2006: 46), and still part of a centralised agenda. In identifying the mechanisms for delivery in the Northern Way, spatial planning at the regional or local level was not explicitly identified as being a means of achieving these changes.

As the Northern Way developed into an organisation with a secretariat and governance structures, it also both led and responded to wider policy interests in the development of city regions as motors of economic change. It found that cities contained much of the concentration of people with poorer skills and without work whilst also creating more sustainable approaches to using existing infrastructure, switching to public transport and also using the concentration of skills and business that already existed in these wider city regions. The Northern Way focussed on developing city regions so that now, with the emergence of city region policy (see below), it has the greatest number of city regions and the first two governance pathfinders lie within its area. In this sense, it has been a successful initiative in developing government policy to support its identified needs but, unlike earlier regional economic policies for underperforming areas, sub-regional initiatives are not confined to areas of regeneration need. A report on the Northern England (OECD 2008) supported the role of the Northern Way in promoting innovation as a way to stimulate a sounder economic basis for the area.

(II) OTHER ENGLISH MEGA REGIONS

Other English mega regions have not developed as quickly as the Northern Way. The Midlands Way was developed in 2005 working across the East and West Midlands. *Smart Growth* (emda 2005) proposed an analysis and action plan of what the two regions needed in order to improve its contribution to gross domestic product, including the identification of specific projects which would support the economy. The role of the Eastern region which was the main location for growth in the Greater South-East and also to support the Cambridge–Ipswich hi-tec axis was kept outside this grouping, although earlier studies had brought the East and East Midlands together in an arc of development, more defined by its relationship with London than any internal coherence. In the South-West, the mega region and region's boundary appear to coincide, although this could change in the future. Little additional specific work has been undertaken on a similar basis to the Northern Way and the Midlands Way, although the region has been at the forefront of an initiative to provide greater input into government spending decisions in the regions through the Regional Funding Advice scheme (HM Treasury 2008) which has brought together regional consideration of priorities and spending.

The South-East region remains a difficult mega region to consider within an English context. Before 1993, the region was identified as the whole area around London. However, as it contained approximately half the population of England and a third of the population of the UK, it was always a problematic concept. The local authorities had reflected the Government definition of the region through the South East Regional Planning Conference (SERPLAN), a voluntary body set up to coordinate the region rather than being a strategic regional planning body. Before SERPLAN was closed in 1996, it was primarily concerned with housing growth and allocation of housing numbers to specific locations. Since the South-East mega region was broken up and distributed between London, the South and Eastern regions, the larger South-East region has been dormant and the large regions within it have their own regional spatial planning approaches. More recently, there has been some interest in discussing this approach again (Musson et al. 2005).

As Glasson and Marshall have identified, the mega regions have 'variable solidity' (2007: 128). The Northern Way continues to make the most progress, although the establishment of functional MAAs and city regions in its areas may shift the main emphasis from the mega region to sub-region. This may be a necessary pathway, sidestepping the regional scale following regionalism's demise in 2004. On the other hand, once the Northern mega region has been populated with functioning sub-regions, it may create a more dynamic leadership and a counterbalance to the South-East. It may also create a region which is similar in scale to the regions emerging in other EU states.

REGIONS

The development of regional spatial policy has been one where institutional conflicts and rivalries have prevented a joined-up focus on delivery that is at the heart of an effective spatial planning approach. Marshall (2004) argues that the development of regional policy reform since 2004 has been directed through a strong policy line from Government but unnoticed by commentators. The need to tackle regional policy in new ways was identified in 2001 (HM Treasury and DTI). In *Productivity in the UK: 3 – the Regional Dimension,* the 'significant and persistent differences in economic performance between and within UK regions' was considered (v). It was pointed out that the least productive regions had a gross domestic product per capital of 40 per cent below that of the richest region, which was London at that time. The report went on to point out that 'both the size of differentials and relative ranking of regions has been persistent. The impact of this untapped potential could be very significant. If all the lagging regions improved their productivity performance at least to that of the current average then the average person in the UK would be around £1000 better off' (ibid.). As a response to this, 'regional economic policy must be focussed on raising the performance of the weakest regions rather than simply re-distributing existing economic activity. Real economic gain for the country as a whole will only come from a process of 'levelling up' (ibid.).

The policy response was the establishment of RDAs through the Regional Development Agencies Act 1999 that also required the RDAs to produce a RES, to be reviewed every three years. However, at the same time, the Planning Green Paper was also published (DTLR 2001b) which sought to address new approaches to regional planning through the creation of RSSs. These were to replace the Regional Planning Guidance system that was introduced in 1994 and was more central government led than locally owned in its processes. These initiatives were not cross-referenced in either report. As the introduction of RSSs was taken forward through the 2004 Planning and Compulsory Purchase Act, the RESs were statutory documents and were intended to be delivery-based approaches for the next 10–20 years in each region (HM Treasury, DTI and ODPM 2004: 44). Once this approach developed, other parts of Government decided that it might be useful to have regionally focussed strategies and those for housing (2003), transport (2006) and culture (2001) followed.

Government was also interested in reforming the approach to the use of EU regional policy as applied to the structural funds and state aid policies which govern where national government can intervene to support specific industries in ways that are not deemed to be anti-competitive. As part of this process, the Government proposed that approaches to developing regional policy should be more flexible and locally determined. This would use 'indigenous strengths' to tackle 'practical weaknesses' in order to promote economic growth (HM Treasury, DTI and ODPM 2004: 3). This paper also recognised that there was a need to draw together existing government investment in the regions in order to 'combine actions to best effect' (ibid.: 4). In the English regions, this joining up was expected to be through a combination of the work of the regional assemblies, the RDAs and the government offices. Regional Planning Guidance, the forerunner of the RSS, was established as part of the process of delivering RESs and 'in providing a long term spatial framework for them' (ibid.: 9). The approach to coordination within regions was also underpinned through a PSA between the three departments of state. It was created in 2002 to be delivered between 2003 and 2008 and set out 'to make sustainable improvements in the economic performance of all English regions and over time to reduce the persistent gap in growth rates' (ibid.: 14). This objective was supported by other PSA targets and agreements for the same period. A Regional Coordination Unit was also established to bring all this together and which was also to manage the government office network.

The publication of the Planning Green Paper (DTLR 2001b) demonstrated that there would be a new approach to regional planning in due course. Catching the mood for change at the regional spatial scale which the Treasury's thinking had engendered, a more integrated approach was proposed and one that was expected to be in the management of local political leaders and other stakeholders rather than led from central government. Changes in regional planning guidance had already been implemented through the PPG 11 (DETR 2000) and, in the Planning Green Paper, this was already proposed to be abandoned and a new approach to RSS developed to replace RPG. RPG was still seen as being insufficiently focussed on the strategic issues and also not integrated with other regional strategies that were emerging, such as the RES. The proposal was to create the RSSs with a statutory status and for LDFs and transport plans to be consistent with it. At the same time, the RSS were expected to identify sub-regions within their areas and the spatial strategies for each of these (DTLR 2001b: §4.42).

The RSS were prepared by their regions as a means through which there could be more ownership of the proposals. It was also a mechanism through which regions could allocate the housing growth that central government had identified would be necessary to meet the country's future economic requirements. Since their introduction, the RSS became as embroiled in the planning disputes and subject of long-running examinations as their predecessor RPGs. The continued focus of the RSS on housing, and the separate roles of the other regional strategies, meant that the RSS have not found their role of strategic regional spatial strategies. Instead of identifying where future investment would be made, they have become political footballs within regional party and place politics. The emphasis on achieving the housing growth through this process also served to increase the role of central government in the RSS process with the result that spatial planning within regions, at all spatial scales, has been put on hold pending the outcomes of these now quasi-national processes.

However, some progress was made in developing their broader spatial purpose, particularly through their role in providing the context for infrastructure planning
and delivery. As part of the development of the RSS for the South-East, a preliminary
assessment of the scale of infrastructure investment required was undertaken. This
concentrated primarily on transport and energy and was made up from existing proposals that had already been identified. This approach was undertaken with Treasury
support and had two key roles. The first was to provide the case for investment in
the South-East which otherwise might have been difficult politically in the face of
evidence of under-provision of infrastructure investment in other parts of the country
(McLean and McMillan 2003). At the same time, it started to create a framework
where public sector infrastructure investment decisions were more transparent and
could be included as part of a wider approach to spatial delivery. This was one of the
original purposes of the new RSS system when originally introduced but one that
had not been developed in a systematic way.

A second approach to infrastructure planning and delivery was developed in
the South-East and South-West, also with Treasury encouragement. In the South-
West, the region set up an infrastructure commission, identifying ways in which
infrastructure could be pre-funded prior to development, partly to overcome local
objections about the pressures that new housing was seen to bring with it. In the
South-East, a study to identify how best to generate funding for infrastructure
through developers' contribution was commissioned by the Regional Assembly.
Both regions were able to use this work to influence central government funding
decisions within the regions through Regional Funding Advice (RFA). In the North-
West, North-East and Yorkshire and Humberside, the approach to infrastructure
planning and delivery was undertaken through the sub-regional strategies that were
part of their economic planning approach. In the Eastern regions, where most population growth was planned, the RDA commissioned four key infrastructure studies
which identified the associated requirements for growth which were usually brought
forward through planning and investment processes.

The approaches taken to identify infrastructure requirements had many similar characteristics. First, they concentrated on physical infrastructure and primarily
on transport, with some telecoms and energy. Second, they all omitted flood risk
prevention which, during the period 2004–2009, became a major new hazard
when considering housing sites, as the proportion of sites suffering first ever floods
increased. Third, the infrastructure programmes were seen to be dependent on additional funding and, in regions with a stronger market, developers' contributions. The
vast proportion of mainstream public sector budgets spent at regional level have
been left untouched outside this process.

The RSS approach lasted for five years, 2004–2009. In this five-year period,
the RSS became a dominant context for LDF production, but continued to be beset

with many of the problems that had faced the previous approach of RPGs. First, the RSS never had the authority of being the 'single' or overarching strategy in the region. The RES barely acknowledged the RSS and led to tensions in each region. This failure of the RSS to fulfil its role undermined its position with other government departments that had moved to create their own regional strategy and governance approaches to promote their own service interests.

Second, the RSS became dominated with single issues and never developed its role. In the South-East, South-West, London, East Midlands and East Anglia, there was a strong skewing towards increased housing provision which was regarded as a continuing constraint on the economic growth in these regions, and this was a Treasury driven policy. The inability of people to buy houses where needed and at a price they could afford spawned two major Treasury Reviews on housing (Barker 2004) and planning (Barker 2006) that set housing growth as the key component and battle ground of the RSS. Despite attempts to find other ways to encourage local authorities to engage in this process in a positive way, through creating 'competitions' for growth area status and small budgets, this continued to be an issue. The Government finally solved this by creating two new approaches to identifying housing requirement and almost removed this from a regional level altogether. The first was to establish its own independent National Housing and Planning Advice Unit in 2006 to undertake population projections and determine housing requirements at the local level. The second was to shift the requirement to deliver housing from the RSS, where local development frameworks had to be in general conformity, to one that was contracted by each local authority through LAAs. These LAA 'delivery contracts' are set prior to assessments of local housing need through LDF processes.

The second key Treasury policy which was emerging for other regions, particularly the North-West, North-East and Yorkshire and Humberside was the dominance of the economic agenda. As we have noted earlier, the development of mega-regional approaches through the Northern Way was already developing an approach to sub-regional economic planning that was largely outside the RSS. Housing was also an issue but policy here was taken forward through another form of competition – this time for housing market area status, where older houses were demolished and redeveloped with newer, more attractive housing stock. The sub-regional economic planning approach immediately moved to delivery mode and became an alternative route to pursue. In these regions, the RSS never had much purchase and the North-West region was the last to have at least one sound LDF. The planning system here was regarded as an irrelevance in the face of the economic agenda.

A third key weakness with the RSS process was that, although set up to be 'owned' by the regional assembly within the region, it still attracted as much criticism and lack of acceptance as the RPGs had before. The transfer of ownership did not reduce the concerns that were faced at local level. Also, the RSS became distorted towards the provision of housing in those regions where this issue was dominant and the development of a spatial strategy and sub-regional approaches were not evolved to their full expression. This also meant that the appropriate context for LDFs was underdeveloped and the over dominance of housing in these regions heavily influenced expectations about the role and purpose of the LDF system and the ToS that accompanied it. For the first four years of LDF, until PPS 12 (CLG 2008c) was reissued in 2008, the overwhelming assumption of those preparing LDFs was that the only important test was that of conformity with the RSS on housing numbers and that all other tests were illusory (Morphet et al. 2007). In fact, the RSS conformity test was one of 27 tests, and a failure to understand this relative role of the RSS housing numbers cost many local authorities dear with unsound or abandoned LDF processes prior to submission. So the new system of RSS did not speed up the process.

Other features of the RSS process did not change from the previous system. Despite the ownership and leadership of the process by the regional assembly, the statutory nature of the RSS meant that it was subject to public examination and a stronger government involvement in this process. Government offices felt unable to change the housing requirements in the RSS in a top down way without having to justify these additional numbers at the local level. The 2001 census was taken at a point when domestic fertility levels were at their lowest point in the cycle. It was also underreporting the number of in-migrants, particularly young workers from the EU A8 countries and, in the subsequent period following accession in 2004, the numbers grew, as did fertility rates. This provided Government with an opportunity to impose housing growth and continue to confirm to local politicians that whatever legislation said, this was not their RSS. Government also continued its practice in the delay and timing of announcing the reviews of the RSS and panel reports. These have become to be viewed as politically sensitive acts with increases in housing numbers in specific locations having devastating political consequences at the national and local level.

So, the RSSs have never fulfilled their mission for a variety of reasons and Regional Strategies are in their third iteration within ten years (CLG and BIS 2010). The new RS will be led jointly by a leaders' board and the RDA. The RS will:

- have no specific model
- should have 15–20 year time horizon
- identify key regional challenges
- have regard to national policy but not repeat it unless there is some specific dimension
- be based on a sound evidence base

- have a deliverable implementation plan
- focus on sustainable economic growth, taking into account environmental considerations, climate change mitigation and adaptation, housing and infra-structure needs
- will have a strong spatial dimension.

The RS may ultimately replicate some of the weaknesses in the current system. However, there are also new pieces of government machinery in place that may moderate this. First, a regional ministerial system has been introduced in a more proactive approach to draw partners together. Although regional ministers combine their regional role with other ministerial responsibilities, they now receive support from government offices and proposals from a think-tank close to Government that has proposed that their role should be extended into a full-time position which would then see the government office become the office of the regional minister (Hope and Leslie 2009).

Second, Parliamentary Select Committees have been established which provide scrutiny for intra-regional affairs. This approach replaces that of regional scrutiny which had been one of the key roles of regional assemblies but had never been established as a significant process. Regional Select Committees mirror those for Scotland and Wales following the failed devolution referenda in 1979 and could be paving the way to develop more specific regional identities and whetting the public appetite for directly elected regional governments in due course.

The third component in this new regional landscape is the Cabinet Committee which is concerned with the cross governmental approaches to investment deci-sions. Currently, almost all decisions are made independently within government departments. The problems created by individual approaches taken by government departments in determining their investment decisions and the way in which they keep data on them was an issue raised by Mclean in 2006 (HM Treasury 2006). The effect of PSA 20 (HM Treasury 2007c) is to embed and normalise housing growth into the government wide agenda as a means of bringing together a more corporate or cross government approach to planning decisions on infrastructure. At the local level, the development of single local area budgets which combine public sector expenditure through a local budget and through the infrastructure delivery programme through the LDF is leading this process. This approach has been devel-oped as Total Place (HM Treasury 2009a) and is supported through Local Spending Reports, a product of the 2007 Sustainable Communities Act.

The final component of change is the creation of the Homes and Communities Agency (HCA) which brings together a range of funding streams at the local level including housing and regeneration. It does not bring this funding under immediate democratic control but through the means of a local 'single conversation' between the HCA and individual local authorities where there are mechanisms for a stronger local input into the decision-making process on public investment. The HCA is organised regionally and will also have a significant contribution to the RS process.

These new approaches will not be without tensions and risk. Marshall describes them as a 'major and very extraordinary reorientation of state policy' (2008: 101). The division of responsibility for the RS between the leaders' board and the RDAs will not be easy. Up to now, these relationships have generally been strong, as RDAs have preferred to deal with more strategic local authorities in each region but a key issue will be the continuing influence that Government will be exerting through RDAs at a regional level. At present, the only counter to this will be by regional Select Committees, although political agendas may see the abolition of RDAs in the future. Second, how strong will the spatial element of the RS be? The planning teams that were put together at the Regional Assembly level seemed likely to be disbanded but they have now been incorporated as part of the new approach and will be used by the leaders' panel as a counterweight to the RDA. There will also need to be other new governance apparatus to make this work at the regional level including the publication of all regional expenditure by government departments. The regions already have a system of providing RFA but, as Hope and Leslie (2009) point out, this only represents five per cent of government expenditure at the regional level. This may need to be increased considerably if this is going to work. They suggest 40 per cent of national regional funding determined within the region should provide a better level of regional ownership.

Once again, regional spatial planning is moving to a new approach. The RS is economic in focus and will be using housing and transport investment as key components of achieving growth in regional GDP. The role of spatial planning is not overtly recognised in this new approach although, in practice, it is likely to have considerable influence in the locations of infrastructure investment and delivery. In effect, the regional tier may drop back in importance and be replaced by sub-regions as the spatial scale of choice for planning and delivery decisions. It is clear that the sub-regional scale, with its new governance model, is emerging to take a leading role in the next five to ten years.

SUB-REGIONS AND CITY REGIONS

The development of sub-regional approaches to spatial planning has been incrementally developing since the mid 1990s. As Le Gales (2002 quoted in Healey 2009) points out, 'the concept of the city region is deeply embedded in ... spatial planning concepts' (832). Healey goes on to state that the city region frequently represents a 'functional reality', whether representing a city and its hinterland or a polycentric area which is connected by space and flows (Davoudi 2003). The terms sub-region and city region are nearly but not quite synonymous. Whilst a city region will always be a sub-region (Neuman and Hull 2009), a sub-region may be polycentric (Darwin 2009) or a natural space, such as that covered by a national park or river basin which has no dominant urban area but which has some unity defined by natural features. Until recently, the notion of sub-regions has been defined as an 'imagined' or 'soft' space that is not represented as an administrative area and there has been much discussion on the issue of defining boundaries (Shaw and Sykes 2005). Any joint working depended on 'thin' informal arrangements which had no direct accountability and required political focus on a limited number of objectives on which the sub-region could agree in order to attract national attention and investment (Turok 2009). Much of the commentary on sub-regions has concentrated not on their functional role but their inability to work.

In 2007 in England, a shift in focus to the economic importance of sub-regions has now led to changes in governance models shifting them from soft to hard spaces (HM Treasury 2007a). As Turok (2009) comments, sub-regions are emerging as a policy tool in areas where economic regeneration is required as well as in areas where growth has to be managed. Sub-regions are appearing in two formats. The first is through sub-regional contractual relationships known as Multi Area Agreements and the second is a hybrid version of this known as the City Region, of which Manchester and Leeds are the first examples (HM Treasury 2009c; CLG 2009d). City regions were first proposed in 2006 (CLGa) and are moving beyond a voluntaristic cooperative relationship to one that is legal and governance based, thus addressing one of the key criticisms of sub-regions as having no democratic mandate for their operation (Morphet 2009b; Roberts and Baker 2004; Marshall 2007).

The trend towards sub-regional spatial planning has come from at least two directions. The first is from the EU where there has been a great interest in the notion of polycentricity as a means of understanding spatial relationships and underpinning strategies of investment (Davoudi 2003; Faludi 2005). Polycentricity is also a means for considering how to promote more sustainable ways of living and working. The EU has also had concerns about the concentration of economic and social investment in capital cities which can run the risk of reducing investment elsewhere in the country or cross border regions (CEC 2007).

In England, a great part of the wider South-East is dominated by London and its economic pull. Within this, there are also sub-systems of integrated market towns and cities which have polycentric characteristics. These groups of places, such as Portsmouth/Southampton and Reading/Oxford, overlap with other areas and in some places form spatial triangles. Outside the South-East, the country works in a more polycentric way than perhaps has hitherto been recognised. Major regional cities create a strong community and cultural centres and provide key transport hubs.

They also operate within sub-regional clusters and patterns. Households move to the suburbs and, in the short term, retain commuting patterns to the major city but, over generations, work and travel habits transfer to their new communities. A second driver has come from the United States where there has been a suggestion that sub-regions are important in generating contributions to national wealth (Lang and Dhavale 2005; Carbonell and Yaro 2005). These are called 'new state spaces' (Brenner 2003; 2004) because they have no democratically accountable governance structures but they represent locations where Government has decided it needs to take some action. The Thames Gateway in London and the South-East could be one of those spaces, as would the M11 corridor from central London to Peterborough.

Over the period since 2000, a range of studies have reviewed the role and place of sub-regions within England. *Prosperous Communities II: Vive la Dévolution* (LGA 2007) identified sub-regions for the whole of England. In 2006, city regions as a future key policy area were proposed (CLG 2006a). City regions have been of long-standing interest to economic geographers as potential generators of growth. They have also now been identified as sustainable units which enable the use of existing infrastructure and efficient use of public transport systems. In 2007, the Sub-National Review of Economic Development and Regeneration (SMR) translated much of this background thinking into policy. This established the role of MAAs as being the policy vehicles for supporting delivery in sub-regional areas. MAAs were expected to address more structural infrastructure investment such as housing, transport planning and regeneration, leaving more personal services and education outside this grouping. However, the SNR did provide the potential route for the MAA to take on other services in due course.

Many groups of local authorities responded to an initial invitation to bid for MAA status − particularly those in the Northern Way that were geared up for this likely change in policy. However, unlike many preceding initiatives of this kind, it was not linked only to the North. Others places such as Leicester and Portsmouth and Southampton (PUSH) were also early adopters. In rural areas, the strategy seems to be to encourage towns and cities to work together and in most rural areas, local government reorganisation appears to be a means to get to the same end.

The development of MAAs is open to all parts of England and it is likely that many more will follow 13 pilots. Earlier experience of LAAs led to a quick transition from pilot to roll out across the whole of England and the same could be expected here.

One of the key issues for the pilots is governance, although the establishment of city region pilots with new governance formats will overcome this objection (CLG 2009d). The development of a spatial planning framework for sub-region remains unclear. At present, there is no guidance to suggest that a new sub-regional plan should be formed. At local levels, the assumption is that Joint Core Strategies should be developed as plans within a common coordinated framework. Is it possible that sub-regional development can take place without an overarching spatial framework? Marshall (2007) argues that sub-regions are the natural successors to structure plans, which were an operational feature of English development planning from 1969 onwards. Structure Plans operated at county level and provided the framework for district or more local plans within them. Structure plans were abolished as part of the introduction of spatial planning in England in 2004. However, structure plans and sub-regional approaches to planning have some differences. First, structure plans were based on administrative boundaries and did not relate to the way in which places functioned. In contrast, sub-regional approaches that have been evolving since 2007 are based on how places work. Around Leeds, for example, 11 local authority areas comprise the city region and these are an amalgamation of local authorities of different types. It would be possible to split local authority areas if necessary and to spread a sub-region across a regional boundary if this represented a spatial reality.

Second, structure plans were only adopted under highly formalised approaches and although originally conceived as delivery plans, in practice they became a tool for the distribution of housing numbers between the authorities within the county boundary. In contrast, the new sub-regional approaches deal with spatial planning but through combining their activities. There is no additional process required, although eventual delivery programmes are likely to require sustainability appraisal. Third, most sub-regions are not set within a formal democratic structure, although as mentioned earlier the 2009 Local Democracy, Economic Development and Construction Act makes provision for sub-regions to have a formalised democratic structure which stretches across administrative boundaries.

The final difference between structure plans and sub-regional plans may be the most important. Structure plans were set within a top down hierarchical model of planning and became primarily the mechanism for the delivery of regional housing requirements. Sub-regions are emerging as the main focal point of delivery. They enable sustainable approaches through the use of existing infrastructure and patterns of movement (Wheeler 2009) and they represent locations that hold some cultural resonance. In 2010, the regional planning system will move to one that is more delivery focussed and, as part of the RS, there will also be a delivery plan which will comprise all of the sub-regional delivery plans (CLG and BIS 2010). There is likely to be further changes in the allocation and use of funding at the regional level to accompany this process (Hope and Leslie 2009) and the emerging regional governance apparatus including regional Select Committees in Parliament will provide greater oversight.

Finally, are city regions likely to become even larger as mega city regions? Hall (2009) argues that the mega city regions are emerging as the dominant form of the twenty-first century. He sees this development in the United States (Carbonell and Yaro 2005; Lang and Knox 2009) and in Europe, as demonstrated through the POLYNET study (Young Foundation: 2006). Hall argues that these mega city regions may not be continuous urban areas or even polycentric but archipelagos: 'a few central islands dominated by the sharp peaks of the core city economies and lower peripheral islands in perpetual danger of economic inundation' (2009: 815). The lack of a democratic mandate for the mega city region can also erode its power (Roy 2009). However, in the English context, this geography of spatial change is now being matched with a governance model which can manage these arrangements with more intent rather than sporadic growth and investment being a by-product of the market.

THE ENIGMA OF LONDON

The role of London is an enigma. It has the population to be a small country. Its governance is through the Mayor who is scrutinised by the Greater London Authority. The government office for London suggests that London is a region and the development of MAAs within London, e.g. for the Olympic boroughs, also suggests that London is a region. Legally, the GLA is a local authority. Perhaps a better way to consider London is as a sub-region. It is larger than a sub-region but it cannot function without working with its immediate partners and these are important in terms of employment, transport and overall investment. The Mayor has the responsibility for the London Plan which is equivalent to the RSS.

Whilst the 2004 Planning and Compulsory Purchase Act removed the two-tier planning process, the system created by the Greater London Authority Act in 1999 reintroduced a two-tier system. The London Plan and borough LDFs together create the spatial planning framework for London. The London Plan is intended as guidance rather than as a plan, and the first version included policies on transport, economic development, housing, retail development, leisure facilities, heritage and facilities for waste management and guidance for particular parts of London (Cullingworth and Nadin 2006: 62). London borough LDFs have to be in general conformity with the Mayor's spatial strategy. Like the other regions, there are also strategies for the delivery of transport, culture and the state of the environment. However, there is a key difference between the arrangements between London and other regions in that much of the public sector investment funding has been devolved to the Mayor. In London, the London Development Agency and Transport for London are answerable to the Mayor rather than delivered through a centrally led RDA or transport funding through the DfT, Highways Agency and other transport operators.

It is likely that the model in London will be replicated in the emerging city region model, with Manchester and Leeds as the pilots, with executive leadership roles such as that exercised by the Mayor of London in these sub-regions (CLG

2009d). The Mayor has much greater control over devolved expenditure than other parts of the UK and, if this model is extended, then it could become a more devolved approach to managing resources at super regional/city regional level.

CONCLUSIONS

The development of regional spatial planning seems to be developing and delivered at the scales above and below the region. The role of the mega region in England seems established and likely to continue, made up of constituent sub-regional delivery programmes as set out in MAAs. Regions remain contested spaces between different government departments with the leadership being unresolved in the current approach to developing Regional Strategies. The approach that will require Regional Strategies to be examined in public will subject all their proposals to wider review and consideration which will be a new approach. They could provide a more integrated approach in general. However, whilst this is going on, the leading roles of mega regional and sub-regional planning can be progressing, despite the regional strategy or as a means of developing it in more detail. The key issue may turn on how many spatial sub-regional plans and LDFs there are, their link to investment and delivery programmes and the extent to which any government department will use a prevailing policy tool to meet their current ends. So at present, the development of more integrated approaches to development and delivery is coming through a range of tiers and levels.

CHAPTER 10

SPATIAL PLANNING IN SCOTLAND, WALES AND NORTHERN IRELAND

INTRODUCTION

The spatial planning systems of England, Scotland, Wales and Northern Ireland are set within individual governance frameworks to deliver better places. They operate at the nexus of vertical and horizontal integration, addressing the twin components of vision and evidence-based need. The development of spatial planning in Wales, Scotland and Northern Ireland has been associated with other changes in governance. In some cases, spatial planning has been identified as part of a process of decentralisation and devolution where:

> devolution to nations and regions may not also be less about the need to develop approaches to deal with local inequalities but rather as a means of creating more territorial cohesion between parts of states that have different cultures and legacies. It can also be a means of adapting to globalisation.
>
> (Rodriguez-Pose and Gill 2005: 408)

In other cases, reform of planning systems towards a more spatial approach has involved a more centralised approach at a sub-regional level (Needham 2005), whilst maintaining a more traditional development planning approach at the local level. Spatial planning systems are influenced by those from other countries.

Effective spatial planning is characterised as part of a wider programme of change which incorporates vision, reductions of the influence of climate change, sustainable development and economic stability and growth and is able to deliver these changes at various spatial scales from national to local levels. Devolution for Scotland and Wales and the restoration of devolved government in Northern Ireland has led to discussion about its consequences for public policy in general and spatial planning in particular. Before devolution, much of the commentary was about the United Kingdom being an over-centralised state with perceptions about the problems that this brought, including the inability to progress local solutions to problems and to prioritise issues that are important at community level (Allmendinger and Tewdwr-Jones 2000; 2006).

Since the implementation of devolution, the discussion has switched to the problems related to a fragmented state (Tewdwr-Jones and Allmendinger 2006; Keating 2006; Davoudi and Strange 2009), where there are differing and diverging approaches, to governance and policies as they are developed and applied at the sub-national level. Another metaphor that has been used is 'hollowing' out of the state which suggests that the central state maintains its 'headquarters' functions but that it no longer has the power to influence what goes on within the multiple scales of governance (Jessop 2002). This is another variant on the centralised state model, although Goodwin *et al.* (2006) argue that in terms of devolution, hollowing out is associated with 'filling in' the governance spaces with alternative governance models, with new versions of 'circumscribed power' (Raco 2006: 326). Are these governance spaces filled with divergent or convergent policies?

In practice, as this chapter will show, it is likely that the state was less centralised than generally considered prior to devolution and that since devolution the divergences have been less. Since the implementation of devolution in Scotland and Wales in 1999, it is likely that there have been fewer commentators interested in the range of solutions across the UK and their similarities and differences than there have been those interested in the implications of devolution within each of the nations. Also, there may be enough differences in priorities for policy and, in this case, spatial planning, to argue that the systems in each of the nations have diverged. This point will be discussed further below but it seems likely that these are variations within a common framework rather than variations between frameworks.

The Scottish Parliament and Welsh Assembly have introduced what are perceived as being differing approaches to planning. Before devolution, Wales, Scotland and Northern Ireland already had separate approaches to planning, although all were within a system of development planning which had common and recognisable characteristics within the United Kingdom. Prior to 1999 in Scotland and Wales, the Scottish and Welsh Offices had developed their own planning policy guidance and advice. In Northern Ireland, the planning system was, and continues to be, run by the Department of the Environment. There have been proposals for planning to be returned to local government as part of the Review of Public Administration that commenced in 2002.

Although since 1999 there has been considerable policy discussion and reform in each administration, it is not yet clear that these represent growing divergences of planning policy or whether they represent a policy fugue where similar policies are introduced but at different times, with differing names and in different sequences. It might be argued that this is because there are other wider and more external forces on UK planning policy which are helping to shape a common system such as globalisation, the effects of the EU, territorial cohesion policies and the focus on the economic role of spatial planning. These all have some force of argument in their favour as there still remains a consistency and coherence in planning policy between the four nations.

If planning policy has been developed in a fugue, then there is case to show that the introduction of new key themes and approaches have been taken by individual nations. One nation has frequently been the lead innovator and instigator of a policy in spatial planning which has then been taken up by the other nations. In addition, the implementation of spatial planning would also suggest more integration between other parts of the public sector, in terms of delivery, funding and governance and more coherent and joint forms of planning and delivery. For spatial planning, this shows itself most clearly in the continuing modernisation of local governance and the role of spatial planning within this as a delivery mechanism. In this chapter, the spatial planning systems in Scotland, Wales and Northern Ireland are reviewed in the context of emerging governance systems and the effectiveness of current practice is considered. This is followed by a discussion of the differences and similarities between these three systems and that of England. This also provides an assessment of the likely next steps for each nation in the further development of the spatial planning approach.

SCOTLAND

The development of spatial planning in Scotland has been a deliberate process both in modernising the system and also ensuring that it addresses distinct Scottish issues (Allmendinger 2001; 2006; Lloyd and Purves 2009). Scotland's continuing debate about separateness (Brown and Alexander 2007; Calman 2009) has some influence in these approaches, particularly in pursuing economic objectives, for Scotland's main contribution to spatial planning practice has been at two spatial scales. The first is through Scotland's approach to national planning, particularly for key infrastructure and the management of rural areas and the second is through city region planning. The national planning framework for Scotland is one that is further advanced than that for England or Northern Ireland and follows on from that of Wales. A new spatial hierarchy for planning was introduced in the Planning White Paper, *Modernising the Planning System* (Scottish Executive 2005), including that of national and local scales.

(I) NATIONAL PLANNING FRAMEWORK (NPF)

The Planning etc. (Scotland) Act 2006 introduced further significant changes including, as Lloyd and Peel argue (2009), the concept of spatial planning. The national scale is where the discussion and decisions about major infrastructure investment for water or waste treatment and transport hubs that had already been previously identified in the Scottish Infrastructure Investment Plan (Scottish Government 2008c) should be taking place. The publication of the National Planning Framework 2 (NPF2) (Scottish Government 2009c) stated that it would concentrate more on delivery, including coordination with major infrastructure providers. As such, the NPF2 is a mechanism for 'integrating and aligning strategic investment priorities and informing inter-regional choice' (Lloyd and Peel 2005: 318). NPF2 also identified development planning at the local level as one of the key means of delivery, including the community plan. However, this integration is more consultative in character, suggesting that the development planning process that will require a whole market perspective and co-ordinated delivery (§77).

When the Scottish Executive published its first NPF in 2004, it had a strong economic focus (Lloyd and Purves 2009) and this was followed by NPF2 in 2009. The differences between the two NPFs is that NPF2 is intended to be far more specific about development priorities (ibid.: 90) and be more specific about imple-mentation. NPF2 is a means through which the spatial consequences of policies for 'economic development, climate change, transport, energy, housing and regen-eration, waste management, water and drainage, catchment management and the protection of the environment' can be considered (Scottish Government 2009c). The foreword to NPF2 also heralds its role in shaping the future approach to ter-ritorial planning in Scotland with the role of spatial planning in aligning strategic investment priorities. Like NPF1, it maintains a strong economic focus and sets out to be the spatial expression of all government policies. It also recognises that it works within the framework of the ESDP and of national spatial policies in other parts of the UK and that it needs to have specific operational relationships with spatial plans from bordering areas such as the North-East region in England. It also creates the contexts for the four city regions, which it states need to develop spatial plans for their areas and concentrates on the need to deliver what is proposed in NPF2 through a variety of delivery agencies and private investment.

NPF2 creates the spatial framework for the future of Scotland. First, it identi-fies a range of key challenges including the economy and its relationship with place. Second, it highlights the challenge of sustainable development including the issues of climate change, transport, energy, waste and new technologies. The third key chal-lenge is to Scotland's people and households, with recent downturns in population being reversed through in-migration and higher fertility rates, with a projected increase in household of 19 per cent by 2031. This has implications for homes, infrastructure and public services. The last challenge to be set out in NPF2 is that of Scotland in the world. It then goes on to identify how these challenges are to be met through a variety of targets, policies and proposals.

NPF2 also contains key proposals for Strategic Transport Corridors, electricity transmission, water and drainage. It also provides spatial perspectives for a series of regional areas within Scotland and their sub-regional components. These provide a framework for both the Strategic Development Plans (SDPs) and Local Development Plans (LDPs) that will follow and, although promised in the Planning White Paper, the NPF does not contain any detail of the way in which it will be delivered other than through the development planning system, as set out in the Development Planning Circular 1 (Scottish Government 2009a).

(II) CITY REGIONS

City regions in Scotland are important as part of the economic future of the country. The development of SDPs for four city regions in Scotland, Aberdeen, Dundee, Edinburgh and Glasgow, is seen as providing national leadership. In the *Review of Scotland's Cities: The Analysis* (Scottish Government 2002), it was stated that 'devolution has provided an opportunity to put Scotland at the forefront of modern integrated approaches to territorial management within the UK' (ibid.: 5). This approach to spatial planning at the sub-regional level can be viewed as a potential forerunner for sub-regional planning within other parts of the UK. The boundaries of the four regions were reviewed in 2002 (Halden 2002) based on transport, housing and retail catchment areas. This was also published at the same time as the analysis of Scotland's City Regions. As Glasson and Marshall (2007: 121) demonstrate, these two reports were set among a long line of studies of the economic role of the city regions.

The proposal that city regions should have their own strategic planning arrangements, which include a number of local authorities in the city region, was made in 2006. The city regions have their own SDPs which bring together development planning and action planning. Glasson and Marshall (2007) also point out the links between this approach and that of Scottish Enterprise's which also promotes the role of Scotland's cities in building future economic success (Scottish Enterprise 2006). This scale was introduced in the 2006 Act and marks the second significant spatial planning initiative in Scotland. Although not mentioned in the 2005 Planning White Paper (Scottish Government 2005), the role of the city regions and the SDPs that will accompany their key role was identified in the 2006 Planning etc. Act. In their focus on the economy and greater interrelationship with economic delivery agencies, these plans can provide a means of planning and delivering investment and infrastructure at this sub-regional scale. On the other hand, they are reliant on a traditional planning approach for their process of development and adoption and there is little difference between the approaches for SDPs and LDPs as set out in Planning Circular 1 (Scottish Government 2009a). There were also proposals for city region plans which would also contain infrastructure requirements for short (five years), medium (ten years) and long term (20 years) (ibid.: §60):

> To work together to prepare a city region plan. Councils on whose a statutory requirement is placed to draw up a city region plan shall establish a joint committee with a mandatory membership. Other councils, key agencies or infrastructure providers should be invited to work with a joint committee where they have a role in delivering the strategy.
>
> (ibid.: §63)

SDPs are now beginning to develop. Edinburgh and South-East Scotland's SDP covers six local authority areas, The Borders, Fife and the four Lothian authorities, and a committee has been set up. In Aberdeen, two of the four local authorities in the city region had been working on a structure plan in the previous system and decided to publish (Aberdeen 2008) this before beginning work on the SDP. In Glasgow, there are eight local authorities that make up the city region. The SDP has been taken forward through the work of an existing joint committee for Glasgow and the Clyde Valley that was previously set up for the structure plan. In Dundee, there are four local authorities, including Fife, which is also part of the Edinburgh city region, and they have set up an organisation called TAYplan to undertake the SDP work. SDPs are in an early stage and seem to represent the only activity at city region level. All the local authorities within the four city regions are also required to develop an LDP for their areas. These will relate to each local authority's community plan. There is no equivalent of the local authority community plan, with its wider interests across each city region and no wider governance model for city regions in Scotland has yet emerged.

(III) DEVELOPMENT PLANNING

In Scotland, despite a plethora of policy reviews and new legislation, it is difficult to argue that there is currently a local system of spatial planning in operation. The Planning etc. Act (2006) has considerable similarities to the 2004 Planning and Compulsory Purchase Act in England, with the same emphasis on the role of evidence, community engagement and a requirement to identify the resources required to deliver the proposals in the plan. However, the system remains resolutely one of more traditional development planning without the integration into the local governance system that has become a defining feature of spatial planning.

The review of national approaches to planning in Scotland, as set out in 2004, had as one of its objectives to make the planning system 'fit for purpose', although the purpose was not then clearly defined. The 2006 Act requires that the new development planning system takes into account the plans and policies of other public agencies and that it should also be consistent with policies in neighbouring local authorities. In 2009, *Development Planning, Planning Circular 1* was published (Scottish Government 2009a) and states that the system should be plan-led. LDPs are to be kept up to date and that there should be a focus on outcomes (ibid.: §5). In addition to setting out requirements for SDPs for the four cities, it focusses on development plans which cover the rest of Scotland. Although defined as a development plan, the approach outlined by *Circular 1* is very similar to that set out in the first version of PPS 1 (ODPM 2005e), in its focus on:

- an evidence base
- a spatial strategy

- a vision statement
- proposals map
- resources available for implementing the plan
- alignments with neighbouring local authorities.

The key differences between the English LDF and the LDP approach being implemented in Scotland are that the LDP:

- is less focussed on delivery of public body strategies
- is not linked with Single Outcome Agreement
- is not part of a public services review
- is not required to do a public assets review
- is not clearly related with Community Planning Partnership (the nearest LSP equivalent)
- has no major landowners group
- has no delivery plan
- examination process is more focussed on planning procedure and less inquisitorial.

Development plans in Scotland have been aligned to the local community plans which have been in place since the 2003 Local Government (Scotland) Act. This relationship between Development Planning and Community Planning, which initially appears to have been strong, seems recently to have been weakened. Following a review by Audit Scotland (2006), Community Planning and Community Planning Partnerships have been moved closer to the delivery of specified and agreed targets across the public sector through Single Outcome Agreements (SOAs) introduced in 2007 (Scottish Government 2007; Scottish Government and COSLA 2007). The role of Community Planning has now been focussed towards a more *transformational* agenda (Scottish Government 2006) which has not yet included planning. However, the SOAs have included house building as one of their key targets, so this relationship between local development planning and SOAs may need to become stronger if they are to be effectively delivered. Although the role of place is mentioned (Scottish Government and COSLA 2009), it does not provide the narrative policy thread that has emerged in England. Similarly, there is no reference to spatial planning in the details of the SOA. In July 2009, Leven, in presenting *Planning Circular 1*, stressed the importance of deliverability as key elements of the development plan process but no further development of this approach has yet been seen.

(IV) FUTURE DIRECTIONS?

Spatial planning in Scotland is expected to develop in time, possibly through closer links to the wider public sector delivery model but there are no current signs that this will occur at the local level. Scotland has continued its approach to national spatial planning. Its concentration on infrastructure is a more positive approach towards improving Scotland's economy than the comparative approach in England through the Infrastructure Planning Commission, which is a regulatory tool rather than focussing on forward national investment. The approach of city regions could also be innovatory and set a model for the rest of the UK.

Why has spatial planning not emerged at the local level in Scotland? Keating has argued that in Scotland, there is more adherence to a 'social democratic model of governance which remains linked to the public service professions' (2005: 461). This may not lead to more integrated approaches but maintenance of professional boundaries. There could also be a policy lag, with Scotland not having the same focus on policy development, as Scottish policies seem to mirror those elsewhere in the UK. In a devolved administration, it could be that Scotland has taken the opportunity to concentrate on reform in other policy areas. Cooke and Clifton argue that Scotland has been more visionary in its economic policy, with the main focus on knowledge being exported and coming into Scotland as the main considerations (2005: 445).

WALES

The introduction of spatial planning in Wales was made through the Spatial Plan for Wales in 2004 and has been focussed at national and sub-national levels. This approach has been separated from development planning in Wales which remains within a traditional development planning model, although some of the new features of the system could move the local planning system closer to spatial planning practice. Early into the life of devolved government, the Welsh Assembly Government decided that spatial planning was an important tool for its own work. Spatial planning is a means of delivery since its inception and although it has developed working at national and sub-national level through sub-national and local partnerships, there is as yet very little evidence of it being used to guide and deliver investment as intended. It was also established to be the context for major infrastructure projects which are on a national scale.

(1) WALES SPATIAL PLAN (WSP)

Devolution in Wales was accompanied by what Harris and Thomas (2009) argue was an innovative approach to spatial planning in the publication of *People, Places, Futures: Spatial Plan for Wales* (Welsh Assembly Government 2004). The 2004 Planning and Compulsory Purchase Act, which covers England and Wales, requires that there should be a Spatial Plan for Wales (WSP) (s60) and that it must be approved by the Assembly. The emphasis within the WSP on inter-sectoral delivery and interrelationships between all policies which have spatial implications makes it a good example of spatial planning in practice. It has a role as part of the architecture of the emerging national state in Wales, and as a delivery mechanism for the Welsh Assembly Government. It has also been seen as part of the new political apparatus (Harris and Hooper 2004). The WSP has allowed a move away from a view of planning as regulatory control and, as such, it is difficult to associate with political choices in its need to demonstrate probity and fairness. Now it has moved to a more integrated approach to spatial planning at least at national and sub-national levels. From the outset, the WSP has been included as a part of the integrated governance, investment and delivery structure for Wales at the national level and this is one of the key distinguishing components of spatial planning.

The development of the WSP was consciously taken within the context of a newly devolved governance system that took the opportunity to align its national planning process with the approach for spatial planning emerging through the EU (Harris *et al.* 2002: 556). The introduction of the ESDP through various stages to publication in 1999 (Faludi 2004), has increasingly provided an underpinning EU policy which had a spatial or territorial dimension. As a significant recipient of EU funding, Wales was concerned to ensure that opportunities were maximised through the adoption of the spatial approaches which were epitomised in the ESDP. Following the introduction of the Wales Assembly Government in 1999, this became an early objective. Before devolution, the EU programmes directly associated with the ESDP had been delivered through INTERREG programmes but, following 2000, the evolution of a more widely integrated approach between EU spending programmes and spatial policy was emerging, not least through a new policy of territorial cohesion. The development of the WSP was an opportunity to create a plan which had Wales as its focus, could identify its key vision for the future for Wales, identify where investment was required to deliver this investment and establish a new relationship with its stakeholders and partners in the process.

The development of the WSP was undertaken by the Assembly through a stakeholder group. The Assembly was able to build on some existing institutional capacity within Wales but also to develop more (Harris *et al.* 2002: 558). At the same time, this needed to be distinctive and able to develop a 'Welsh way' of doing things. Even after devolution, Wales was seen to be heavily reliant on policy development and research commissioned by English departments of state (Powell 2001), which at that time were more concerned with the development of the Planning Green Paper (DTLR 2001b) and the introduction of spatial planning at local authority levels rather than planning at a national scale for Wales.

If Wales wanted to introduce spatial planning at a national level, it would need to forge its own approach. In part, it looked to the other nations for experience. Northern Ireland has a more spatial approach to planning, integrating economic development approaches with infrastructure planning. There were also links with

Scotland. Other models included Regional Planning Guidance in England, although this was undergoing a parallel process of reform. The Assembly commissioned research to identify the common components of spatial planning methodologies (Harris *et al.* 2002: 561) to advise the process. Reviewing this with hindsight, the research does not contain any of the key features which would now distinguish a spatial planning approach, i.e. integration, delivery and investment. However, although not operationalised into a methodology, the key identifying features were emerging, particularly through the recognition of the spatial consequences of policy making. Although a major move outside the role of the development planning system at the time, these first steps towards spatial planning seem tentative and passive. This may be due to the reducing role of planning within local governance during the 1980s and 1990s which have left it in a regulatory and marginalised mode. It could also be that the emerging role of spatial planning, as a means of delivery, was still not yet explicitly expressed although subliminally beginning to be understood.

The objectives for Wales that were set by the WAG after devolution were sustainable development, tackling social disadvantage and ensuring equal opportunity (Welsh Assembly Government 2000) and these were the main focus and drivers of the WSP. It was also the 'spatial expression of the policies and programmes of the National Assembly of Wales and others' (Welsh Assembly Government 2001: 2, quoted in Harris and Hooper 2004). The WSP had thus a policy coordination role across all the other sectors including transport, economy, environment and culture (Harris and Hooper 2004: 154). The development of the WSP has drawn on the policy documents and plans that have been prepared for Wales as a whole and has also developed a sub-national approach to policy development and delivery. In identifying its four key functions of the WSP, spatial planning emerges. The functions of the WSP were:

1   The establishment of the spatial context for all policies in Wales.
2   To provide a strategic framework for investment.
3   To provide a means of assessing the impact of WAG policies under consideration.
4   To express the different functional areas and their characteristics within Wales.

(Harris *et al.* 2002: 563–4)

This approach is interesting in that it does not suggest that the WSP stands on its own with a separate vision and agenda but is a tool for delivery. It also does not suggest that the plan should have its own evidence base but should use that which has been established for the Assembly as a whole. It also introduces the concept of 'functional area' which is now being used across other parts of the UK to recognise the difference between administrative areas and those which work together through economic or environmental geography, and has frequently been seen in urban areas in England and other parts of the EU.

These functions and features of the WSP represent significant differences in approach which had not been seen before in practice. As a new approach, the Assembly could argue a common use of evidence and the need to represent existing places rather than to create a separate vision. These represent essential components of spatial panning as a delivery mechanism. However, the use of spatial planning to provide an assessment tool for the spatial implications of policy and the economy is one that has not yet been fully developed in other parts of the United Kingdom. It is also noticeable that the assessment of the spatial implications for policy and delivery was based on sustainable principles.

The development of the WSP as a coordinating document was initially to draw from the identification of the explicit spatial elements of the other key plans and strategies. However, some of the key strategies had no explicit spatial references and this required an assessment of implicit spatial references (Harris and Hooper 2004: 154). This work extended to all the specific plans and strategies which helped to identify specific loca-tional requirements for facilities such as waste, areas of spatial interest such as rural areas and locations where specific investment was identified or proposed, particularly in the Plan for Wales (2001) (Harris and Hooper 2004).

The update on the WSP, *People, Places, Futures* (Welsh Assembly Government 2008) re-emphasises the role of the spatial approach in Wales as being 'a key mechanism in joining up our activities: nationally, regionally and locally' (ibid.: 2). On delivery, it states that the WSP presents 'a better chance of aligning the investments that *all* organisations make, whether in the public, private or third sectors' (ibid.: 3). That is done through 'delivery frameworks'. 'However, these delivery frameworks are not regarded as either being commitments to delivery or inclusive of all projects ...' (ibid.: 4). However, ministerially-led Spatial Plan Area groups have been set up for sub-national areas. The WSP update in 2008 is specifically addressing horizontal and vertical integration across current issues in policy terms but is weaker on the delivery element, albeit that it states that one of the key roles is to align investment.

The WSP update demonstrates its clear underpinning on evidence which is drawn from statistical information, commissioned and independent studies. At this stage, it does not especially include consultation feedback as an evidence strand in decision making, although it does have strong commitments to consultation and involvement elsewhere in the document. The governance of the WSP is set out as being at national, regional and local levels. At the national level, the lead is held with the Finance Minister, at regional level it is through the ministerial chaired boards and at the local level it is through the community strategies developed by the Local Strategic Boards. The local development plans are identified as one of the key deliv-ery mechanisms of the WSP and community strategies at the local level. Delivery of investment is through EU funds, regeneration funds and capital projects funded by the WAG, through a Strategic Capital Investment Board. They do not explicitly include the capital investment of other bodies such as health, local authorities or universities that may be making strategic investment decisions outside this framework.

The WSP update is made up of five interconnected thematic approaches and then area-based frameworks. The five themes are:

1   Building sustainable communities (which includes housing and health).
2   Promoting a sustainable economy (which includes infrastructure).
3   Valuing our environment (includes climate change.
4   Achieving sustainable accessibility.
5   Respecting distinctiveness.

Harris and Thomas argue that the WSP represents more a 'direction of travel' statement (2009: 57) than a detailed series of actions but it has been translated through sub-national delivery boards. This suggests that it will be shaping investment and is developing a co-production model for delivery.

(II) SUB-NATIONAL AREA STRATEGIES

The WSP is being delivered through six sub-national area strategies that concentrate on establishing a vision for the area. They then address each of the five key themes within the area and each also has a section on 'working with our neighbours' to deal with cross-boundary issues. Each of the areas has a board chaired by a WAG minister who is supported by a WAG official and a manager for the area. The action plans have been developed through ministerial led meetings and the publication of interim statements. The commitment to delivery has been through the development of initial delivery frameworks for each of the six areas and the progress towards achieving these outcomes will be through the annual report of the WSP. Progress on individual delivery plans is shown as agenda items on the six-monthly ministerial meeting agendas, although they are not shown on a common format. At present, these delivery programmes do not show any clear relationship with the WSP, although the annual report may develop this link when it is published. The delivery programmes appear to be focussed on more traditional regeneration projects rather than taking an overview of all investment in each area but this is difficult to assess as the formats vary.

(III) DEVELOPMENT PLANNING

By December 2008, there were no LDPs prepared for any part of Wales and the former UDP system which existed prior to 2004 was still being delivered with UDPs being adopted in Swansea and Neath Port Talbot – both in late 2008. Some parts of Wales have no updated plans since the 1980s, e.g. for the Caerphilly Basin or

1987 for the Menaii Strait. In some parts of central Wales, there are no approved development plans at all.

The development of integrated local governance in Wales has been focussed primarily on external objectives and internal performance. There has been a key concern to enhance the economic performance of Wales within the EU and beyond. The local focus is on the economy of Wales and there will be annual delivery reports from 2009. Whilst the WSP has been established as a formal context, the operation of the planning system in Wales at local authority level has remained within a pre-spatial mode. The introduction of UDPs was brief and was never established as a common mode of development planning. Whilst the *Planning: Delivering for Wales* (Welsh Assembly Government 2002) introduced the LDP system, the operational system has remained within a structure and local plans model. The LDP system was set up as a means of creating a single plan at local authority level with a CIS. The programme for developing the LDP must be agreed with the Assembly (Cullingworth and Nadin 2006).

Within the public services in Wales, there has been considerable pressure to focus on service improvement and greater local integration between services. In contrast to approaches to public services in England, there has long been a view in Wales that improvement was more likely to be generated through cooperative rather than competitive models of delivery, which are represented by outsourcing, performance league tables and outcome targets. The reasons for developing this approach were cultural and related to the geography of Wales which offered fewer opportunities for alternative sources of service provision than in a more urbanised England. The collaborative model for public resources in Wales has been both horizontal and vertical in its character. At the local level, there is a focus on potential co-location and sharing of back office services between public bodies such as health, police and local authorities (Andrews and Martin 2007: 150). The vertical integration has been through the relationship between the WAG and local authorities and other partners as expressed through activities such as the sub-national partnerships expressed through the WSP.

The development of more integrated working at the local level has been developed through the introduction of Local Service Boards (LSBs) in 2006, following the Beecham Review (2006). The role of the LSB is to bring together the local leaders in any area, from the public, private and voluntary sectors and together they will have 'joint responsibility for connecting the whole network of public services in their area'. LSBs are 'based on the area's community and, from this, the boards will agree, and ensure delivery of, a set of priority joint actions to achieve this. These actions will be expressed as local delivery agreements' (Welsh Assembly Government 2006). The LSBs also have lead officials from the WAG sitting on them. The LSBs meet regularly with ministers to discuss the WSP but there seems little if any interconnection with development planning at this level (Welsh Assembly Government 2009). However, Swansea has a draft delivery agreement for the LDP (2009). This agreement focusses on two uses of the role of delivery. The main thrust is an outline of how the LDP is to be delivered by the local authority and similarly to LDFs in England. The second element of delivery that is addressed is that of the delivery of key service strategies prepared by the authority and the delivery of their land-use implications, including the Community Plan, the Children's and Young People's Plan and the health social care and well-being strategy.

(IV) FUTURE DIRECTIONS?

The WSP is seen as a significant corporate tool in the future of Wales and this has been recognised through the shift of responsibility for the plan to the Strategy Division of the Assembly from the Planning Division (Cullingworth and Nadin 2006). As the WSP was expected to have a key role in influencing and representing the spatial implications of other key strategies in Wales, is there evidence that this has been achieved? Harris and Hooper point out that there has been some reluctance to do this and that the plan still remains disconnected from development planning at the local level (2006: 47). Although the WSP includes infrastructure investment and delivery as one if its key functions, this role is underdeveloped and not fully connected to funding programmes (ibid.: 143). The disconnection between the WSP and its delivery approach through area strategies on one hand and development plans on the other is significant. It seems as if there is no practical integration and this may be problematic in the longer term. It could be that the intention to develop a sub-national approach in Wales as in Scotland and England and will ease this problem in time. At present, development plans in Wales can be described as being regulatory rather than spatial or integrated and delivery focussed although, as Swansea illustrates, they might be moving forward into local spatial planning.

NORTHERN IRELAND

It can be argued that Northern Ireland was the first part of the UK to develop a systematic approach to spatial planning in *Shaping Our Future* (DRD 2001). The need to develop a more strategic approach to planning in Northern Ireland emerged alongside the new opportunities provided by the EU Peace and Reconciliation Fund, awarded in 1994. At the local level, the role of area, local and subject plans, which were introduced in 1972, continued, with the plans being prepared by the Department of Environment for Northern Ireland (DOENI), rather than by local authorities. Pressure for reform of the development planning system came following a report of the House of Commons Northern Ireland Affairs Committee on *The Planning System in Northern Ireland* in 1996 (Cullingworth and Nadin 2006: 124) but changes in response to this have been overtaken by the Review of Public

Administration. This was launched in 2002 with the objective of rescaling responsibilities within the state, including planning, and returning many functions to a newly
established local government tier.

(1) NATIONAL PLANNING

The development of a spatial planning approach in Northern Ireland was included
in the Belfast Agreement (1998). As Neill and Ellis state, 'the Agreement was novel
in that for the first time, spatial planning was acknowledged as having a crucial and
constitutionally recognised role in preparing the region for what was hoped to be
an enduring peace' (2006: 133). It also represented a significant break with the
planning processes which, up to that time, had 'a long history of almost slavishly
following policy practices in Britain' (McEldowney and Sterrett 2001: 47), but as
Morrissey and Gaffikin argue, for reshaping the structural weaknesses in the economy and social distribution of services, a spatially led approach was appropriate
(2001: 66). They go on to argue that this break with the structure and practices
of the existing planning system was fundamental to any successful changes (69).
An approach which is integrated, partnership-based, coordinated and focussed on
social cohesion (ibid.) would represent spatial planning as distinct from traditional
development plan approaches which had prevailed in Northern Ireland since 1972.

However, some of the thinking in advancing a spatial planning approach
to developing a programme for Northern Ireland had begun before this (Morphet
1996). Consideration of the emerging integrated approach to territorial cohesion
and the wider changes in approaches to EU structural funding, of which the whole
of Ireland had been a significant beneficiary, was a key stimulus. Changes in EU programmes were being implemented for urban and rural areas (Morphet 1998: 147),
both of which would have significant implications for existing funding streams. The
development work on the RDS that was undertaken in the late 1990s was significantly and consciously informed by a spatial planning approach. It also represented
a conscious effort in achieving a 'joined-up governance' approach between three
government departments (Berry et al. 2001: 785). The development of the RDS
was one of the first spatial planning documents to straddle the emerging relationship
between the European Spatial Development Perspective and the EU's Structural
Funds Programme (Neill and Gordon 2001: 33),[1] and there was always an intention
to develop and establish a model for European 'good practice' in spatial planning
(Morrison 2000: 8–9).

Shaping Our Future: the Regional Development Strategy for Northern Ireland (RDS)
was published in 2001 by the Northern Ireland Department of Regional Development
(DRD). The RDS was focussed on delivery at regional and sub-regional levels, across a
range of agencies and delivery vehicles. The sub-regional approach was seen as one that

would underpin the restoration of local government in due course. This focus on delivery and shaping the funding that would be available in a cross-sectoral way, integrating the range of a programmed investment for physical, social and economic change, fulfilled the spatial planning approach as identified in the Belfast Agreement. The leadership of the process from the DRD emphasised, perhaps ten years before this occurred in England, the strong leading role of the economic component in the spatial plan.

The RDS has many of the key components of an effective spatial plan. It is based on evidence; it has a vision, and a spatial strategy based on urban hubs, corridors, clusters and gateways. The process of developing the RDS was also highly participative (Murray and Greer 2002; Murray 2009). It is also set within a global-to-local context and within a social, economic and environmental framework. The RDS translates this spatial vision at the sub-regional level. Although geared towards implementation, the lack of a detailed implementation and delivery plan with identified funding, programmes and accountable delivery agencies might now be regarded as a weakness in the RDS, although the delivery element of the RDS is strong and well defined. It has subsequently been followed through with regular monitoring reports and five-year reviews.

The resources which were made available to implement the RDS were provided through the funding that the Belfast Agreement delivered through the EU in the Peace and Reconciliation Programme. This was initially established from 1994, but was boosted as part of the Agreement. The approach to this package was multiple. It promoted cross border working between Northern Ireland and the Irish Republic, and it prompted infrastructure investment, rural development and community-based projects at the local level. A cross-sectoral Civic Forum was established in Northern Ireland to manage and steer the process of change and investment. This work continues with the EU's PEACE III Programme which, under a range of key thematic programmes, is primarily aimed at building positive relations at the local level, acknowledging and dealing with the past, creating shared space and developing key instructional capacities with a programme of €333m.

The examination of the RDS was through a public process that was themed and based on an inquisitorial approach rather than one that was adversarial. It also included a 'challenge' by the panel examining the RDS (Murray and Greer 2002: 204). This was put through the chair of the panel rather than through a cross examination of those raising questions. As with proposed Regional Strategies in England, the RDS was subject to Examination in Public (Murray and Greer 2002: 199–201) and so the influence of the RDS in the shaping the reception of spatial planning processes at regional scale continues.

There are various views about the success of the RDS, which Ellis and Neill believe has been greatly exaggerated (2006: 130). Their criticism relates to an initial 'optimism bias' which they see in the original document which, in their view, did not deal with the substantive issues for Northern Ireland in a fundamental way. As Berry *et al.* (2001) point out, there were tensions from the outset in central government. The three government departments which were brought together to create the RDS had, just until that point, all been part of the same department. There were potential issues of fragmentation and reforming, although the process was tied into to the wider delivery programmes of these new departments through their PSAs (ibid.: 785–6). One of the key weaknesses in hindsight could be the lack of a more detailed delivery plan which identified which government department or agency had the responsibility for specific delivery (ibid.: 788). Murray has also argued that although a technically confident, positivist approach was taken, the RDS deals less well with issues of 'identity, segregation, interconnections and potential' (2009: 126).

Since its publication, the RDS has been the subject of a monitoring report each year with the first years' report entitled the *First Implementation and Monitoring Report September 2001–March 2003.* Subsequent annual reports have lost the implementation focus and been either annual reports or annual monitoring reports, which have been outcome focussed assessments of progress against objectives and targets rather than of the delivery of components of the RDS. So it is possible to assess the outcomes from the delivery of the RDS but not to view the extent to which it has been used as a means of sharing funding and investment decisions within Northern Ireland as a delivery programme.

(II) DEVELOPMENT PLANNING

At the local level, development planning in Northern Ireland has been largely unreconstructed from the model that was established in 1972, although recommendations have been made for changes over time. However, following the publication of the RDS, there was a growing recognition of the need for a relationship between the RDS and the local development plan as a delivery mechanism. The discontinuity between the RDS and the development plan system, particularly when making decisions on particular applications, came to a head in 2005 when a joint ministerial statement was issued between the DRD and DOENI. In this, the slow progress in reviewing the development plans was recognised as a threat to 'the successful implementation of the RDS' (DRD and DOENI 2005: §16). As a result, the statement confirmed that decisions on planning applications would be made within the context of the RDS and confirmed that all development plans had to be in conformity with the RDS.

Much of the delay in the changes to the system have been dependent on the Review of Public Administration which commenced in 2002 and which has been focussing on the rescaling of responsibilities within Northern Ireland. A key feature of this has been the development of a new model of local government delivered through 11 newly formed local authorities. Planning has always been a key component of these reforms with the expectation that a new system would be delivered through the local authorities. In 2007, the Northern Ireland Assembly Government invited Professor Greg Lloyd to provide advice to them on the reform of the land-use planning system within Northern Ireland (Lloyd 2008).

The terms of reference for Lloyd's report and its subsequent recommendations did not suggest the wider introduction of spatial planning at the local level. Instead, it reaffirms a separate land-use planning system which is not connected with the wider planning and delivery responsibilities of the new local authorities when they are set up. Further, it proposed the insertion of a new regional tier of planning without any reference to the relationship with the RDS and it does not make these relationships clear. The consistent references to land-use planning in Lloyd's report serves to identify its separation from a spatial planning approach which would be more integrated. Although development control is proposed to be changed into development management, it is not clear how its delivery role will be implemented. In Northern Ireland, for the time being at least, capital planning is being conducted at a regional, i.e. national scale, and at the local level there is a reaffirmation of a separate traditional development planning system.

The ministerial response to Lloyd's paper, however, may move planning closer to the spatial planning agenda at the local level. In the report on *Planning Reform: Emerging Proposals* (DOENI 2008), one of the key purposes of the new local plan led system is the coordination of public and private investment within the overall framework of supporting economic and social needs of communities within Northern Ireland (8). Like Scotland, Wales and England, local authorities will have to produce and present a management scheme for development preparation and there will also be a Statement of Community Involvement. This approach has been confirmed in the consultation of the *Reform of the Planning System in Northern Ireland* published in July 2009 (DOENI). The objectives of the new planning system will, like Scotland, Wales and England, be to promote economic growth and proposes that development planning and development management will be undertaken by the 11 new local authorities. Significant applications will be determined centrally in the same way as Scotland and England and regional policy will also be developed centrally.

The new approach to local development planning is focussed on speed and stakeholder engagement. A Plan Strategy will be developed in association with Site Specific Policies and Proposals and these will be the two separate components of the LDP. Additionally, the development plan will be closely allied to the community plan developed by the district councils, similar to approaches in Scotland and England. The role of the LDP in identifying and supporting delivery is contained in the functional objectives as set out in §3.7. The examination of the plan documents will move from an adversarial to an inquisitorial process and the plan will be examined against ToS with English and Welsh models being provided as examples (DOENI 2009: annexes 4 and 5). The LDP will need to be in general conformity with regional policy, although this is to be interpreted at the local level. It will also have a focus on delivery and be required to include measures for implementing the plan which can also include delivery agreements and master plans (ibid.: §3.44–3.45).

(III) FUTURE DIRECTIONS?

The introduction of spatial planning through the RDS was a significant national innovation and this work has informed all subsequent practice. Its links with the development of the economy and EU funding foreshadow later developments in Wales and England. At the local level, the introduction of LDPs that move away from stand-alone, traditional development plan approaches will be challenging. Much of the success of these changes will relate to the extent to which cultural change, which needs to be multi-dimensional, can be achieved. This issue is acknowledged (DOENI 2009: 119). A range of measures is proposed for training and development support for planners and other stakeholders to support this culture change including the use of student bursaries, community aid and a version of a Planning Delivery Grant. The transfer of power for local development planning from central government is going to be difficult, not least as this will be within the context of new local authorities with wider ranging powers. On the other hand, the scale of such change could make it easier for spatial planning to be established in a new integrated format from the outset rather than encountering the difficulties faced by inserting it into an existing system.

Although there are no specific linkages between the proposed development planning system and the rest of local governance and delivery, it is clear that the delivery of the new approach to planning within local authorities will engage a far wider range of interests than those in the planning service. So spatial planning at the local level in Northern Ireland looks as if it will be underway in much the same framework as the rest of the UK after 2011.

CONCLUSIONS: DIVERGING OR CONVERGING SYSTEMS OF SPATIAL PLANNING?

The conclusion that can be drawn from this review of the UK nations' spatial planning systems is that ten years on from devolution, the systems remain similar, with the same characteristics and requirements, albeit with different names and delivered in different time frames. Each of the four nations has developed an approach to spatial planning which has focussed on a different spatial scale. There has also been knowledge transfer between the four nations. The innovation of the RDS in Northern Ireland informed the WSP, which also set out to be innovative. The WSP has developed this approach further by being defined as a major tool in the delivery of the whole of the Welsh agenda that has some spatial implications. It has also been used to evaluate the spatial implications of potential policy considerations. The WSP has also had a clear approach to delivery through the sub-national boards. This approach has also been taken up in Scotland through the city regions but their delivery mode has yet to be fully developed. If sub-national approaches derive from spatial planning in Wales and Scotland, in England they are emerging from economic policy through city regions and MAAs and here the spatial planning underpinning is coming through LDFs at the local level.

The development of spatial planning in Northern Ireland informed the regional reform process in 2004 in England, when the RSS was introduced, and tensions apparent between government departments representing the economy, planning/ local government and rural affairs in Northern Ireland are also apparent in England. In Wales, the decision to bring the WSP into the centre of government under the Finance Minister has addressed this issue and in Scotland the focus of NPF2 on national infrastructure has much the same effect.

In Scotland, there has been leadership in the development of strategic plans for each of four city regions. Although in Wales, there are sub-national spatial planning areas, these are larger than city areas and they cover the whole of the territory of Wales. SDPs in Scotland may be nearer in scope and intention to the range of city region pilots emerging in England, whereas the sub-national approach in Wales may represent what is likely to occur in other sub-regions in England as an outcome of the implementation of the Sub-National Review of Economic Development and Regeneration (SNR) (HM Treasury 2007a; CLG 2009d and e) that will be redeveloped and delivered through MAAs between the state and the locality. In England, these sub-regional approaches are developing without a specific spatial planning component, although some local authorities are joining up their LDFs in a common process or through a single Joint Core Strategy.

In England, the delivery of spatial planning has been at the local level through LDFs which are required to be prepared for each local authority area in England and at present, although the local planning systems in Scotland, Wales and Northern Ireland all have similar delivery objectives set within them, these have yet to be activated operationally. There was a similar delay in England between 2005 and 2008 so the focus on local delivery may emerge in due course.

In reviewing spatial planning approaches across the four nations of the UK, a number of similar themes emerge and these are shown in Box 10.1. They are developing within different time scales and in each nation a different scale seems to be more predominant. Once the lead has been 'tested' in one nation, then the pattern is that it is then applied in the other nations. The four nations meet regularly to discuss planning systems and operation and this cross influence may be one of the results of this continued dialogue. The shaping factors on spatial planning in England will be equally influential; in the other nations comparing ways of responding to these is not surprising.

Box 10.1   Common themes in national spatial planning within the UK

The common themes emerging for spatial planning within the four UK nations are:

- a primary focus on the economy as a key outcome of spatial planning;
- the identification of national infrastructure investment and ways that it should be implemented;
- national/regional, sub-regional and local spatial scales are all emerging as operational levels for spatial planning;
- an emphasis at all scales on delivery;
- spatial planning approach is being observed through integrated delivery models;
- assessment of spatial planning at the local level is moving from adversarial to inquisitorial mode;
- at the local level, horizontal integration is developing, albeit at different rates.

Source: The author

A second key conclusion that can be drawn from this review of the spatial planning systems in Wales, Scotland and England is the similarity between their formal processes and the wording that is used for each of them and their components. The main differences are emerging through application and implementation of these processes. Hence, English LDFs were required, through the ToS, to provide evidence of their deliverability. At the outset, this was assumed to be concerned with the deliverability of the planning documents rather than the infrastructure and investment required to deliver the plan (Morphet *et al.* 2007). The role of the LDF as a means of achieving delivery was subsequently reaffirmed through a revision to PPS 12 (CLG 2008c). The development of local delivery plans in Wales is primarily focussed on the delivery of the plan documents and not with the outcomes of the plan.

Another area where similarities can be found is in the reforms to the architecture of local governance. These reforms relate to all the spatial scales and are associated with the development of spatial planning in each nation as identified above. The development of strategic development plans in Scotland includes a grouping of local authorities that make up a city region in much the same way as a sub-regional grouping for an MAA in England. At local level, all administrations have systems of local targets and outcome agreements between the central and local state, although the names differ. In England, there are Local Area Agreements, in Scotland, Single Outcome Agreements and in Wales, Local Delivery Agreements. At the local level, all have cross-sectoral boards which have been established to develop a joint vision based on evidence and to find ways of instituting better ways of joining up service delivery to improve the focus on service users, efficiency and improvement. In Scotland, these are community partnerships, in England, LSPs and in Wales, Local Service Boards. Finally, all four nations have a form of community planning which is increasingly at the heart of the planning and delivery process and which forms the context for spatial planning.

CHAPTER 11

SPATIAL PLANNING IN EUROPE, NORTH AMERICA AND AUSTRALIA

INTRODUCTION

The development of spatial planning is an international phenomenon (OECD 2001). At the international level, spatial planning remains a generic and slippery term which is relational in its local definition and application. Yet everywhere, spatial planning is understood as something that is more than land-use planning and that is integrated with other policies to deliver interventions within and between different spatial scales. This book has concentrated primarily on spatial planning at the local scale because this is a particularly strong feature of English spatial planning. In other parts of the UK, spatial planning is more dominant and developed at other scales. In this chapter, there is a focus on spatial planning in Europe, the United States and Australia. The purpose of this is to provide the context for the English system of spatial planning, to demonstrate some of its antecedents and to indentify any potential trends for the future in spatial planning policy and practice. Spatial planning is a dynamic activity that seeks out approaches and solutions to the challenges that it confronts from a variety of locations.

The business of reviewing spatial planning approaches and practices in other countries is immediately beset by issues of comparing approaches within different cultures (Friedmann 2005; Sanyal 2005). Comparative studies can focus on different aspects of national planning systems and then consider differences and similarities within them. This is an 'input' method. It is also possible to consider if there are comparable outcomes from spatial planning. Does spatial planning in different countries deliver similar outcomes although through different culturally bound means? This second approach is more likely to be used in Europe. The overarching spatial planning framework in Europe creates similarities in individual spatial planning systems, albeit that they operate within different governmental traditions. In Europe, regions are also a predominant governance scale, whilst at the local level, local authorities are more likely to have legal autonomy than in England. This chapter identifies some of the European spatial planning commonalities and how these are influencing the English system, both now and as it continues to develop in the future. One of the conclusions of this discussion is that English spatial planning lies centrally in the heart of European approaches.

Beyond Europe, there are also frameworks that bind together approaches to spatial planning and delivery. These come through organisations such as the OECD which has taken an interest in spatial planning as part of its economic localism agenda (OECD 2001). There are also strands of policy from other institutions such as the World Bank. Governments are hungry for new policy ideas, particularly if these have worked in other cultures (Cabinet Office Strategy Unit 2009). Governments are less concerned about the cultural provenance of successful initiatives and have more interest in the type of mechanism they may represent. They continue to search for approaches that can be transplanted or translated, albeit approximately. For English spatial planning, the dominant influences outside Europe have been from the United States and Australia.

The combination of these European, American and Australian influences on frameworks and approaches leads to an essentially hybrid system of spatial planning in England. The extent of these influences may reflect a significant turn in the development of spatial planning in England; there has been an expectation of influencing international planning practice rather than drawing from it. There has been some discussion about how far this new approach to spatial planning represents a paradigm shift from earlier English planning practice (Sanyal 2005; Shaw and Lord 2007; Morphet 2009b). Taylor (1999), for example, argues that there is no paradigm shift but rather that there are a number of potential elements of English spatial planning which suggest that its new approach represents a significant break with immediate past practice. The paradigm shift may not be in the context of spatial planning (Sanyal 2005) but rather in its process (Morphet 2009b). The 'communicative turn' in planning is much spoken of where planners have advocated a more deliberative approach to planning (Healey 2006). In contrast to this model, there is a spatial planning reality (Newman 2009) set by legislation and developed through practice. As Booth suggests (2005; 2009), it is the interconnection between the system, set within its cultural context and the influences on it, from whatever quarter, that creates the process that is in use. It is this approach to English spatial planning, influenced by Europe, the United States and Australia, that this chapter will focus on.

THE CHARACTERISTICS OF SPATIAL PLANNING IN EUROPE

Spatial planning in England operates within an integrated local governance model and its prime focus is delivery within this context. The focus on developing an integrated approach to planning has a strong economic driver behind it, particularly in the delivery of housing and infrastructure. This economic imperative is drawn from the United States and from the EU, neither of which have a common system of spatial planning, although there is a meta-narrative which provides the context and framework within which spatial planning operates (Morphet 2006). The ways in which spatial planning operates within the EU as a whole are discussed in detail in other texts such as Faludi and Waterhout (2002), the *EU Compendium of Spatial Planning Systems and Policies* (CEC 1997) and Duhr *et al.* (2010). The European dimensions of spatial planning provide a context for English spatial planning. Europe also provides an arena within which English spatial planning can perform.

As Cullingworth and Nadin (2006) demonstrate, the development of an approach to spatial planning within the EU has been slow but steady. In the early years of policy development, the movement towards creating a more integrated approach was largely hidden or brushed aside in the UK, at a time when anti-EU politics were dominant (Tewdwr-Jones and Williams 2001; Jensen and Richardson 2006). This ignored the growing role of EU legislation in key areas of domestic policy such as transport, the environment, public health and competition policy and has left a knowledge vacuum at the heart of English planning practice. In place of this understanding, a distraction emerged that perceived the EU as a primary provider of funding. Duhr *et al.* (2010) show the extent of the influence of this pan-EU legislative platform within which all spatial decisions within the EU are now located.

A key driver for the EU approach to spatial planning, which has been one of voluntaristic cooperation rather than an area within any treaty, was the development of the Single European Market in 1992. This was instigated as a mechanism to ensure that the fragmented regulatory regimes that existed in the EU were not disadvantaging Europe in an era of global competition. There were perceived to be no similar barriers to trade in large economies such as the United States and Canada. The drive to include spatial planning as part of this consideration came from three different directions. The first was a concern about the costs and potential intra-EU benefits from different regimes for planning regulation. The maintenance of different planning and building regulation regimes was seen to be creating a financial burden which could be addressed. The simplification of planning application processes in England has been one of the outcomes of this approach, not least since this was identified as one of the key processes to be available through e-government methods in 2000 (CEC 2000).

The second driver for more concerted action was that of competition to attract mobile business between different parts of the EU. The use of spatial designations together with other incentives could make it easier for businesses to move short distances across national borders in order to gain more favourable operating conditions such as easier planning consent. The high proportion of land borders in Europe made this a real threat and a component of internal competition when the focus should be competition in the world markets. On the other hand, administrative boundaries seldom reflect the reality of places as people understand and use them. They often have common underlying geographies and boundaries which have owed more to political rather than cultural divides. Borders have also been places of conflict. The potential role of common approaches to territory, including planning, have been considerations in overcoming these divides through specific territorial programmes such as INTERREG (Diez and Hayward 2008).

The third approach to spatial planning in the EU represents a fundamental and underlying shift. As Duhr *et al.* (2010) demonstrate, the whole programme of spatial planning has been set within a programme of *cohesion.* The context for this was Europe 2000+ (1994), which showed common interests in Europe not by member states but through relational geographies. Programmes such as INTERREG have been set up to encourage cross-border working in Europe and within these geographies in order to foster this principle of cohesion, now retermed *territorial cohesion.*

However, this approach to cross-border working also underpinned a fundamental shift in the way that the EU worked. This was a move from a spatially selective approach to interventions to one that included all parts of the territory. In retrospect, the 25-year period when the EU focussed its spatial attention on economic and social interventions in lagging regions was stepping out of a longer-term direction rather than resetting an approach. Before the UK joined the EU in 1973, territorial policy had reflected that in France and Germany which was inclusive of all places. This can be seen in the term *amenagement du territoire,* that suggests 'public action envisioning the spatial disposition of people, activities and physical structure based on a balanced notion reflecting the geographical and human situation within the space under consideration' (Dupuy 2000: 11, quoted in Faludi and Waterhout 2002: 30). Faludi and Waterhout point out that this phrase has not had a specific translation into English that captures its full meaning and that the economic components of the French concept of spatial planning are never understood within the English context.

In joining the EU, the UK was keen to have a major portfolio and to bring some of its own policy interests into influence in the EU. Without a more specific, spatially interventionist approach, the contributing support that the UK gave to its lagging regions would soon be in danger, whilst other major portfolios were already allocated (Young 1998; Grant 1994). The French had long held the lead on agriculture, and the Spanish, who entered at the same time as the UK, were keen to lead on transport given the scale of national modernisation required in their own infrastructure (Faludi and Waterhout 2002). The UK was given the regional economic portfolio and this selective policy approach was inserted into EU working. This gave life to the structural funds and their major impact on infrastructure spending in the following period.

The withdrawal of this more selective approach to regional assistance and its replacement with a more 'holistic' approach to 'economic and social development' was proposed by the then President of the Commission, Jacques Delors at the first meeting on spatial planning in Europe in Nantes in 1989 (Faludi and Waterhout 2002: 36). By the time that the Maastricht Treaty was signed in 1992, a deal negotiated by the then UK Prime Minister, John Major, ensured that the structural funds package would be the last of the existing style. Following this, there would be a return towards a full territory model. In political terms, this was partly argued as a responsible response to EU enlargement, when it would not be possible to support accession states with the same levels of structural funds. It also represented the return of the pre-1973 model of territorial working.

As part of this 1992 funding package, Trans European Networks (TENS) were further supported. These have created major transport corridors across European and helped to improve some of the major transport linkages. Schemes that have benefited for this funding have been new rail investment as well as roads. The TENS also support telecommunications and other utility grids as part of a major programme of improvement. They have started to form economic development corridors on the back of this new infrastructure investment. By 2005, Polverari and Bachtler could write that the basis of EU territorial policies was the geography of place and those that lived there (2005: 37). This approach is now being copied by the United States. As part of the Obama package for stimulating the economy, investment in infrastructure is a key priority. The Regional Plan Association is leading this work (Carbonell and Yaro 2005).

Spatial planning in the EU is emerging as a key component in EU policy development such as Territorial Policy Integration (TPI) (Schout and Jordan 2007: 836; Faludi 2004). In this approach, spatial planning is now seen to be an important component in integrating layered spatial policies within delivery programmes which have EU funding such as INTERREG or within a national context, an indirect EU source such as Neighbourhood Renewal or transport projects. The development of a more 'balanced' approach to territorial cohesion has left some challenges to consider how competitive approaches between regions can be turned into more cooperative behaviours, particularly when investment is coming from outside the EU. As Tewdwr-Jones and Mourato (2005) point out, the attraction of this type of investment does not generally relate to planning policy but other financial invectives that are available to regions where the economy is lagging. A shift to an approach which promotes the whole area and reduces the funding support to economically lagging areas will leave them more dependent on their ability to offer skilled labour at competitive prices. Much business now takes a global view of locations and the most attractive locations may now well be in China or India. This details a switch away from chasing footloose but incentive-hungry companies to developing sustainable business to serve more local markets within Europe and will require different approaches to economic growth within localities.

The spatial planning approach for the EU has been set out in the ESDP that was agreed in 1999. Its main purpose is 'to work towards a balanced and sustainable development of the territory of the European Union … through achieving the three fundamental goals of European policy in all regions of the EU:

*   economic and social cohesion
*   conservation and management of natural resources and the cultural heritage
*   more balanced competitiveness of the European territory'.

(CEC 1999: foreword)

As Faludi and Waterhout state, the ESDP is no 'masterplan' (2002: 159) because although it is described as a framework, it does not have a role in determining decisions in member states. However, it exerts some influence and power in the convergence of policy and there are examples of where these approaches are already emerging. In England, for example, the development of urban–rural partnerships (CEC 1999: 25) in order to support rural communities and strengthen the functionality of regions is already emerging through MAAs. Other groups of local authorities have also set up growth partnerships, e.g. Cheltenham, Gloucester and Tewksbury which relate to the urban areas and their rural hinterland. Leicester and Leicestershire have established an MAA as a partnership between a city and the surrounding area which is part commuter belt and part deep rural hinterland. Parity of access for information (CEC 1999: 26) has been developed through Broadband Britain (HM Treasury 2009d) which seeks to enhance coverage and speed all over England. Another key element was the proposal that infrastructure should be better used and incorporated more within the spatial planning system (CEC 1999: 28), with much greater cooperation between transport provider policies within specific areas. The new approaches to Local Transport Planning and its integration into LDFs is an example of this occurring in England (DFT 2009).

The interrelationship between the ESDP and INTERREG funding has begun to have some outcomes in bringing places together. The EU mega regions have provided a means for regions within their areas to come together in a positive way to explore and compare policy responses to issues. Dabinett (2006) illustrates through the VISP (see www.vispnet.org) programme within the North Sea Region that the European approach has also promoted the notion of more integrated approaches through spatial planning. As Kidd has pointed out (2007), this has been growing. This integration is occurring in three ways:

*   horizontal integration – between place
*   vertical integration – between spatial scales
*   organisational integration.

Horizontal integration between sectors, organisations or localities may be a more familiar approach within mainland Europe. Within England, vertical integration has remained the dominant form in planning, although increasingly less so in wider public policy since 2000. In much of Europe, horizontal policy integration may be important between adjoining areas which are located on borders. In England, horizontal integration has been concentrated on organisational integration within localities primarily through the local LSP, SCS and LAA.

As spatial planning has developed, it is possible to see the emergence of its integrated reforms in local government and set more firmly within the local governance architecture as a delivery mechanism. In France, as Booth shows, spatial planning has 'deliberately been seen as a means of consolidating reform of local government' (2009). The development of a *schema de coherence territoriale* introduced in France in 2000 as a means of representing an approach to planning in urban areas (Booth 2005) has some similarities with the LDF system proposed in the Planning Green Paper (DTLR 2001b) and then introduced in England in 2004. As in England, the reforms of planning and local government in France were 'intended to be mutually reinforcing' (Booth 2005). Booth identifies these changes at the local and sub-regional level, where local authorities have been encouraged to work together to deliver 'contracted' outcomes, similar to MAAs in England and city regions in Scotland. Booth questions whether the English and French systems of spatial planning are converging and, although he believes that there is no argument to support this, he does see what he describes as a 'common thread' between the two systems (2005: 283).

The reforms on local government in Northern Ireland has been undertaken at the same time as the reform of the planning system (see Chapter 10) and Amdam discusses this integration in Norway (2004). In Denmark, at the local level, the spatial plan is often integrated with local authority plans for the economy, health and culture and the reform of local government in 2007 has elevated the municipal plan to be the overarching plan for the area and any local plans must operate within it (Danish Ministry of the Environment 2007). Sehested (2009) has described this as a hybrid form of planning where planners are at the nexus of local delivery and place within a governance framework.

Although Dabinett (2006) has described working together within the EU across different countries as primarily a learning model, where institutional and policy processes can be compared, experience suggests that its influence is stronger than this in practice. The development of project-based working at the local level is an essential feature of cultural change and learning which supports a journey to a more common approach but not the destination. In England, the influence of the EU in the practice of spatial planning is multi-faceted and includes:

- horizontal policy integration at the local level;
- consistency and coherence between spatial policies in all spatial scales;
- the focus on city regions (although this may also be a US influence on EU policy);

- the increasing informal designation of Functional Urban Areas (FUAs) which are sub-regions that can be developed as a means of extending the EU's potential for growth outside its economic centre;
- the development of mega regional approaches within England, e.g. the Northern Way;
- fair access to services and facilities for all citizens within a spatial context for delivery.

As Faludi and Waterhout (2002) indicate, the ESDP has not developed much beyond its agreement in 1999. Does this mean that spatial planning in Europe has come to an end? Although there have been fewer explicit outcomes since 1999, there have been other initiatives which suggest that the spatial planning approach set out in the ESDP is being developed further. There is also evidence that this integrated approach to spatial planning is being implemented within member states. If this is to happen, then there needs to be some stability in the centrally led development of policy. One of the main arguments against the continuing role of spatial planning has been that the borders and states within the EU are becoming increasingly fuzzy so that state-based, regulatory planning systems are no longer applicable. However, as Faludi (2009) argues, the EU now presents 'a range of spatial contexts within which planners can exercise their skills' (ibid.: 37) and that the role of spatial planning will continue to develop. This might be confusing but already represents the overlapping and interleaved approaches that spatial planning seeks to integrate at present.

(I) THE EMERGING ROLE OF TERRITORIAL COHESION

Although the notion of territorial cohesion has been developing in the EU over a long period of time, it has now become a dominant determinant of policy and delivery. It is also a mechanism for promoting almost any policy initiative: 'cohesion' is an elastic concept and can be pulled in any direction required as a justification for action. It also creates a platform for networked models of governance (Bevir and Rhodes 2003) which blur the boundaries of institutions and organisations. Territorial cohesion has also been included in the consultation on the future direction of the EU (Jensen and Richardson 2006) which has been embodied in the Lisbon Treaty, which has been agreed but not yet ratified across Europe. As Zonneveld and Waterhout (2005) state, territorial cohesion 'should not be used as a synonym for spatial planning policy', although Schon asks if it is the new 'buzzword' for spatial planning (2005: 390). Rather spatial planning is one of the mechanisms for delivering territorial cohesion. The policy outcomes for territorial cohesion are critically concerned with fairness which is measured through a range of outcome indicators. Viewed in this way, spatial planning is an input to achieving outcomes, not an outcome in itself (Schafer 2005).

There is a continuing debate about the role of spatial planning. Healey sees it as the 'shaper' (2007), Mazza (2003) as the hinge between plans and places, whereas it may be more like a handle, a means to open up and deliver change. The role of the territorial cohesion policy within the EU is being reviewed as part of the implementation of the Lisbon Treaty to be introduced in 2013. The Barca review has been undertaken as part of this process. It argues that 'there is a strong case for allocating a large share of the EU budget to a place-based development strategy' (Barca 2009: vii). The underlying drivers for this assertion are similar to those being seen in England for spatial planning through its transformative role that is to 'reduce the persistent underutilisation of potential inefficiency' including assets or people. It also sees the future in 'bundles of integrated public goods and services' (ibid.: 25). The case for this approach is supported by the need to promote sustainable approaches and managing cross border interdependencies.

In the Barca review, the risks of place-based strategies are set out and reflect the disadvantages of the UK's approach to more selective interventions in the period 1973 onwards until the policy reforms started in 1988. These risks are set out by Barca as:

*   sheltering regions from markets
*   creating a dependency culture
*   fueling rent – extracting machines at the local level
*   failing to give enough certainty to businesses or individuals who invest in the process
*   prevent agglomerations.

The processes working in English Regional and sub-regional policy are all addressed to resolving these issues as part of their intervention strategies.

In the review, Barca recommends five key elements to a strategy for the future as shown in Box 11.1.

Box 11.1   The Barca recommendations 2009

Review of EU's Territorial Cohesion Policies – the recommendations of the Barca review

1   Concentrating resources on priorities, e.g. for social exclusion, children, migrants, economic issues.
2   Orientating grants to results:
     a Establishing new European Strategic Development Frameworks to be used to assess investment and outcomes.

b   Establishing a new 'contract' relationship between EU and member states at the regional level.

c   Strengthening governance for the delivery of core priorities.

d   A system of performance monitoring through the use of targets and monitoring.

e   A scoreboard approach to outcomes.

f   Promoting innovation through some flexibility.

3   Mobilising and learning:

a   Developing evidence of what works – i.e. evidence-based policy making.

b   Promoting counterfactual impact evaluation.

4   Strengthening the European Commission:

a   Making staff more responsible for achieving delivery.

b   Linking personal progressing to performance.

c   Promoting inter directorate working to achieve joined-up outcomes.

5   Reinforcing political checks and balances through increased assessment and scrutiny of contact and outcomes.

Source: Barca 2009

(II) How is EU policy influencing spatial planning in England?

There are considerable similarities between the Lisbon Treaty, the Barca review and the policy processes implemented in England including LAAs, the duty to promote the economy, transformation and performance management in places through CAAs. However, it is difficult to say at this point whether England is leading EU policy or preparing for the changes that these might bring post-2013. There could also be the stimulus for a reinvigoration of the ESDP, which might be part of or allied to the proposed *European Strategic Development Framework.*

EU policy has had a shaping influence on England's spatial planning policy in a variety of ways. It has to conform to the frameworks that are incorporated into the EU's competences. These are primarily for environmental standards including waste and also for major transport investments through the TENs. There are also other policy areas such as public health which are having a major influence on policy and delivery at the local level in reducing obesity and environmental actions to reduce other disease (NICE 2008). The application of the territorial cohesion policy also has implications for investment and support for declining economies, whilst the rural development policies are a major instigator of interventions in rural areas.

In a European context, the planning system in England has been regarded as primarily regulatory and concerned with land use. In this way, it has similarities with other European states and uses similar tools such as developers' contributions to contribute towards infrastructure (Ache 2003). However, how far is now true since the implementation of spatial planning? The outcomes of spatial planning inevitably bind on the protection and investment of place and there are also wider components contained within the LDF process that go beyond regulatory approaches to land-use planning. One example of this is the remodeling of public sector services to ensure that they are best located to meet the needs of the communities that they service (CLG 2008c) which appears to be an almost complete transportation of the requirements of territorial cohesion policies. Janin Rivolin (2005) argues that the UK has always been a performing rather than a conforming system as it has not developed strong approaches to zoning land or adopting building codes.

In addition to those policies of 'conformity', Janin Rivolin also identified a series of European policies which are performative in their nature. Through these policies, which are not part of the EU's competencies, member states including the UK initiate change and policy initiatives which are not required but nevertheless 'perform the agreed collective strategy' (2005: 168). Janin Rivolin cites spatial planning as one these 'performing' policy areas where initiatives are not 'implemented' but rather 'applied'. There can be some debate about whether planning in England is a performing or conforming model. Planning practitioners would be surprised to see that the system that they work in is not considered a 'conforming' one. They would cite the strong vertical pressures that exerted on them in a hierarchical way and the need to undertake a version of environmental assessment as part of the development permission system. Perhaps a better way of describing this would be to determine whether this conformity is in the process.

The conditions that are required to implement spatial planning also need to be created and this takes time. The development of the integrated approach to local governance structures in England creates the conditions within which spatial planning can operate effectively. The development of city planning in Scotland is another example of the approaches being developed in other parts of the European Union, e.g. Bilbao, Dublin, Lille and Munich. In Wales, sub-regional planning has moved away from a traditional land-use approach to one which is integrated with the delivery of public funding initiatives including the structural funds, which are still available to meet economic and social issues.

One outstanding issue in relation to spatial planning in Europe is how far it is converging. There is now a formal agreement to deliver a more unified spatial planning system across the member states, although the Lisbon Treaty makes greater convergence inevitable. These converging forces are shown in Box 11.2.

Some of these influencers are worth discussing in more detail. When nations are working within a common framework but have their own power of initiative, the policy process represents a fugue where the themes and initiatives have strong

Box 11.2   Forces of conformity in European spatial planning

A spatial dimension to policy development and evaluation
- Programmed and regular spending reviews that target priorities for change.
- Evaluation of interventions at the local level.

Forms of development
- Corridors – with development being associated with transport investment.
- Polycentricity – the associations of groups of smaller towns to provide a sustainable solution.
- City regions.

Environmental
- Policies and action on climate change create a common baseline.
- The application of a common approach to Environmental Impact Assessment on all projects, plans and programmes.
- Through specific activities including waste management, mineral extraction, biodiversity, water quality.

Economic
- The recent economic crisis forcing a closer view on reducing regular operating costs of businesses.
- The need for the EU to be more competitive in the global market.
- Structural reforms in member state economies.
- Longer-term development of the internal market.

Transformational governance
- Reduction in fixed operating costs of public bodies.
- Fairer and more sustainable access to local services.
- The development of integrated investment programmes delivered through spatial planning processes.
- Cross-border working between adminstrative and political areas within and between states.

Source: The author

common features and objectives, but the manner and timing of their delivery will depend on national choice. The same policy fugue is apparent in the EU albeit on a larger scale. The pattern of elections, cultural differences in the way that initiatives are introduced and delivered does not disguise their similarity in provenance and intent. The 'spatiality' of policy making which has been introduced into EU approaches through both the ESDP and territorial cohesion policies have begun to make their way into England (Hope and Leslie 2009). In the ESDP, this is promoted through cross-border working and the INTERREG programme but the same approach is developing within England through sub-regional working in MAAs and between regions in the Northern Way. The implementation of the LDF system within that of the joined-up governance structure provides further example of this approach at the local level.

Polycentricity describes how many German cities interoperate with each other. German cities are generally smaller than the more major cities in other countries and the interdependency between them creates attractive places to live on a scale which supports more sustainable lifestyles. As Faludi has also shown (2005), the adoption of a polycentric approach to territorial cohesion has also been part of a wider EU approach to global economic competition. Polycentricity is a concept that works for much, although not all, of England. In the larger urban centres, the pull of London or Birmingham feels overwhelming. However, around major cities such as Manchester or in West and South Yorkshire, there are networks of towns which work on an interdependent basis for services, culture and employment. Polycentricity is also apparent in more rural regions such as the East Midlands, where Nottingham, Leicester and Derby are close together and all play leading roles. In the South-West, major regional bodies and facilities are distributed between Bristol, Taunton, Exeter and Plymouth (ODPM 2003a).

Another key area where European influence is at its strongest in spatial planning is through the EU's environmental directives and regulations. These are apparent in a number of ways and many of them form the requirements of the evidence base for spatial planning. As Schout and Jordan have pointed out (2008b), the environmental integration has been a key objective of the EU since the Fifth Environmental Action Plan (CEC 1992; Morphet 1992). Since then, the progress towards the development and application of standards has progressed steadily. The EU's environmental agenda is likely to be increased through the standards that are applied as it deals with climate change but also because the progress towards the implementation of integrated environmental regulation has not worked as well as had been anticipated (Schout and Jordan 2008a: 959). The changing position of the United States post Obama's election means that the fears of environmental regulation leading to uncompetitive economic outcomes is now reduced and allows a more international approach to be developed.

As always, where similar initiatives are rolled out, there is always a question of why this occurs. Is it planned? Does a good idea in one place just 'catch on' somewhere else? Are governmental policy machines constantly hungry for new approaches to solving problems? Are policy initiatives another form of fashion? The answers to all of these questions may all be positive to some degree. Knowledge transfer works in many ways. As Janin Rivolin and Faludi (2005) have suggested:

> British perspectives have cast light on the crucial but complex link between
> spatial planning and land-use planning. Consequently, they have paved the way

for a conception of European spatial planning as embedded in a multi-level governance system that could reach from the supranational to a local level.

(2005: 211)

SPATIAL PLANNING OUTSIDE EUROPE

Although the context provided by spatial planning practices in the EU, including the ESDP, have been important for the development of English spatial planning, these have not been the only influences. The role of the United Sates in the manner in which its planning system has been strongly focussed on the economy has had some influence and may have been responsible for the economic turn in the focus of English spatial planning that has been growing cumulatively since 1997. Achieving sound economic growth is not only the aim of the planning system in England but in Wales, Scotland and Northern Ireland as well. If the US focus on the economy has had a marked influence on the objectives of spatial planning in England, the Australian focus on spatial planning as a means of delivery has had an equal influence. In Australia, the infrastructure turn (Dodson 2009) is having an equally significant role at the operational level. The hybridity of the English spatial planning system may reduce some of the objections about this approach in Australia. In the English system, infrastructure delivery is being used as a means of horizontal integration at the local level rather than primarily about the private sector. The way in which these approaches have become infused within English spatial planning are now discussed in more detail.

(I) PLANNING IN NORTH AMERICA

A major influence on the role of spatial planning in England post-2004 has been economic (Bennett *et al.* 2004). This can be seen as part of an international trend in promoting economic growth through spatial competitiveness and governance. It is an increasing intertwining between public and private sector approaches to development where, as Teitz argues, the sharp divides between the public and private sectors have softened to the point where public–private entities can easily be established to reflect developer planning objectives (2002: 195). As Brenner states, this can be understood as 'an outcome of complex, cross-national forms of policy transfer and ideological diffusion' (2003: 306) and, although Brenner relates this approach primarily to Western Europe, it is also a key policy strand of the OECD through their Local Economic and Employment Development Programme (LEED).

Planning in the US is described by Birch as being 'often messy' (2005: 332). Planning operates within a federal structure, where the individual states cede power to the centre. In planning, the federal government has some powers over transportation and water which can have implications for planning decisions. In turn, the states cede their power to the municipalities, that create planning commissions and bring together comprehensive planning for areas with provisions for implementation including zoning and capital investment (ibid.: 333). The transition of planning in the US from one that had sharp divisions between the public sector and the private sector has also seen a change in the role of the professional planner. As Teitz points out, the planner's new emphasis on communication, transparency and meaningful participation has led to other changes in the role of planners and their value systems, 'one in which the professional is less an autonomous designer-hero than a creative intermediary, translator and technical resource in a process that truly empowers its participants' (2002: 197). This may be an oversimplified view, as Teitz admits, but it represents the supporting role of planners rather than as those with the answers.

In North America, there has been an emphasis on 'smart growth' which has focussed the sustainable role on existing urban areas. Although this is based on using existing infrastructure more effectively, there is an interest in building more infrastructures where this can support sustainable lifestyles. As Neuman (2009) points out, effective infrastructure that is green and well managed can provide cities with competitive advantages. The new economy needs a new approach. For the US, infrastructure planning and delivery is at the heart of strategic and spatial planning. Neuman also points out that leading planners in the American Planning Association are 'spearheading' infrastructure 'to raise infrastructure to a new strategic level in the planning profession' (ibid.: 210).

In Canada, the economic impetus has also had an important role as local authorities have increasingly used charges on developers to fund infrastructure. As Wolfe (2002) sets out, these have become an important and growing source of capital funding for hard and soft costs both on and off site. Like the United States, Canada has also engaged in initiatives for 'smart growth' to achieve more compact forms of urban development and directing its locations. As Wolfe states, the problem of managing growth has been one of perceived fragmentation, where a number of local authorities have difficulty in coordinating growth. Canada, like France, has been pursuing an amalgamated approach to municipalities to cover urban areas, although this has been through formal reorganisation rather than more informal, softer working arrangements. In Canada, there has been a joined-up approach to local infrastructure planning and delivery for capital investment although as Bradford (2005) suggests, this would benefit from an approach associated with the provision of a more cultural and community infrastructure. However, there is a pressure to move to more project-based approaches which cross tiers of governance with multi-level agreements to support strategic approaches.

(II) PLANNING IN AUSTRALIA

The last and least recognised key influence on the role of spatial planning post-2004 is that deriving from the late-Blair approach to public services. This asks the question of how much 'worth' public services are delivering (HMG 2007a). Much of the focus of this delivery discussion has been on education and health services, but the continued focus on planning delivery, particularly housing, has been a key concern of Government since 1997. It has started to view the role of planning in a different light, frustrated by what was regarded as planning's poor performance in determining planning applications and its seeming failure to produce enough land for government-projected housing requirements.

In England, this third approach has been translated into a consideration of what contribution planning makes in exchange for the public funding that it receives (Morphet 2007b). This has generally been interpreted as being a more detailed consideration of how the planning process maintains property values, protects specific environments and identifies land for new housing. Planning is now being asked 'what is its public worth?' In this approach, an assessment of the financial investment in planning through public support for staff and democratic processes is being weighed against greater measurement of the financial and community returns which flow from planning activity.

This new evaluation of planning has led to it being given a more proactive role, i.e. in the use of existing assets and resources. At present, there is no calculation of the value of annual capital investment at the local level from the public, private and voluntary sectors and this is now emerging as a key interest for the integrated spatial planning task. Up to now, planning's main role in this process has been through the development control process, where it has been central to achieving developers' contributions, although this has been more of a sporadic process than is generally recognised, with only 14 per cent of new dwellings generating development contributions (Audit Commission 2008b). The deliverability role of spatial planning is concerned with the management of local investment, including the public sector, whilst development contributions are becoming a more systematised part of the process through the adoption of the CIL or through more standardised applications of current approaches.

The approach towards making better use of existing assets and investment is also being implemented at central government level, where government departments are now being required to report on their asset use on a quarterly basis as set out in PSA 20 (HM Treasury 2007c). This process is designed to bring greater alignment and integration to government spending and has profound effects on public sector funding streams.

Planning is not only being asked to deliver change on the ground through its normal processes of plan making and development regulation but has now to go beyond this in two ways. The first is to manage infrastructure delivery in a more integrated and 'transformational' way where public sector land and buildings are reviewed as part of the LDF (CLG 2008c: §2.5). The second is to achieve a more consistent level of contributions from private sector investors. This has now been developed based on practice in Australia and New Zealand. Planning is being asked to add value through regulation. This has also been marked through the introduction of 'development management' to replace 'development control' in English practice.

Planning in Australia is state based and is derived from a system largely inherited from the UK. It is argued by Gleeson and Low (2000) that the Australian system has been one based on shared values that have used the regulation of property rights as a mechanism for wider community benefit. The introduction of a more neo-liberal approach to planning, which has included a greater focus towards the private sector together with a more urbanised society has frequently been compared with the US but, as Gleeson and Low point out, the difference between the outcomes in the US and Australia have largely been based on the differences in the regulatory frameworks that have remained in Australia despite its neo-liberal turn. In Australia, new urban development remains within a wide sustainable framework and reducing other outcomes such as social segregation. On the other hand, some of the state governments have blamed the planning system for inhibiting new investment (Hamnett and Lesson 1998). Another contributor to the problems of investment has been the privatisation of the public sector as part of the implementation of the GATT Agreement on world trade and public services in 1992.

In the Australian system, Priority Infrastructure Plans (PIPs) have to be drawn up for all areas, although there is an assumption of a priority towards designated growth areas. The provision of new development is closely related to the contribution of new infrastructure to go with it and the concept of 'green infrastructure' relates primarily to that provided in association with greenfield site development. The provision of infrastructure as part of the development permission process is also in effect in metropolitan areas. Dodson argues that this process is now regarded as a solution to urban problems (2009: 109) and goes on to point out the risks of seeing cities through an 'infrastructure frame' (ibid.: 110). However, as described by Dodson in a Melbourne case study, the infrastructure planning process has not been integrated within the spatial planning system but operates separately from it. In some ways, this represents the negotiated approach to developers' contributions in England which, because of the way in which the legislation is being used, relate to the development but not necessarily to the place as a whole.

The approach that integrates mainstream public sector budgets with developers' contributions for the delivery of infrastructure is typical of planning practice in Australia and New Zealand where local authorities use Development Contributions Plans for all development (Christchurch (City of) 2007; Wilmoth 2005). In Australia, the role of 'the planning profession is specifically concerned with shaping cities, towns and regions by managing development, infrastructure and services' (Planning Institute of Australia). In New South Wales, for example, 'state infrastructure is funded by the NSW government using state infrastructure contributions and general revenue' (www.planning.nsw.gov.au). Development Contributions Plans are made under s94 of the Environmental Planning and Assessment Act 1979 (Dollery et al. 2000; Lang 1990; McNeill and Dollery 1999). The objectives of the Development Contributions Plans are to provide an administrative framework which will ensure that contributions can be made to ensure that public facilities are provided to address the cumulative demand from new development and ensure that the existing community is 'not burdened by the provision of public amenities and public services required as result of future development' (Sydney (City of) 2006: 15).

The Development Contributions Plan is set at a baseline so that current standards are maintained or are improved. The infrastructure requirements in specific areas are identified and 'the works in the Contributions Plan are apportioned over all new development, large and small' (ibid.: 16). The Contributions Plan also includes a management charge for administration. The New South Wales Government has recently reviewed its system and in Circular PS 08–017, issued in December 2008, the purpose of this review was stated as 'to ensure that infrastructure levels are consistent with the Government's plans to boost housing supply and affordability as well as support business and provide a stimulus to the construction industry' (ibid.: 1). In reviewing the approach to raising infrastructure levies, the timing is important and the package of measures in the circular reflect both a wish to stimulate construction and to reduce costs on some types of development. As a consequence of the reforms, the state is making a larger contribution of infrastructure planning than hitherto, whilst local authorities' ability to raise levies has been curtailed. However, the system will still be in effect despite the downturn.

The approach to infrastructure planning in Australia has been viewed in a variety of ways. Sandercock argues that this approach comes from a period when most of the state capital investment infrastructure was going to support 'private sector resource development projects' (2005: 325), leaving little for urban areas, whereas Dodson (2009) argues that this approach has skewed development within urban areas. Gleeson and Low (2000) criticise this approach as being a strategy that has left little space for projects to support communities, whilst Maginn and Rofe argue that it is the disenfranchisement of many of the peri-urban communities that has driven the need to provide more infrastructure alongside the growth to ensure that most Australians are not exiled from 'the heart of rural Australia' (2007: 204). Low Choy *et al.* (2007) argue that there needs to be greater integration between urban and peri-urban planning processes to bring together governance with investment in these peri-urban growth areas.

In England, this approach is being translated into the LDF process, which will identify what infrastructure is required and how it will be funded using mainstream budgets. Added to this will be competitive funding bids, and private and voluntary sector investment. The role of developers' contributions, through the introduction of a CIL will complement this process as a funding stream. It will focus developers' contributions more systematically on pre-determined requirements as identified through the LDF rather than being one-off negotiations. It will also encourage a more systematic use of developers' contributions than has been the case hitherto, with many local authorities failing to collect contributions on the basis that they are uncertain about the legal position or being concerned that the application of a contributions policy will deter development. The implementation of CIL at the local level will depend on having a sound Core Strategy (CLG 2008c), in an echo of the system in New South Wales where a Contributions Plan has to be in place before developers' contributions can be collected (Dollery *et al.* 2000: 311).

CONCLUSIONS

The international development of spatial planning inevitably leads to cross fertilisation of ideas and practices. Some of these are shaped by overriding economic forces and others by new trends in governance. The approach to spatial planning in England is drawn from a range of practices. The focus on integration has strong European ties, not least where this is with local government structures. Where this integration has been more vertical between governance scales, it is moving to one that is more balanced between horizontal and vertical models. This inevitably has the effect of encouraging institutional and organisational integration. These local structures appear to be in transitions to ones that have a greater cross sectoral approach, with mixed economies and early evidence of organisational reverse engineering, where the local takes over the responsibilities of other spatial scales further up the hierarchy.

CHAPTER 12

SPATIAL PLANNING: WHAT DOES IT ALL ADD UP TO?

INTRODUCTION

Spatial planning in England has, until recently, provided an opportunity for integrated delivery to change places. Planning has only been able to identify what needs to be done but then has had to rely on others to exercise the power of initiative. It has not had a leadership role in developing and delivering systematic programmes of change in places over periods of time. It has often not been engaged in proactive approaches to regeneration, location of major new facilities such as community hubs or extended schools. Spatial planning reasserts this delivery role again. Spatial planning has the powers and the tools now to achieve these changes in ways that work through the use of evidence, consultation and with partners. The provision of additional housing remains an important focus of spatial planning but we now see this within the context of existing communities, facilities and wider infrastructure. Strategic sites are new pieces of townscape that need to integrate with existing areas, add quality to them and secure their futures.

The introduction of spatial planning provides both opportunities and challenges. The opportunities for place shaping, coordination and enhancement of communities are considerable and the power of place as a leading narrative for our times cannot be underestimated. Spatial planning also provides a way of bringing together discussion between organisations about plans, to break down silos of difference and the competitive approaches that they sometimes bring. It presents ways of working within the ambit of the LSP and to deliver social, green and physical requirements for any area. Spatial planning is mainstream not peripheral. It is concerned with the investment budgets that are spent locally. These can frequently be hundreds of millions of pounds in a local authority area. The investment of two new schools, a health clinic and some flood defences can be considerable. Planning has moved from having a marginal, although important role in generating additional resources through developers' contributions to a central role in the whole budget. As Table 12.1 demonstrates, spatial planning now has an integrated role which is horizontal and vertical, it is at the heart of delivery and supporting the economy. This is very different from land-use planning and demonstrates the shift that spatial planning represents in practice.

This also provides some challenges. Planners need to extend their informal, negotiating and networking skills in order to ensure that they are effective in

Table 12.1 Integrated spatial planning: characteristics and implementation

Characteristic of integrated spatial planning	Manifestation in the post-2004 system	Delivered through
Horizontal integration	**LDF Tests of Soundness** Consistency and coherence with neighbouring authorities Duty to cooperate Joint Core Strategies Sub-regional partnerships/Multi Area Agreements	Tests of Soundness Voluntary arrangements Voluntary and legislative
Vertical integration	National planning policies Regional planning policies	Tests of Soundness
Organisational integration	**LAAs** **CAA** Duty to cooperate	Central government contracts
Local economic growth	New duty to assess economic conditions Sub-regional economic Improvement boards	As yet to be determined
Infrastructure delivery	**LSP** oversight of resources Existing public sector funding Fees and charges Asset maximisation Transformation Community Infrastructure Levy **CAA**	Audit Commission

Source: the author

operating the spatial planning system. This has presented some initial tensions as understanding has been developing. However, once the opportunities of spatial planning are recognised, planners report that they find this 'exciting', 'what they came into planning to do', 'fascinating' and 'enthusing'. Communicating this more widely will also take time but partners and infrastructure providers recognise the strength of working together and some have said 'at last! This is the final piece of the jigsaw for working together'. English spatial planning has developed at the local scale and can contribute this experience to others. It can also learn from others at different spatial scales whether in Europe, Australia, South Africa or North America.

THE SEVEN CS OF SPATIAL PLANNING

Can spatial planning be distilled into some key principles? In this section, seven Cs of spatial planning are identified which encompass spatial planning and how it is practised. The introduction of spatial planning has created a larger, more central and important role for planning which is concerned with delivery. It has an extended scope and has a fundamental position in the delivery of investment – whether public, private or voluntary – at all spatial scales. Its emerging importance will make it likely that it will be a more corporate activity, taken into the centre of organisations such as local authorities. Identification of infrastructure investment requirements will have a leading role in place shaping, locating future investment and ensuring that this investment can be delivered in a timely and appropriate way. This important role suggests some key implications for the delivery of spatial planning:

1 CORPORATE

The development of new approaches to spatial planning is likely to be more corporate in its nature. The development of spatial delivery programmes which will see the combined use of capital funding across the full range of public agencies suggests an activity that will be central to the core of any public organisation. This is a particularly important role for local authorities, who also have the convening role for all bodies at the local level through the LSP and for orchestrating delivery through partners and associated bodies. The role of spatial planning in identifying social, physical and green infrastructure requirements with service providers and other private and community investors is central to the local task but not one that can be done without the involvement of other departments and activities.

2 COOPERATIVE

The development of a spatial planning approach requires more cooperation than has been the case for land-use planning preparation and processes hitherto. The land-use planning process has frequently been seen as legalistic and process driven and which takes some time to complete. For those wishing to achieve key change in localities, including public services, other tools such as master planning, or special organisational delivery vehicles have been used with a regeneration lead.

Now that spatial planning embraces the full range of infrastructure investment activity, it requires that those leading on the planning component need to undertake this work in a more cooperative framework. The LSP has no powers to compel different public sector organisations to spend their budgets in ways that are mutually supportive, so much of the development and delivery of infrastructure plans and programmes will need to be undertaken in a new way. This cooperation can take place within an LSP delivery sub-committee or other similar arrangements where places that have changing demography, intensified populations or which are newly developed can all be considered in a joined-up way.

Spatial planning is the process that draws all this together and the planners can support the development and delivery of these plans and monitor their implementation. They can also seek investment through proactive development management. They can advise on change and assess the potential locations for this investment, including the addition of co-location or service realignment through restructuring the use of land and building assets to everyone's benefit.

3 CONTRACTUAL

The nature of spatial planning is now contractual. The role of LAAs and MAAs as contracts between the locality and the state bring with them a different relationship for the delivery of investment. Before 2009, the delivery of housing through development planning that was identified in the relevant RSS was regarded as a contextual and allied process between the regional and local levels. Under the new 'contractual' system, implemented through LAAs, each local authority area is contracted to deliver a certain number of houses, affordable homes and/or housing sites ahead of the adoption of the development plan. The number of housing units that is included in the 'contract' is based on the regional assessment but these can be subject to local drifting. Also, this leaves the local authority no room to renegotiate the housing numbers once they have reached the submission stage of the development plan. The 'contracted' numbers could precede the findings of the evidence through local studies such as SHLAA and SHMAA and may not give much room for manoeuvre. One consideration is that the economic downturn has meant that all housing numbers identified in the LAA may be difficult to attain in the period 2009–2012. However, the shift to a contractual basis for housing delivery is an important one.

4 CONSULTATIVE

Planning has always been consultative and the introduction of spatial planning has brought with it both a more developed approach to involving stakeholders, partners, landowners and communities through the preparation of a SCI and the duty to involve. Initially, the process used to underpin the SCI was an issue to be considered at the same time as the development plan was considered to be sound. The implementation of the 2007 Local Government and Public Involvement in Health Act has moved the consultation approach for spatial planning into the wider sphere of the LSP. Instead of consultation being undertaken and considered for the development plan alone, it now is part of a wider cross authority and partner consultation approach which ensures that all consultation activity can be considered together as part of the plan-making process. Spatial planning will reposition the role of consultative approaches and bring them to the heart of its concerns.

5 COHESIVE

The process of spatial planning is concerned with social, community and territorial cohesion. In its relationship to spatial and community cohesion, the application of the principles of spatial planning through delivery, whether by the private, public or voluntary sectors, has distributional effects that need to be considered. The selection of areas for action to promote regeneration or development can have a significant effect and implications. These may receive attention, investment and general uplift; other areas can be more stable with less change. There may be community concerns that there is less investment in these areas and this can cause resentment. Some areas are never quite bad enough for action or not quite good enough for investment. Taking an overall view of infrastructure requirements and deficiencies enables every area to be considered against a set of local standards and actions to be considered that address these local issues.

Spatial planning is aligned with the delivery of territorial cohesion. This is an EU policy that has been included in the Lisbon Treaty. This represents a similar shift towards 'place' in EU policy making and focus. It has similar characteristics to the more culturally centred approaches to regeneration through communities and sub-regions that has been the basis for English policy since 2004. Territorial cohesion works through the power of difference and accepts that to achieve beneficial ends for any area, different approaches are needed to achieve positive outcomes. It has some already familiar characteristics. It suggests a contractual relationship between places and scales which is based on specific objectives, the use of resources within an overarching strategy. It is led within a partnership framework and the achievement of core priorities would require a reinforced reporting framework. It would be based on local priorities and expertise. Barca states: 'In a place-based policy, public interventions rely on local knowledge and are verifiable and submitted to scrutiny' (2009: vii).

Within England, sub-regions have been selected as the spatial scale where cultural differences can be recognised. Within these, local areas and communities make the multiple contributions that propel places forward. Will the EU approach to territorial cohesion have an influence in England at the local level? Spatial planning's focus on identifying vision and deficiencies and how to deliver change is at the forefront of territorial cohesion approaches. The English model of local spatial planning promotes territorial cohesion.

6 CLIMATE CHANGE

Spatial planning has a key role in supporting the delivery of solutions to reduce the impacts of climate change. In the coming decade, the need to deal with adaptation and mitigation of climate change is likely to be a main driver of policy and delivery of strategy. The climate change themes will work their way through into practical delivery through spatial planning. In addition to supporting international action and change in developing countries, in England they will mean the enforcement of carbon budgets to cap emissions, greater low carbon energy generation and preparing for flood risk. In many areas, this will represent a retrofitting programme for drainage and energy systems and energy production through recycling. It may mean a major programme for all types of housing to bring it up to acceptable standards. Climate change will also have an influence on the design of buildings and homes. Spatial planning has the role of bringing together more sustainable ways of living and working and identifying areas at risk from climate change (DECC 2009).

At the local level, spatial planning will be identifying opportunities to support low carbon activities and helping communities capture the benefits that they may bring. LAAs include a range of low carbon targets and 97 per cent of local authorities have adopted one of these targets (CLG 2009d). These will need to be delivered through the LDF. In the longer term, more detailed approaches may be developed.

7 CAPITAL PROGRAMMES

Capital programmes make up the last key component of spatial planning because they represent the means of achieving delivery. Capital programmes are formal accounting tools that demonstrate how any organisation is investing in its long-term future. They are required to be shown on the balance sheet of all organisations in ways that help to identity specific projects or programmes. In the private sector, they may be used to assess the worth of a company.

Capital programmes in the public sector are a product of a range of funding sources and legacy approaches. The size of any capital programme budget will depend on an organisation's assets, a willingness to borrow and its effectiveness in capturing funding from competitive sources. Some capital programme projects may depend on the delivery of new government initiatives and policies, including polyclinics and Building Schools for the Future.

Some public sector agencies undertake joint capital ventures with other organisations and the private sector. There may be a pooling of assets and risks to support development. Local authorities may use their compulsory purchase powers to assemble sites that can be used to support major redevelopment. The extent to which any organisation has capital assets is almost accidental and for local authorities there have been major transfers at times of local government reorganisation. In 1974, the transfer of assets was primarily from district councils to county councils. In the later round of the creation of unitary councils, these transfers have been from county councils to new unitary councils or a redistribution of assets between local authorities. Each local authority takes a different approach to capital investment. Some local authorities take pride in being 'debt free' which means that they will only fund any investment from within their own resources and not take on any borrowing. Others will trade their property assets and raise loans in order to be able to redevelop the town centre, build a swimming pool or a theatre. Many other local bodies own assets that can contribute to these opportunities.

Spatial planning is concerned with the use of capital at the local level by all organisations. Initiatives such as Total Place, Total Capital and the publication of Local Spending Reports will make this a more routine process. Spatial planning's role is to work with those who make these investment decisions at an early stage to ensure that this investment is made in effective and efficient ways that support the community's future.

WHAT'S NEXT FOR SPATIAL PLANNING?

Spatial planning in England was established in 2004. In the first five years since its introduction, there has been a transition in understanding of the major differences with the system that preceded it and the opportunities that it provides. To some extent, spatial planning has been awaiting other governance reforms that are now in place and can enable it to operate in an integrated framework and turn its full focus on delivery. The coming period will see this further embedded. As spatial planning develops, it is likely to turn its attentions to other spatial scales, most notably sub-regions. Here, the concerns for transport, housing and regeneration make spatial planning's integrating role a central part of the sub-regional project. Sub-regions may cover the whole of England by 2020 and, by that time, spatial planning may have returned its attentions to regions again. Spatial planning will develop and respond to changes in the coming years, whilst its roots will remain in shaping and delivering places.

NOTES

CHAPTER 1

1   www.localpriorities.communities.gov.uk.

2   http://www.ogc.gov.uk/better_asset_management.asp.

CHAPTER 4

1   A more detailed description of flooding types is set out in Annexe C of PPS 25 (CLG 2009j).

CHAPTER 6

1   CAA Guidance www.audit-commission.gov.uk.

CHAPTER 10

1   At the time, the balance of EU structural funding programmes was beginning to switch from areas that were economically lagging through the application of the structural funds, to an approach which was more 'edge to edge' across all of the EU's territory and emerged as a policy of territorial cohesion and an expanding of the INTERREG programme. This process continues to rebalance the allocation of EU programme resources.

REFERENCES

6, P., D. Leat, K. Seltzer and G. Stoker, (2002) *Towards Holistic Governance: The New Agenda in Government Reform*, (Basingstoke: Palgrave Macmillan).

Aberdeen, City and Shire Strategic Development Plan Authority (2008) *Structure Plan* (Aberdeen: SDPA).

Ache, P., (2003) 'Infrastructure Provision and the Role of Planning in the Ruhr Region', in Ennis, F., (ed.), (2003b) *Infrastructure Provision and the Negotiating Process*, (Aldershot: Ashgate), 135–54.

Albrechts, L., (2006) 'Bridge the Gap: From Spatial Planning to Strategic Projects', *European Planning Studies*, 14:10, 1487–500.

Aldridge, S. and D. Halpern, with S. Fitzpatrick, (2002) *Social Capital: A Discussion Paper*, (London: PIU/Cabinet Office).

Alexander, E., (2009) 'Dilemmas in Evaluating Planning, or Back to Basics: What is Planning For?', *Planning Theory and Practice*, 10:2, 233–44.

Allmendinger, P., (2001) 'The Head and the Heart: National Identity and Urban Planning in a Devolved Scotland', *International Planning Studies*, 6:1, 33–54.

Allmendinger, P., (2006) 'Escaping Policy Gravity: The Scope for Distinctiveness in Scottish Spatial Policy', in Tewdwr-Jones, M. and P. Allmendinger, (eds), *Territorial Identity and Spatial Planning: Spatial Governance in a Fragmented Nation*, (Abingdon: Routledge), 153–66.

Allmendinger, P. and G. Haughton, (2006) 'The Fluid Scales and Scope of Spatial Planning in the UK', *Project paper 2*.

Allmendinger, P. and G. Haughton, (2007) 'The Fluid Scales and Scope of UK Spatial Planning', *Environment and Planning (A)*, 39:6, 1478–96.

Allmendinger, P. and M. Tewdwr-Jones, (2000) 'Spatial Dimensions and Institutional Uncertainties of Planning and the "New Regionalism"', *Environment and Planning (C)*, 16:6, 711–26.

Allmendinger, P. and M. Tewdwr-Jones, (2006) 'Territory, Identity and Spatial Planning', in Tewdwr-Jones, M. and P. Allmendinger, (eds), *Territorial Identity and Spatial Planning: Spatial Governance in a Fragmented Nation*, (Abingdon: Routledge), 3–21.

Amdam, R., (2004) 'Spatial Planning as a Regional Legitimating Process', *European Journal of Spatial Development*, 11, 1–22.

Amin, A., N. Thrift and D. Massey, (2003) *Decentering the Nation: Radical Approach to Regional Inequality*, (London: Catalyst).

Anderson, B., (2006) *Imagined Communities*, (new edition), (London: Verso).

Andrews R., and S. Martin, (2007) 'Has Devolution Improved Public Services?' *Public Money and Management*, 27:2, 149–56.

Ashworth, R., (2003) *Evaluating the Effectiveness of Local Scrutiny Committees, ESRC report on award R000223542*, (Swindon: ESRC).

Atkins, (2008) *Local Development Frameworks: Evidence Bases*, (London: PAS).

Audit Commission, (2002) *A Force for Change*, (London: Audit Commission).

Audit Commission, (2004) *People, Places and Prosperity*, (London: Audit Commission).

Audit Commission, (2006a) *Securing Community Benefits Through the Planning Process*, (London: Audit Commission).

Audit Commission, (2006b) *The Planning System: Matching Expectations and Capacity*, (London: Audit Commission).

Audit Commission, (2008a) *In the Know*, (London: Audit Commission).

Audit Commission, (2008b) *Positively Charged*, (London: Audit Commission).

Audit Commission, (2008c) *A Mine of Opportunities*, (London: Audit Commission).

Audit Commission, (2009a) *Comprehensive Area Assessment*, (London: Audit Commission).

Audit Commission, (2009b) *Is There Something I Should Know?*, (London: Audit Commission).

Audit Commission, (2009c) *Draft Strategic Approach to Housing (KLOE)*, (London: Audit Commission).

Audit Commission and IDeA, (2002) *Acting on Facts: Using Performance Measurement to Improve Local Authority Services*, (London: Audit Commission).

Audit Scotland, (2006) *Community Planning: An Initial Review*, (Edinburgh: Audit Scotland).

Baker, M. and S. Hincks, (2009) 'Infrastructure Delivery and Spatial Planning: The Case of English Local Development Frameworks', *Town Planning Review*, 80:2, 173–99.

Baker, M., J. Coaffee and G. Sherriff, (2006) 'Achieving Successful Participation in the New UK Planning System', *Planning Practice and Research*, 22:1, 79–93.

Balls, E., (2003) 'Foreword', in Corry, D. and G. Stoker, (eds), *New Localism*, (London: NLGN).

Barca, F., (2009) *An Agenda for a Reformed Cohesion Policy: A Place-based Approach to Meeting European Challenges and Expectations*, (Brussels: CEC).

Barker, K., (2004) *Review of Housing Supply*, (London: HM Treasury).

Barker, K., (2006) *Review of Land-use Planning*, (London: HM Treasury).

Barnes, M., (2008) 'Passionate Participation: Emotional Experiences and Expressions in Deliberative Forms', *Critical Social Policy*, 28:4, 461–81.

Beecham, J., (2006) *Making the Connections: Delivering Beyond Boundaries: Transforming Public Services in Wales*, (Cardiff: Welsh Assembly Government).

Bennett, R.J., C. Fuller and M. Ramsden, (2004) 'Local Government and Local Economic Development in Britain: An Evaluation of Developments Under Labour', *Progress in Planning*, 62, 209–74.

Beresford-Knox, T., (2003) 'Good Management in Planning Departments', *Planning*, 18 July, 21.

Berry, J., L. Brown and S. McGreal, (2001) 'The Planning System in Northern Ireland Post-devolution', *European Planning Studies*, 9:6, 781–91.

Bevan, G. and C. Hood, (2006) 'What's Measured is What Matters: Targets and Gaming in the English Public Health System', *Public Administration*, 84:3, 517–38.

Bevir, M. and R. Rhodes, (2003) *Interpreting British Governance*, (Abingdon: Routledge).

Bevir, M. and F. Trentmann, (eds), (2007) 'After Modernism: Local reasoning, Consumption and Governance', *Governance, Consumers and Citizens Agency and Resistance in Contemporary Politics*, (Basingstoke: Palgrave Macmillan).

Birch, E.L., (2005) 'U.S. Planning Culture Under Pressure: Major Elements Endure and Flourish in the Face of Crises', in Sanyal, B., (ed.), *Comparative Planning Cultures*, (New York: Routledge), 331–57.

Bishop, J., (2008) Presentation to PAS event for councillors, Warwick University Business School, 30 January.

Bishop, K., M. Tewdwr-Jones and D. Wilkinson, (2000) 'From Spatial to Local: The Impact of the European Union on Local Authority Planning in the UK', *Journal of Environmental Planning and Management*, 43:30, 309–34.

Blears, H., (2002) *Communities in Control*, (London: Fabian Society).

Boaz, A., L. Grayson, R. Levitt and W. Solesbury, (2008) 'Does Evidence-based Policy Work? Learning from the UK experience', *Evidence and Policy*, 4:4, 233–53.

Boddy, M., J. Lovering and K. Bassett, (1986) *Sunbelt City? A Study of Economic Change in Britain's M4 Growth Corridor*, (Oxford: Clarendon Press).

Bogdanor, V., (2009) 'Straw has wasted his chance to wield the reformer's broom', *The Guardian*, 21 July, 26.

Booth, P., (2005) 'The Nature of Difference: Traditions of Law and Government and Their Effects on Planning in Britain and France', in Sanyal, B., (ed.), *Comparative Planning Cultures*, (New York: Routledge), 259–83.

Booth, P., (2009) 'Planning and the Culture of Governance: Local Institutions and Reform in France', *European Planning Studies*, 17:5, 677–95.

Bounds, A., (2009) 'Manchester heads council revolution', *Financial Times*, 23 July, www.ft.com.

Brabham, D.C., (2009) 'Crowdsourcing: The Public Participation Process for Planning Projects', *Planning Theory*, 8:3, 242–62.

Bradford, N., (2005) *Place-based Public Policy: Towards a New Urban and Community Agenda for Canada*, (Ottawa: Canadian Policy Research Network).

Brenner, N., (2003) 'Metropolitan Institutional Reform and the Rescaling of State Space in Western Europe', *European Urban and Regional Studies*, 10:4, 297–324.

Brenner, N., (2004) *New State Spaces: Urban Governance and the Rescaling of Statehood*, (Oxford: Oxford University Press).

Brown, G., (2009) *Prime Ministerial Statement on Constitutional Reform*, 10 June, (London: Hansard).

Brown, G. and D. Alexander, (2007) 'Stronger Together: The 21st Century Case for Scotland and Britain', *Fabian Ideas 621*, (London: The Fabian Society).

Brownill, S. and J. Carpenter, (2007) 'Increasing Participation in Planning: Emergent Experiences of the Reformed Planning System in England', *Planning Practice and Research*, 22:4, 619–34.

Bruce-Lockhart, S., (2004) *Innovation Forum Kent Public Service Board*, (London: ODPM).

Burgess, G. and S. Monk, (2007) *The Provision of Affordable Housing Through s106: The Situation in 2007*, (London: RICS Education Trust/Joseph Rowntree Foundation).

Burrows, R., N. Ellison and B. Woods, (2005) *Neighbourhoods on the Net: The Nature and Impact of Internet-based Neighbourhood Information*, (Bristol: The Policy Press).

CABE, (2006) *Physical Activity and the Green Environment*, (London: CABE).

Cabinet Office, (2008) *The Pitt Review: Lessons Learned from the 2007 Floods*, (London: Cabinet Office).

Cabinet Office Strategy Unit, (2009) *Power in People's Hands: Learning from World Class Public Services*, (London: Cabinet Office).

Calman, K., (2009) The Calman Commission on Scottish Devolution, (London: The Swiftland Office).

Cameron, D., (2009) Speech to Open University, Milton Keynes, 26 May.

Carbonell, A. and R. Yaro, (2005) 'American Spatial Development and the New Megalopolis', *Land Lines*, 17, 1–4.

Carmona, M. and L. Sieh, (2005) 'Performance Management Innovation in English Planning Authorities', *Planning Theory anLuxd Practice*, 6:3, 303–33.

Carmona, M., S. Marshall and Q. Stevens, (2006) 'Design Codes: Their Use and Potential', *Progress in Planning*, 65, 209–89.

CEC, (1992) *Towards Sustainability: The Fifth Environmental Action Plan*, (Brussels: CEC).

CEC, (1994) *Europe 2000+ Cooperation for European Territorial Development*, (Brussels: CEC).

CEC, (1997) *The EU Compendium of Spatial Planning Systems and Policies*, (Luxembourg: CEC).

CEC, (1999) *European Spatial Development Perspective: Towards Balanced and Sustainable Development of the Territory of the European Union*, (Brussels: CEC).

CEC, (2000) *Common List of Basic Public Services for a Government*, (Brussels: CEC).

CEC, (2007) *Growing Regions, Growing Europe: Fourth Report on Economics and Cohesion*, (Luxembourg: CEC).

Centre for Public Scrutiny, (2007) *The Good Scrutiny Guide*, (London: CfPS).

Centre for Public Scrutiny, (2008) *Community Engagement Library Monitor 7*, (London: CfPS).

Christchurch, City of, (2007) *Development Contributions Policy 2007–2009*, (Christchurch, New Zealand: City of Christchurch).

Clark, J. and E. Hall, (2008) 'Will the Lessons be Learned? Reflections on Local Authority Evaluations and the Use of Research Evidence', *Evidence and Policy*, 4:4, 255–68.

Clarke, J., (2005) 'New Labour's Citizens: Activated, Empowered, Reponsibilized, Abandoned?' *Critical Social Policy*, 25:4, 447–63.

Clarke, J., (2007) '"It's Not Like Shopping": Citizens, Consumers and the Reform of Public Services', in Bevir, M. and F. Trentmann, (eds), *Governance, Consumers and Citizens Agency and Resistance in Contemporary Politics*, (Basingstoke: Palgrave Macmillan), 97–118.

CLG, (2006a) *Strong and Prosperous Communities: Local Government White Paper, vol. 1*, (London: CLG).

CLG, (2006b) *Planning for Sustainable Waste Management: Companion Guide to PPS 10*, (London: CLG).

CLG, (2006c) *Planning Policy Statement 3: Housing*, (London: CLG).

CLG, (2007a) *Planning Policy Statement 3 (PPS 3): Housing*, (London: CLG).

CLG, (2007b) *MAAs announcement*, (London: CLG).

CLG, (2007c) *Development of the New LAA Framework: Operational Guidance*, (London: CLG).

CLG, (2007d) *Strategic Housing Market Assessments*, (London: CLG).

CLG, (2007e) *Strategic Housing Market Assessments: Annexes*, (London: CLG).

CLG, (2007f) *Housing Green Paper*, (London: CLG).

CLG, (2007g) *Identifying Sub-regional Housing Market Areas*, (London: CLG).

CLG, (2007h) *Strategic Housing Land Availability Assessments: Participative Guidance*, (London: CLG).

CLG, (2007i) *Using Evidence in Spatial Planning*, (London: HMSO).

CLG, (2007j) *Planning Green Paper*, (London: CLG).

CLG, (2007k) *Planning Policy Statement: Planning and Climate Change, Supplement to PPS 1*, (London: CLG).

CLG, (2008a) John Healey's statement on new rules for creating parishes, 15 February.

CLG, (2008b) *How to Develop a Local Charter*, (London: CLG).

CLG, (2008c) *Planning Policy Statement 12: Local Spatial Planning*, (London: CLG).

CLG, (2008d) *Creating Strong, Safe and Prosperous Communities: Statutory Guidance*, (London: CLG).

CLG, (2008e) *Community Infrastructure Levy*, (London: CLG).

CLG, (2008f) *Stakeholder Involvement: Spatial Plans in Practice*, (London: CLG).

CLG, (2008g) *Participation and Policy Integration in Spatial Planning: Spatial Plans in Practice*, (London: CLG).

CLG, (2008h) *Reporting Performance Information to Citizens*, (London: CLG).

CLG, (2008i) *Neighbourhood Statistics, Vacant Dwellings*, (London: CLG).

CLG, (2009a) *Planning Together 2*, (London: CLG).

CLG, (2009b) *Planning Policy Statement: Planning for Sustainable Economic Growth*, (London: CLG).

CLG, (2009c) *Places Survey*, (London: CLG).

CLG, (2009d) *Strengthening Local Democracy*, (London: CLG).

CLG, (2009e) *Policy Statement on Regional Strategies and Guidance on the Establishment of Leaders' Boards*, (London: CLG).

CLG, (2009f) *Infrastructure Planning Commission Implementation Route Map*, (London: CLG).

CLG, (2009g) *Community Infrastructure Levy*, (London: CLG).

CLG, (2009h) *National and Regional Guidelines for Aggregates Provision in England 2005–2020*, (London: CLG).

CLG, (2009i) *PPS 25 Companion Guide*, (London: CLG).

CLG, (2009j) *Housing and Planning Delivery Grant (HPDG): Consultation or Allocation Mecanisam for Year 2 and Year 3*, (London: CLG).

CLG, (2010a) *Planning Policy Statement 25: Development and Flood Risk*, (London: CLG).

CLG, (2010b) *Community Infrastructure Levy: An Overview* (London: CLG).

CLG and BERR, (2008a) *Taking Forward the Sub National Review of Economic Development and Regeneration*, (London: CLG).

CLG and BERR, (2008b) *Taking Forward the Sub National Review of Economic Development and Regeneration: The Government Response to Public Consultation*, 25 November, (London: CLG).

CLG and BIS, (2009) *Local Democracy, Economic and Construction Bill Policy Document on Regional Strategies*, (London: CLG).

CLG and BIS, (2010) *Policy Statement on Regional Strategies*, (London: CLG).

CLG and LGA, (2008) *Housing and Planning: The Critical Role of the New Local Performance Framework*, (London: CLG).

Collins, P., (2009) 'Successful Policy Relies on Failure and Mistakes', *The Times*, 20 July, 15.

Conservative Party, (2009) *Control Shift Returning Power to Local Communities: Responsibility Agenda Policy Green Paper no 9*, (London: The Conservative Party).

Conservative Party, (2010) *Open Source Planning*, (London: The Conservative Party).

Corry, D., (2004) 'Introduction', *Choice Cuts: Essays on the Improvement of Local Public Services*, (London: New Local Government Network), 7–10.

Cooke P., and N. Clifton, (2005) 'Visionary, Precautionary and Constrained "Varieties of Devolution" in the Economic Governance of the Devolved UK territories', *Regional Studies*, 39:4, 437–51.

Counsell, D., P. Allmendinger, G. Haughton and G. Vigar, (2006) '"Integrated" Spatial Planning: Is it Living up to Expectations?', *Town and Country Planning*, September, 243–6.

Cowell, R., (2004) *Sustainability and Planning: A Scoping Paper for the RTPI*, (London: RTPI).

Crook, A., J.M. Henneberry, S. Rowley, R.S. Smith and C. Watkins, (2008) *Valuing Planning Obligations in England: Update Study for 2005–2006*, (London: CLG).

Cuff, N. and W. Smith, (2009) *Our Towns, Our Cities: The Next Steps for Planning Reform*, (London: The Bow Group).

Cullingworth, B. and V. Nadin, (2006) *Town and Country Planning in the UK*, (14th edition), (Abingdon: Routledge).

Dabinett, G., (2006) 'Transnational Planning: Insights from Practices in the European Union', *Urban Policy and Research*, 24:2, 283–90.

Danish Ministry of the Environment, (2007) *Spatial Planning in Denmark*, (Copenhagen: Ministry of the Environment).

Davies, P., (2004) *Is Evidence-based Government Possible?*, (London: Cabinet Office).

Darwin, N., (2009) 'Devolution for Smaller Cities', in Hope, N., (ed.), *Cities, Sub-regions and Local Alliances, MAA Forum Essay Collection*, (London: NLGN), 28–32.

Davis Smith, J. and P. Gay, (2005) *Active Ageing in Active Communities: Volunteering and the Transition to Retirement*, (York: Joseph Rowntree Foundation/The Policy Press).

Davoudi, S., (2003) 'Polycentricity in European Spatial Planning: From an Analytical Tool to a Normative Agenda', *European Planning Studies*, 11:8, 979–1000.

Davoudi, S. and I. Strange, (2009) 'Space and Place in Twentieth-century Planning: An Analytical Framework and an Historical Review', *Conceptions of Space and Place in Strategic Spatial Planning*, (Abingdon: Routledge), 7–42.

DCSF, (nd) *New Pupil Places (Basic Need) Allocation and the Safety-valve: 2006–2007 and 2007–2008, Annex A*, (London: DCFS).

DECC, (2009) *The Road to Copenhagen: The UK Government's Case for an Ambitious International Agreement on Climate Change*, (Norwich: TSO).

Defra, (2007a) *Guidance on Water Cycle Studies*, (London: Defra).

Defra, (2007b) *Integration of Parish Plans into the Wider Systems of Local Government*, (London: Defra).

Defra, (2009) 'Hilary Benn announces decisions on water company plans', press statement, 3 August.

DETR, (1998) *Modern Local Government: In Touch with the People*, (London: HMSO).

DETR, (2000) *Planning Policy Guidance Note 11: Regional Planning*, (London: DETR).

Development Trusts Association, (2006) *Bonds and Bridges: A DTA Practitioner Guide to Community Diversity*, (London: DTA).

DFT, (2009) *Statutory Guidance to Support Production of Local Transport Plans*, (London: DFT).

DH, (2007) *Guidance on Joint Strategic Needs Assessment*, (London: DH).

DH, (2008) *JSNA Core Indicators*, (London: DH).

Dickert N. and J. Sugarman, (2005) 'Ethical Goals of Community Consultation in Research', *American Journal of Public Health*, 95:7, 1123–7.

Diez, T. and K. Hayward, (2008) 'Reconfiguring Spaces of Conflict: Northern Ireland and the Impact of European Integration', *Space and Polity*, 12:1, 47–62.

Doak, J. and G. Parker, (2005) 'Networked Space? The Challenge of Meaningful Participation and the New Spatial Planning in England', *Planning Practice and Research*, 20:1, 23–40.

Dodson, J., (2009) 'The "Infrastructure Turn" in Australian Metropolitan Spatial Planning', *Space and Polity*, 14:2, 109–23.

DOENI, (2008) *Planning Reform: Emerging Proposals*, (Belfast: DOENI).

DOENI, (2009) *Reform of the Planning System in Northern Ireland: Your Chance to Influence Change: Consultation Paper*, (Belfast: DOENI).

Dollery, B., A. Witherby and N. Marshall, (2000) 'Section 94 Developer Contributions and Marginal Cost Pricing', *Urban Policy and Research*, 18:3, 311–28.

DRD, (2001) *Shaping Our Future*, (Belfast: DRD).

DRD and DOENI, (2005) 'Development Plans and Implementation of the Regional Development Strategy', a statement by John Spellar MP, Minister for Regional Development and Angela Smith MP, Minister for the Environment, 31 January.

DTLR, (2001a) *Strong Local Leadership: Quality Public Services*, (London: Cm 5237).

DTLR, (2001b) *Planning: Delivering a Fundamental Change – The Planning Green Paper*, (London).

Dryzek, J. and P. Dunleavy, (2009) *Theories of the Democratic State* (Basingstoke: Macmillan).

Duhr, S., C. Colomb and V. Nadin, (2010) *European Spatial Planning and Cooperation*, (Abingdon: Routledge).

Durning, B., (2004) 'Planning Academics and Planning Practitioners: Two Tribes or a Community of Practice?', *Planning Practice and Research*, 19:4, 435–46.

Durning, B., (2007) 'Challenges in the Recruitment and Retention of Professional Planners in English Planning Authorities', *Planning Practice and Research*, 22:1, 95–110.

EC, (2008) 'PEACE III', monthly progress report to Programme Monitoring Committee, December.

Eddington, R., (2006) *Understanding the Relationship: How Transport Can Contribute to Economic Success*, (London: HM Treasury and Department for Transport).

Ellis, G. and W.J.V. Neill, (2006) 'Spatial Governance in Contested Space: The Case of Northern/North of Ireland', in Tewdwr-Jones, M. and P. Allmendinger, (eds), *Territorial Identity and Spatial Planning: Spatial Governance in a Fragmented Nation*, (Abingdon: Routledge), 123–38.

emda (2005) *Smart Growth* (Nottingham: emda).

Ennis, F., (ed.), (2003) 'Infrastructure Provision and the Urban Environment', *Infrastructure Provision and the Negotiating Process*, (Aldershot: Ashgate), 1–18.

Entec, (2007) *Local Development Frameworks: Effective Community Involvement*, (London: PAS).

Enticott, G., (2006) Modernising the Internal Management of Local Planning Authorities: Does it Improve Performance? *Town Planning Review*, 77(2): 147–72.

Faludi, A., (2004) 'European Spatial Development Perspective in North-West Europe: Application and the Future', *European Planning Studies*, 12:3, 391–408.

Faludi, A., (2005) 'Polycentric Territorial Cohesion Policy', *Town Planning Review*, 76:1, 107–18.

Faludi, A., (2009) 'A Turning Point in the Development of European Spatial Planning? The "Territorial Agenda of the European Union" and the "First Action Programme"', *Progress in Planning*, 71, 1–42.

Faludi. A. and B. Waterhout, (2002) *The Making of the European Spatial Development Perspective: No Masterplan*, (Abingdon: Routledge).

Fiedler, F., (1967) *A Theory of Leadership Effectiveness*, (New York: McGraw-Hill).

French, D. and M. Laver, (2009) 'Participation Bias, Durable Opinion Shifts and Sabotage Through Withdrawal in Citizen's Juries', *Political Studies*, 57:2, 422–50.

Friedmann, J., (2005) 'Planning Cultures in Transition', in Sanyal, B., (ed.), *Comparative Planning Cultures*, (New York: Routledge), 29–44.

Gallent, N. and D. Shaw, (2007) 'Spatial Planning, Area Action Plans and the Rural–Urban Fringe', *Journal of Environmental Planning and Management*, 50:5, 617–38.

Galloway, T.D. and R.G. Mahayuni, (1977) 'Planning Theory in Retrospect: The Process of Paradigm Change', *Journal of the American Planning Association*, 43:1, 62–71.

Gershon, P., (2003) *Releasing the Resources to the Front-line*, (London: HM Treasury).

Gibb, K. and C.M.E. Whitehead (2007) 'Towards the More Effective Use of Housing Subsidy: Mobilisation and Targeting Resources', *Housing Studies*, 22:2, 183–200.

Gibson, T., (1979) *People Power, Community and Work Groups in Action*, (London: Penguin).

Gibson, T., (1998) *The Doers Guide to Planning for Real*, (London: Neighbour Initiatives Foundation).

Gibson, T., (2008) *Streetwide Worldwide: Where People Power Begins*, (Chipping Norton: Jon Carpenter).

Giddings, B. and B. Hopwood, (2006) 'From Evangelistic Bureaucrat to Visionary Developer: The Changing Character of the Master Plan in Britain', *Planning Practice and Research*, 21:3, 337–48.

Glasson, J. and T. Marshall, (2007) *Regional Planning*, (Abingdon: Routledge).

Gleeson, (1998) 'The Resurgence of Spatial Planning in Europe', *Urban Policy and Research*, 16:3, 219–25.

Gleeson, and N. Low, (2000) 'Revaluing Planning: Rolling Back Neo-liberalism in Australia', *Progress in Planning*, 53:2, 83–164.

GMGU, (2008) *Joint Waste Planning in Metropolitan and Unitary Authorities: Evidence Gathering and Review*, (Manchester: GMGU Urban Vision).

Goodsell, T.L., C.J. Ward and M.J. Stovell, (2009) 'Adapting Focus Groups to a Rural Context', *Community Development*, 401, 64–79.

Goodwin, M., M. Jones and R.A. Jones, (2006) 'The Theoretical Challenge of Devolution and Constitutional Change in the United Kingdom', in Tewdwr-Jones, M. and P. Allmendinger, (eds), *Territorial Identity and Spatial Planning: Spatial Governance in a Fragmented Nation*, (Abingdon: Routledge), 35–46.

GovMetric, (2009) Newsletter 8, www.govmetric.com.

Grant, C., (1994) *Delors: Inside the House that Jacques Built*, (London: Nicholas Brealey).

Greed, C., (2005) 'An Investigation of the Effectiveness of Gender Mainstreaming as a Means of Integrating the Needs of Women and Men into Spatial Planning in the United Kingdom', *Progress in Planning*, 64, 243–321.

Guy, S., S. Marvin and T. Moss, (2001) 'Conclusions: Contesting Networks', in Simon, G., S. Marvin and T. Moss, (eds), *Urban Infrastructure in Transition Networks: Buildings Plans*, (London: Earthscan), 197–206.

Hague, C. and P. Jenkins, (eds), (2005) *Place Identity, Participation and Planning*, (Abingdon: Routledge).

Halden Consultancy, D., (2002) *City Region Boundaries Study*, (Edinburgh: Scottish Stationery Office).

Hall, P., (1973) *The Containment of Urban England: The Planning System, Objectives, Operations, Impacts*, (London: Allen and Unwin).

Hall, P., (2009) 'Looking Backward, Looking Forward: The City Region of the Mid-21st Century', *Regional Studies*, 43:6, 803–17.

Hamnett, S. and M. Lesson, (1998) 'Metropolitan Plan Making in Australia', in Spoehr, J., (ed.), *Beyond the Contract State: Ideas for Social and Economic Renewal in South Australia*, (Adelaide: Wakefield Press).

Hampton, P., (2005) *Better Regulation*, (London: HM Treasury).

Harris, N. and A. Hooper, (2004) 'Rediscovering the "Spatial" in Public Policy and Planning: An Examination of the Spatial Content of Secotoral Policy Documents', *Planning Theory and Practice*, 5:2, 147–69.

Harris, N. and A. Hooper, (2006) 'Redefining the Space that is Wales: Place, Planning and the Spatial Plan for Wales', in Tewdwr Jones, M. and P. Allmendinger, *Territorial Identity and Spatial Planning: Spatial Governance in a Fragmented Nation*, (Abingdon: Routledge), 139–52.

Harris, N. and H. Thomas, (2009) 'Making Wales: Spatial Strategy Making in a Devolved Context', in Davoudi, S. and I. Strange, (eds), *Conceptions of Space and Place in Strategic Spatial Planning*, (Abingdon: Routledge), 43–70.

Harris, N., A. Hooper and K. Bishop, (2002) 'Constructing the Practice of "Spatial Planning": A National Spatial Planning Framework for Wales', *Environment and Planning (C)*, 20:4, 555–72.

Haughton, G. and P. Allmendinger, (2007) 'Growth and Social Infrastructure in Spatial Planning', *Town and Country Planning*, November, 388–91.

Haughton, G. and P. Allmendinger, (2008) 'The Soft Spaces of Local Economic Development', *Local Economy*, 23:2, 138–48.

Haughton, G., P. Allmendinger, D. Counsell and G. Vigar, (2010) *The New Spatial Planning*, (Abingdon: Routledge).

Healey, P., (2006) *Collaborative Planning*, (2nd edition), (Basingstoke: Palgrave Macmillan).

Healey, P., (2007) *Urban Complexity and Spatial Strategies: Towards a Relational Planning for Our Times*, (Abingdon: Routledge).

Healey, P., (2009) 'City Regions and Place Development', *Regional Studies*, 43:6, 831–43.

Henry, M., (2009) 'Holding onto our Long-term Vision', *Active in Adversity: Councils Respond to Recession*, (London: Solace Foundation Imprint/The Guardian), 16–18.

HCA, (2009) *Investment and Planning Obligations: Responding to the Downturn*, (London: HCA).

HCA, (2010) *Single Conversation: Futher Inflammation of Local Investment Plan*, (London: HCA).

HMG, (2007a) *Building on Progress: Public Services*, (London: Prime Minister's Strategy Unit).

HMG, (2007b) *Building on Progress: the Role of the State*, (London: Prime Minister's Strategy Unit).

HMG, (2007c) *PSA Delivery Agreement 7: Improve the Economic Performance of all English Regions and Reduce the Gap in Economic Growth Rates Between Regions*, (London: HMG).

HMG, (2009a) *Building a Better Britain*, (London: HMG).

HMG, (2009b) *The UK Low Carbon Industrial Strategy*, (London: HMG).

HMSO, (1965) *The Future of Development Plans*, (London: HMSO).

HMSO, (1970) *Development Plans Manual*, (London: HMSO).

HM Treasury, (2003) *UK Membership of the Single Currency: An Assessment of the Five Economic Tests*, (London: HM Treasury).

HM Treasury, (2004) *Devolved Decision Making 2: Meeting the Regional Economic Challenge: Increasing Regional and Local Flexibility*, (London: HM Treasury).

HM Treasury, (2006) *Devolved Decision Making 3: Meeting the Regional Economic Challenge: The Importance of Cities to Regional Growth*, (London: HM Treasury).

HM Treasury, (2007a) *Review of Sub-National Economic Development and Regeneration*, (London: HM Treasury).

HM Treasury, (2007b) *The Transformation Agreement*, (London: HM Treasury).

HM Treasury, (2007c) *Public Service Agreement 20*, (London: HM Treasury).

HM Treasury, (2007d) *The Budget*, (London: HM Treasury).

HM Treasury, (2008) *Regional Funding Advice: Guidance on Preparing Advice*, (London: HM Treasury).

HM Treasury, (2009a) *Operational Efficiency Programme: Final Report*, (London: HM Treasury).

HM Treasury, (2009b) *Operational Efficiency Programme: Property – The Carter Report*, (London: HM Treasury).

HM Treasury, (2009c) *The Budget*, (London: HM Treasury).

HM Treasury, (2009d) *Building Britain's Future*, (London: HM Treasury).

HM Treasury and Cabinet Office, (2007) *The Future Role of the Third Sector in Social and Economic Regeneration: Final Report Cm 7189*, (London: HMSO).

HM Treasury and Communities and Local Government, (2009) *Business Rate Supplements: A Consultation on Draft Guidance to Local Authorities*, (London HM Treasury).

HM Treasury and DTI, (2001) *Productivity in the UK: 3 – The Regional Dimension*, (London: HM Treasury).

HM Treasury, DTI and ODPM, (2004) *Devolved Decision Making: 2 – Meeting the Regional Economic Challenge: Increasing Regional and Local Flexibility*, (London: HM Treasury).

Hood, C., (2007) 'Public Service Management by Numbers: Why Does it Vary? Where Has it Come From? What Are the Gaps and the Puzzles?', *Public Money and Management*, 27:2, 95–102.

Hood, C., O. James, G. Jones and T. Tavers, (1998) 'Regulation Inside Government: Where New Public Management Meets the Audit Explosion', *Public Money and Managment*, 18:2, 61–98.

Hood, C., O. James and C. Scott, (2000) 'Regulation of Government: Has it Increased, is it Increasing, Should it be Diminished?', *Public Administration*, 78:2, 283–304.

Hood, C., and G. Peters, (2004) 'The Middle Aging of New Public Management: Into the Age of Paradox?', *Journal of Public Administration Research and Theory*, 14:3, 267–83.

Hope, N. and C. Leslie, (2009) *Challenging Perspectives: Improving Whitehall's Spatial Awareness*, (London: NLGN).

House of Commons, (2004) *Choice, Voice and Public Services: Fourth Report of Session 2004–2005*, (London: House of Commons Public Administration Committee).

House of Commons, (2009) *Select Committee on CLG, Report on Planning Skills.* (London: House of Commons).

HUDU, (2007a) *Health and Urban Development Toolkit*, (London: NHS London Healthy Urban Development Unit).

HUDU, (2007b) *Delivering Healthier Communities in London*, (London: NHS London Healthy Urban Development Unit).

HUDU, (2009a) *Planning fo Health in London: The Ultimate Manual for Primary Care Trusts and Boroughs*, (London: NHS London Healthy Urban Development Unit).

HUDU, (2009b) *Integrating Health into the Core Strategy: A Guide* (London: NHS London Healthy Urban Development Unit).

HUDU, (2009c) *Watch Out For Health: A Checklist For Assessing the Health Impact of Planning Proposals*, (London: NHS London Healthy Urban Development Unit).

Hughes, M., C. Skelcher, P. Jas, P. Whiteman, D. Turner, (2004) *Learning from the Experience of Recovery: Paths to Recovery – Second Annual Report*, (London: ODPM).

Imrie, R., and M. Raco, (2003) *Urban Renaissance?: New Labour, Community and Urban Policy*, (Bristol: The Policy Press).

Janin Rivolin, U., (2005) 'Cohesion and Subsidiarity', *Town Planning Review*, 76:1, 93–106.

Janin Rivolin, U. and A. Faludi, (2005) 'The Hidden Face of European Spatial Planning: Innovations in Governance', *European Planning Studies*, 13:2, 195–215.

Jensen, O.B., and T. Richardson, (2006) 'Towards a Transnational Space of Governance? The European Union as a Challenging Arena for UK Planning', in Tewdwr-Jones, M. and P. Allmendinger, (eds), *Territory, Identity and Spatial Planning*, (Abingdon: Routledge), 47–63.

Jessop, B., (2002) *The Future of the Capitalist State*, (Cambridge: Polity Press).

Johnson, K. and W. Hatter, (nd) *Realising the Potential of Scrunity* (London: New Local Government Network and Centre for Public Scrutiny).

Jones, E., (2001) 'Liveable Neighbourhoods', paper to conference *Australia: Walking the 21st Century*, Perth, 20–22 February.

Kearns, A., (2003) 'Social Capital, Regeneration and Urban Policy', in Imrie, R. and M. Raco, (eds), *Urban Renaissance? New Labour, Community and Urban Policy*, (Bristol: The Policy Press), 36–60.

Keating, M., (2005) 'Policy Convergence and Divergence in Scotland Under Devolution', *Regional Studies*, 39:4, 453–63.

Keating, M., (2006) 'Nationality, Devolution and Policy Development in the United Kingdom', in Tewdwr-Jones, M. and P. Allmendinger, (eds), *Territorial Identity and Spatial Planning: Spatial Governance in a Fragmented Nation*, (Abingdon: Routledge), 22–34.

Kidd, S., (2007) 'Towards a Framework of Integration in Spatial Planning: An Exploration from a Health Perspective', *Planning Theory and Practice*, 8:2, 161–81.

Killian, J. and D. Pretty, (2008) *The Killian Pretty Review: Planning Applications – A Faster and More Responsive System: Final Report*, (London: CLG).

Kitchen, T., (2007) *Skills for Planning Practice*, (Basingstoke: Palgrave Macmillan).

Kondra, A.Z and D.C. Hurst, (2009) 'Institutional Processes of Organizational Culture', *Culture and Organization*, 15:1, 39–58.

Kuhn, T.S., (1969) *The Structure of Scientific Revolutions*, (2nd edition), (Chicago: University of Chicago Press).

Lang, J., (1990) 'The Provision of Infrastructure in New Urban Developments in Three Australian States', *Urban Policy and Research*, 8:3, 91–104.

Lang, R. and D. Dhavale, (2005) 'America's Megapolitan Areas', *Land Lines*, 17, 3.

Lang, R. and P.K. Knox, (2009) 'The New Metropolis: Rethinking Megalopolis', *Regional Studies*, 43:6, 789–802.

Lawless, P., (1989) *Britain's Inner Cities*, (London: Paul Chapman Publishing).

Lawrie, G., I. Cobbold and J. Marshall, (2003) *Design of a Corporate Performance Management System in a Devolved Governmental Organisation*, (Maidenhead: 2GC Active Management).

Leach, S., C. Skelcher, C. Lloyd-Jones, C. Copus, E. Dunstan and D. Hall, (2003) *Strengthening Local Democracy: Making the Most of the Constitution*, (London: ODPM).

Le Gales, P., (2002) *European Cities: Social Conflicts and Governance*, (Oxford: Oxford University Press).

Leven, R., (2009) 'Priorities for New Development Plans', *Development Plan Workshop*, 13 July, (Edinburgh: Scottish Executive).

Lewisham's Citizen's Jury, (2004) *To What Extent Should the Car Fit into Lewisham's Future Transport Plans?* (London: L.B. Lewisham).

LGA, (2007) *Prosperous Communities II: Vive la Dévolution*, (London: LGA).

LGA, (2009) *Counting Cumbria*, (London: Leadership Centre for Local Government).

Lloyd, G., (2008) *Planning Reform in Northern Ireland: Independent Report to the Minister of the Environment*, (Belfast: DOENI).

Lloyd, G. and D. Peel, (2005) 'Tracing a Spatial Turn in Planning Practice in Scotland', *Planning Practice and Research*, 20:3, 313–25.

Lloyd, G. and D. Peel, (2009) 'New Labour and the Planning System in Scotland: An Overview of a Decade', *Planning Practice and Research*, 24:1, 103–18.

Lloyd, G., and G. Purves, (2009) 'Identity and Territory: The Creation of a National Planning Framework for Scotland', in Davoudi, S. and I. Strange, (eds), *Conceptions of Space and Place in Strategic Spatial Planning*, (Abingdon: Routledge), 71–94.

Low Choy, D., C. Sutherland, S. Scott, K. Rolley, B. Gleeson, J. Dodson and N. Sipe, (2007) *Change and Continuity in Peri-Urban Australia: Peri Urban Case Study: South East Queensland Monograph 3*, (Brisbane: Griffith University).

Lucci, P. and P. Hildreth, (2008) *City Links*, (London: Centre for Cities).

Lyons, M., (2004) *Well Placed to Deliver Shaping the Pattern of Government Service*, (London: HM Treasury).

Lyons, M., (2007) *Place Shaping: A Shared Ambition for Local Government*, (London: HM Treasury).

MacLeod, G. and M. Jones, (2006) 'Mapping the Geographies of UK Devolution: Institutional Legacies, Territorial Fixes and Network Topologies', in Tewdwr-Jones, M. and P. Allmendinger, (eds), *Territorial Identity and Spatial Planning: Spatial Governance in a Fragmented Nation*, (Abingdon: Routledge).

Maginn, P.J. and M.W. Rofe, (2007) 'Urbanism and Regionalism Down Under: An Introduction', *Space and Polity*, 11:3, 201–8.

Marshall, T., (2004) 'Regional Planning in England: Progress and Pressures since 1997', *Town Planning Review*, 75:4, 447–72.

Marshall, T., (2007) 'After Structure Planning: The New Sub-regional Planning in England', *European Planning Studies*, 15:1, 107–32.

Marshall, T., (2008) 'Regions, Economies and Planning in England after the Sub-national Review', *Local Economy*, 23:2, 99–106.

Massey, D., A. Amin and N. Thrift, (2003) *Decentering the Nation*, (London: Catalyst Forum).

Masterman, M., (1970) 'The Nature of a Paradigm', in Lakatos, I. and A. Musgrave, (eds), *Criticism and the Growth of Knowledge*, (3rd edition), (Cambridge: Cambridge University Press), 59–89.

Mayo, E. and T. Steinberg, (2007) *The Power of Information: An Independent Review*, (London: Cabinet Office).

Mayor of London, (2007) *Health Issues in Planning: Best Practice Guidance*, (London: Mayor of London).

Mayor of London, (2009) *London City Charter*, (London: Mayor of London and London Councils).

Mazza, L., (2003) 'Dalla città diffusa alla città diramata, 7. Nuove forme di pianificazione urbanistica a Milano', edited by Detragiache, A., (Rome: Franco Angeli).

McEldowney, M. and K. Sterrett, (2001) 'Shaping a Regional Vision: the Case of Northern Ireland', *Local Economy*, 16:1, 38–49.

McLean, I and A. McMillan, (2003) 'The Distribution of Public Expenditure Across the UK Regions', *Fiscal Studies*, 24:1, 45–72.

McNeill, J. and B. Dollery, (1999) 'A Note on the Use of Developer Charges in Australian Local Government', *Urban Policy and Research*, 17:1, 61–9.

Mintrom, M., (2003) 'Market Organizational and Deliberative Democracy Choice and Voice in Public Service Delivery', *Administration and Society*, 35:1, 52–81.

Morphet, J., (1992) *Towards Sustainability: The EU's Fifth Action Programme*, (Luton: LGTB).

Morphet, J., (1993) *Local Authority Chief Executives: Their Function and Role*, (Harlow: Longman).

Morphet, J., (1994) 'The Committee of the Regions', *Local Government Policy Making*, 20:5, 556–60.

Morphet, J., (1996) *Emergent Trends in EU Spatial Systems*, paper for DOENI, unpublished.

Morphet, J., (1998) 'Local Authorities', *British Environmental Policy and Europe*, (Abingdon: Routledge), 138–52.

Morphet, J., (2004) *RTPI Scoping Paper on Integration*, (London: RTPI).

Morphet, J., (2005) 'A Meta-narrative of Planning Reform', *Town Planning Review*, 76:4, iv–ix.

Morphet, J., (2006) 'Global Localism: Interpreting and Implementing New Localism in the UK', in Tewdwr-Jones, M. and P. Allmendinger, (eds), *Territorial Identity and Spatial Planning: Spatial Governance in a Fragmented Nation*, (Abingdon: Routledge), 305–19.

Morphet, J., (2007a) 'The New Decision Making Process within Local Government', *Journal of Planning and Environment Law*, (special edition), 1–9.

Morphet, J., (2007b) *Delivering Inspiring Places*, (London: National Planning Forum).

Morphet, J., (2008) *Modern Local Government*, (London: Sage).

Morphet, J., (2009a) *A Steps Approach to Infrastructure Planning and Delivery for Local Strategic Partnerships and Local Authorities*, (London: PAS).

Morphet, J., (2009b) 'Local Integrated Spatial Planning: The Changing Role in England', *Town Planning Review*, 80:4, 383–415.

Morphet, J., (2009c) 'Delivering Joined up Public Services', *Planning*, 7 August, 1830, 23.

Morphet, J., N. Gallent, M. Tewdwr-Jones, B. Hall, M. Spry and R. Howard, (2007) *Shaping and Delivering Tomorrow's Places: Effective Practice in Spatial Planning (EPiSP)*, (London: RTPI, CLG, GLA and JRF).

Morrissey, M. and F. Gaffikin, (2001) 'Northern Ireland: Democratizing for Development', *Local Economy*, 16:1, 2–13.

Morrisson, B., (2000) 'Staying Ahead of the Game on the Quality Front', *Planning*, Special Irish Supplement, 8–9 June.

Mullins, C., (2009) *A View from the Foothills*, (London: Profile Books).

Murray, M., (2009) 'Building Consensus in Contested Spaces and Places? The Regional Development Strategy for Northern Ireland', in Davoudi, S., and I. Strange, (eds), *Conceptions of Space and Place in Strategic Spatial Planning*, (Abingdon: Routledge), 125–46.

Murray, M. and J. Greer, (2002) 'Participatory Planning as Dialogue: The Northern Ireland Regional Strategic Framework and its Public Examination Process', *Policy Studies*, 23:3/4, 191–209.

Musson, S., A. Tickell and P. John, (2005) 'A Decade of Decentralisation? Assessing the Role of the Government Offices for the English Regions', *Environment and Planning A*, 37:8, 1395–1412.

Nadin, V., (2007) 'The Emergence of the Spatial Planning Approach in England', *Town Planning Review*, 22:1, 43–62.

Needham, B. (2005) 'The New Dutch Spatial Planning Act: Continuity and Change in the Way in Which the Dutch Regulate the Practice of Spatial Planning', *Planning Practice and Research*, 20:3, 327–40.

Neill, W.J.V., (2004) *Urban Planning and Cultural Identity*, (Abingdon: Routledge).

Neill, W.J.V. and M. Gordon, (2001) 'Shaping Our Future? The Regional Strategic Framework for Northern Ireland', *Planning Theory and Practice*, 2:1, 31–52.

Neuman, M., (2009) 'Spatial Planning Leadership by Infrastructure: An American View', *International Planning Studies*, 14:2, 201–17.

Neuman. M. and A. Hull, (2007) 'The Futures of the City Region', *Regional Studies* 43:6, 777–87.

Neuman, P., (2008) 'Strategic Spatial Planning: Collective Action and Moments of Opportunity', *European Planning Studies*, 16:10, 1371–84.

NHS, (2007a) *A Guide to Town Planning for NHS Staff*, (London: NHS).

NHS, (2007b) *A Guide to the NHS for Local Planning Authorities*, (London: NHS).

NICE, (2008) *Promoting and Creating Built or Natural Environments that Encourage and Support Physical Activity*, (London: NICE).

Nokes, S. and S. Kelly, (2007) *The Definitive Guide to Project Management: The Fast Track to Getting the Job Done on Time and on Budget*, (Financial Times Series), (London: Financial Times/Prentice Hall).

NRU, (2002) *The 'Learning Curve': Developing Skills and Knowledge for Neighbourhood Renewal.* (London: ODPM).

O'Brien, M., S. Clayton, T. Varag-Atkins and A. Qualter, (2008) 'Power and the Theory-and-practice Conundrum: The Experience of Doing Research with a Local Authority', *Evidence and Policy*, 4:4, 371–90.

ODPM, (2002) *Sustainable Communities: Delivered Through Planning*, (London: HMSO).

ODPM, (2003a) *Polycentricity Scoping Study*, (London: ODPM).

ODPM, (2003b) *Sustainable Communities: Building for the Future*, (London: ODPM).

ODPM, (2004a) *Learning from the Experience of Recovery*, (London: ODPM).

ODPM, (2004b) *The Egan Review: Skills for Sustainable Communities*, (London: ODPM).

ODPM, (2004c) *Community Involvement in Planning*, (London: ODPM).

ODPM, (2005a) *Planning Policy Statement 10: Planning for Sustainable Waste Management*, (London: ODPM).

ODPM, (2005b) *Sustainability Appraisal of Regional Spatial Strategies and Local Development Documents*, (London: ODPM).

ODPM, (2005c) *Annual Monitoring Report (AMR) – FAQs and Seminar Feedback on Emerging Best Practice 2004/05*, (London: ODPM).

ODPM, (2005d) *Local Development Framework Monitoring: A Good Practice Guide*, (London: ODPM).

ODPM, (2005e) *Planning Policy Statement 1: Delivering Sustainable Development*, (London: ODPM).

ODPM, (2005f) *Circular 05/05 Planning Obligations*, (London: ODPM).

OECD, (2001) *Towards a New Role for Spatial Planning*, (Paris: OECD).

OECD, (2008) *North of England: Review of Regional Innovation*, (Paris: OECD).

Office of Government Commerce, (2009) PRINCE 2, (London: OGC).

OPSR, (2005) *Choice and Voice in the Reform of Public Services*, (London: Cabinet Office).

Osborne, D. and T. Gaebler, (1993) *Reinventing Government*, (London: Penguin).

Osborne, D. and P. Hutchinson, (2004) *The Price of Government*, (New York: Basic Books).

Page, B., (2009) *Understanding People, Perceptions and Place*, (London: Ipsos MORI).

Page, B. and M. Horton, (2006) *Lessons in Leadership*, (London: IDeA/Ipsos MORI).

Parker, G., (2008) 'Parish and Community-led Planning, Local Empowerment and Local Evidence Bases: An Examination of West Berkshire', *Town Planning Review*, 79:1, 61–85.

Planning Advisory Service, (2007a) *Delivering the Difference: Annual Report 2006/07*, (London: PAS).

Planning Advisory Service, (2007b) *Open for Business: Changing the Way that Local Authorities Work with Developers*, (London: PAS).

Planning Advisory Service, (2007c) *Local Development Frameworks: Guidance on Sustainability Appraisal*, (London: PAS).

Planning Advisory Service, (2008a) *Prevention is Still Better than Cure*, (London: PAS).

Planning Advisory Service, (2008b) *Plan and Deliver: How Partners are Working in Partnership to Create Better Places*, (London: IDeA).

Planning Advisory Service, (2008c) *Development Management Guidance and Discussion Document*, (London: ILGA).

Planning Advisory Service, (2008d) *Finding the Flow: Re-engineering Business Processes for Planning*, (London: IDeA).

Planning Advisory Service, (2008e) *Positive Engagement: A Guide for Planning Councillors, updated version*, (London: PAS).

Planning Advisory Service, (2008f) *Equality and Diversity: Case Studies*, (London: IDeA).

Planning Advisory Service, (2008g) *Waste Content of Core Strategies*, www.pas.gov.uk, (accessed 4 May 2009).

Planning Advisory Service, (2009) *Planning Together: Case Studies*, (London: PAS).

Planning Inspectorate National Service, (2005) *Development Plans Examination: A Guide to the Process of Assessing the Soundness of Development Plan Documents*, (Bristol: PINS).

Planning Inspectorate National Service, (2007) *Local Development Frameworks: Lessons Learnt Examining Development Plan Documents*, (Bristol: PINS).

Planning Inspectorate National Service, (2008) *Tests of Soundness*, (Bristol: PINS).

Planning Inspectorate National Service, (2009a) *Local Development Frameworks: Examining Development Plan Documents – Procedure Guidance*, (Bristol: PINS).

Planning Inspectorate National Service, (2009b) *Local Development Frameworks: Examining Development Plan Documents, Learning from Experience*, (Bristol: PINS).

Planning Inspectorate National Service, (2009c) *General Advisory Guidance*, (Bristol: PINS).

Planning Inspectorate National Service, (2009d) *Brief Guide to Examining Development Plan Procedure*, (Bristol: PINS).

Planning Institute of Australia, 'About Planning', www.planning.org.au (accessed November 2009).

Pollitt, C. and G. Boockaert, (2004) *Public Management Reform: A Comparative Analysis*, (2nd edition), (Oxford: Oxford University Press).

Polverari, L, and J, Bachtler, (2005) 'The Contribution of European Structural Funds to Territorial Cohesion', *Town Planning Review*, 76:1, 29–42.

POS, (2008) *Strategic Housing Land Availability Assessment and Development Plan Document Presentation*, (London: PAS).

Powell, K., (2001) 'Devolution, Planning Guidance and the Role of the Planning System in Wales', *International Planning Studies*, 6:2, 215–22.

Power, M., (1997) *The Audit Society*, (Oxford: Oxford University Press).

Prince's Foundation for the Built Environment, (2005) *Sherford New Community Enquiry by Design, 4–6 October, 2004 Summary Report*, (London: the Prince's Foundation for the Built Environment).

Prince's Foundation for the Built Environment, (nd) *Enquiry by Design*, (London: Prince's Foundation for the Built Environment.

Prior, A., (2005) 'UK Planning Reform: A Regulationist Interpretation', *Planning Theory and Practice*, 6:4, 465–84.

Putnam, R., (2000) *Bowling Alone*, (New York: Simon and Schuster).

Raco, M., (2003) 'New Labour: Community and the Future of Britain's Urban Rennaissance', in Imrie, R. and M. Raco, *Urban Renaissance?: New Labour, Community and Urban Policy*, (Bristol: The Policy Press).

Raco, M., (2006) 'Building New Subjectivities: Devolution, Regional Identities and the Re-scaling of Politics', in Tewdwr-Jones, M. and P. Allmendinger, (eds), *Territorial Identity and Spatial Planning: Spatial Governance in a Fragmented Nation*, (Abingdon: Routledge), 320–34.

Rader Olsson, A., (2009) 'Relational Rewards and Communicative Planning: Understanding Actor Motivation', *Planning Theory*, 8:3, 263–81.

Raynsford, N., (2004) *Developing a Ten-Year Vision for Local Government*, (London: ODPM).

Reeves, D., (2005) *Planning for Diversity: Policy and Planning in a World of Difference*, (Abingdon: Routledge).

Roberts, P. and M. Baker, (2004) 'Sub-regional Planning in England', *Town Planning Review*, 75:3, 265–86.

Rodriguez-Pose, A. and N. Gill, (2005) 'On the "Economic Dividend" of Devolution', *Regional Studies*, 39:4, 405–20.

Rowlandson, K. and S. McKay, (2005) *Attitudes to Inheritance in Britain*, (York: Joseph Rowntree Foundation/The Policy Press).

Roy, A., (2009) 'The 21st Century Metropolis: New Geographies of Theory', *Regional Studies*, 43:6, 819–30.

RTPI, (2007) *Extra Care Housing: Development Planning, Control and Management*, (London: RTPI).

RTPI, (2009a) *Delivering Healthy Communities, RTPI Good Practice Note 5*, (London: RTPI).

RTPI, (2009b) *Planning to Live with Climate Change Action Plan*, (London: RTPI).

Sandell, M., (2009) *The Reith Lectures*, (London: BBC).

Sandercock, L., (2003) *Cosmopolis II, Mongrel City*, (London: Mansell).

Sandercock, L., (2005) 'Picking the Paradoxes: A Historical Anatomy of Australian Planning Cultures', in Sangal, B., *Comparative Planning Cultures*, (New York: Routledge), 309–30.

Sanyal, B., (2005) 'Hybrid Planning Cultures: The Search for the Global Cultural Commons', in Sanyal, B., (ed.), *Comparative Planning Cultures*, (New York: Routledge), 3–25.

Schafer, N., (2005) 'Co-ordination in European Spatial Development', *Town Planning Review*, 76:1, 43–56.

Schon, P., (2005) 'Territorial Cohesion in Europe', *Planning Theory and Practice*, 6:3, 389–400.

Schout, A. and A. Jordan, (2007) 'From Cohesion to Territorial Policy Integration (TPI): Exploring the Governance Challenges of the European Union', *European Planning Studies*, 15:6, 835–51.

Schout, A. and A. Jordan, (2008a) *EU-EPI, Policy Co-ordination and New Institutionalism*, (Barcelona: l'Instituit Universitari d'Estudios Europeus).

Schout, A. and A. Jordan, (2008b) 'The European Union's Governance Ambitions and its Administrative Capacities', *Journal of European Public Policy*, 15:7, 957–74.

Scottish Enterprise, (2006) *Scottish Enterprise Operating Plan 2006–2009*, (Edinburgh: Scottish Enterprise).

Scottish Executive, (2005) *Modernising the Planning System*, (Edinburgh: Scottish Executive).

Scottish Executive, (2006) *Transforming Public Services*, (Edinburgh: Scottish Executive).

Scottish Government, (2002) *Review of Scotland's Cities: The Analysis*, (Edinburgh: Scottish Stationery Office).

Scottish Government, (2005) *Modernising the Planning System: White Paper*, (Edinburgh: Scottish Government).

Scottish Government, (2006) *Community Planning Advice Note 4*, (Edinburgh: Scottish Government).

Scottish Government, (2007) *Scottish Budget Spending Review*, (Edinburgh: Scottish Government).

Scottish Government, (2008a) *Scottish Planning Policy Parts 1 and 2*, (Edinburgh: Scottish Government).

Scottish Government, (2008b) *National Planning Framework 2: 2008 Proposed Framework*, (Edinburgh: Scottish Government).

Scottish Government, (2008c) *Infrastructure Investment Plan*, (Edinburgh: Scottish Government).

Scottish Government, (2009a) *Planning Circular 1: Development Planning*, (Edinburgh: Scottish Government).

Scottish Government, (2009b) *Scottish Planning Policy Part 3: Consultative Draft*, (Edinburgh: Scottish Government).

Scottish Government, (2009c) *National Planning Framework for Scotland 2*, (Edinburgh: Scottish Government).

Scottish Government and COSLA, (2007) *Concordat*, (Edinburgh: Scottish Government and COSLA).

Scottish Government and COSLA, (2009) *Concordat on Single Outcome Agreements*, (Edinburgh: Scottish Government).

Sehested, K., (2009) 'Urban Planners as Network Managers and Metagovernors', *Planning Theory and Practice*, 10:2, 245–63.

Shaw, D. and O. Sykes, (2005) 'Addressing Connectivity in Spatial Planning: The Case of the English Regions', *Planning Theory and Practice*, 6:1, 11–33.

Shaw, D. and A. Lord, (2007) 'The Cultural Turn? Culture Change and What it Means for Spatial Planning in England', *Town Planning Review*, 22:1, 63–78.

Shipley, R. and J.L. Michela, (2006) 'Can Vision Motivate Planning Action?', *Planning Practice and Research*, 21:2, 223–44.

SIP, (2009a) *Surrey Infrastructure Capacity Study, Part 1A: Demographic Analysis, Governance, Funding Outlook*, (Kingston: Surrey Improvement Partnership).

SIP, (2009b) *Surrey Infrastructure Capacity Study, Part 1B: Infrastructure Baseline and Future Needs Analysis*, (Kingston: Surrey Improvement Partnership).

Skeffington, A., (1969) *People and Planning: Report of the Committee on Public Participation in Planning*, (London: HMSO).

Snape, S. and P. Taylor, (2000) *Realising the Potential of Scrutiny: A Hard Nut to Crack*, (London: NLGN).

Snape, S. and S. Leach, (2002) *The Development of Overview and Scrutiny in Local Government*, (London: ODPM).

Soja, E.W., (1996) *Thirdspace*, (Oxford: Blackwell).

Spencer, K., A. Taylor, B. Smith, J. Mawson, N. Flynn and R. Batley, (1986) *Crisis in the Industrial Heartland*, (Oxford: Clarendon Press).

Stern, N., (2009) *A Blueprint for a Safer Planet*, (London: The Bodley Head).

Swansea, City and County of, (2009) *Draft Delivery Agreement for Local Development Plan*, (Swansea: City and County of Swansea).

Sweeting, D. and H. Ball, (2002) 'Overview and Scrutiny of Leadership, Bristol City Council', *Local Governance*, 28:3, 201–12.

Sydney, City of, (2006) *Development Contributions Plan*, (Sydney, Australia: City of Sydney).

Sykes, R., (2003) *Planning Reform: A Survey of Local Authorities*, (London: Local Government Association).

Taylor, M., (2008) *Transforming Disadvantaged Places: Effective Strategies for People and Places*, (York: Joseph Rowntree Foundation).

Taylor, M., M. Kingston and S. Thake, (2002) *Networking Across Regeneration Partnerships: A National Study of Regional Approaches*, (York: Joseph Rountree Foundation).

Taylor, N., (1999) 'Anglo American Town Planning Theory Since 1945: Three Significant Developments but no Paradigm Shifts', *Planning Perspectives*, 14:4, 327–45.

Teitz, M.B., (2002) 'Progress and Planning in America over the Past 30 Years', *Progress in Planning*, 57, 179–203.

Tett, G., (2009) Speech to RTPI Planning Convention, June.

Tewdwr-Jones, M. and R. Williams, (2001) *The European Dimension of British Spatial Planning*, (London: Spon Press).

Tewdwr-Jones, M. and J.M. Mourato, (2005) 'Territorial Cohesion, Economic Growth and the Desire for European "Balanced Competitiveness"', *Town Planning Review*, 76:1, 69–80.

Tewdwr-Jones, M. and P. Allmendinger, (eds), (2006) *Territorial Identity and Spatial Planning: Spatial Governance in a Fragmented Nation*, (Abingdon: Routledge).

Turok, I., (2008) 'A New Policy for Britain's Cities: Choices, Challenges and Contradictions', *Local Economy*, 23:2, 149–66.

Turok, I., (2009) 'Limits to the Mega-City Region: Conflicting Land and Regional Needs', *Regional Studies*, 43:6, 845–62.

Turok, I. and P. Taylor, (2006) 'A Skills Framework for Regeneration and Planning', *Planning Practice and Research*, 21:4, 497–509.

UNECE, (2002) *Convention of Access to Information: Public Participation in Decision Making and Access to Justice in Environmental Matters*, (Geneva: UNECE).

Van de Walle, S. and T. Bovaird, (2007) *Making Better Use of Information to Drive Improvement in Public Services*, (Birmingham: Inlogov).

Varney, D., (2006) *A Better Service for the Citizens and Businesses: A Better Deal for the Taxpayer*, (London: HM Treasury).

Wainwright, H., (2003) *Reclaim the State Adventures in Popular Democracy*, (London: Verso).

Wates, N., (2000) *The Community Planning Handbook: How People can Shape Their Cities, Towns and Villages in any Part of the World*, (Hastings: Earthscan).

Welsh Assembly Government, (2000) *Better Wales*, (Cardiff: WAG).

Welsh Assembly Government, (2002) *Planning: Delivering for Wales*, (Cardiff: WAG).

Welsh Assembly Government, (2004) *Spatial Plan for Wales*, (Cardiff: WAG).

Welsh Assembly Government, (2006) *Local Delivery Agreements*, (Cardiff: WAG).

Welsh Assembly Government, (2008) *People, Places, Futures: The Welsh Spatial Plan 2008 Update*, (Cardiff: WAG).

Welsh Assembly Government, (2009) *LSB update*, June, (Cardiff: WAG).

Western Australia Government, (2003) *The Enquiry-by-Design Workshop Process: A Preparation Manual*, (Perth: The Government of Western Australia, Department for Planning and Infrastructure).

Wheeler, S., (2009) 'Regions, Megaregions and Sustainability', *Regional Studies*, 43:6, 863–76.

Wicks, M., (2009) *Energy Security: A National Challange in a Changing World*, (London: BIS).

Williams, P., (2002) 'The Competent Boundary Spanner', in *Public Administration*, 80:1, 103–24.

Wilmoth, D., (2005) 'Urban Infrastructure Planning: Connection and Disconnection', paper presented to *State of Australian Cities Conference*, Brisbane, 30 November– 2 December.

Wolfe, J.M. (2002) 'Reinventing Planning: Canada', *Progress in Planning*, 57, 207–35.

Wong, C., (2006) *Indicators for Urban and Regional Planning: The Interplay of Policy and Methods*, (Abingdon: Routledge).

Wood, C., (2008) 'Progress with Development Plan Documents: Lessons Learnt in England?', *Journal of Planning and Environment Law*, March, 265–74.

Woodman, C.L., (1999) 'The Evolving Role of Profession in Local Government', *Local Governanace*, 25:4, 211–220.

Wright, T. and P. Ngan, (2004) *A New Social Contract: From Targets to Rights in Public Services*, (London: The Fabian Society).

Young Foundation, (2006) *The Polycentric Metropolis: Learning from Mega-city Regions in Europe*, (London: The Young Foundation).

Young, H., (1998) *This Blessed Plot: Britain and Europe from Churchill to Blair*, (London: Overlook Press).

Zonneveld, W. and B. Waterhout, (2005) 'Visions on Territorial Cohesion', *Town Planning Review*, 76:1, 15–27

INDEX